Simone
de Beauvoir,
Nathalie
Sarraute,
Marguerite
Duras,
Monique
Wittig,
and Maryse
Condé

BY LEAH D. HEWITT

University of Nebraska Press: Lincoln & London

Auto-bio-graph-ical Tight-ropes

Publication of this book was
assisted by a grant from The
Andrew W. Mellon Foundation

Library of Congress
Cataloging in Publication Data
Hewitt, Leah Dianne.
Autobiographical tightropes :
Simone de Beauvoir,
Nathalie Sarraute, Marguerite
Duras, Monique Wittig,
and Maryse Condé /
Leah D. Hewitt.
p.   cm.   Includes bibliograph-
ical references.
ISBN 0-8032-2354-4 (alk. paper)
ISBN 0-8032-7258-8 (pbk.)
1. French prose literature –
Women authors – History and
criticism. 2. Auto-
biographical fiction, French –
Women authors –
History and criticism. 3. Wom-
en novelists, French –
20th century – Biography –
History and criticism.
4. Feminism and literature –
France – History –
20th century. 5. Women and
literature – France –
History – 20th century.
6. Autobiography – Women authors. I. Title.
PQ629.H49   1990
840.9′9287 – dc20
89-29319   CIP

⊛

FOR MY PARENTS

Contents

ACKNOWLEDGMENTS

I would like to thank the National Endowment for the Humanities and Amherst College for their generous financial support during the writing of this book.

I want to express my warmest gratitude to Marie-Hélène Huet and Jay Caplan for their enduring intellectual and moral support. Marie-Hélène's suggestions and gentle criticisms were particularly valuable. Her cogent commentaries on the overall shape of my argument were instrumental as I began to map out my concluding remarks. I cannot thank her enough. I am also grateful to Ann Smock, whose wonderful comments and thoughts on Sarraute rekindled my enthusiasm in the later stages of writing.

Finally, I especially want to thank Kevin Clark, whose daily emotional support and encouragement sustained me through it all.

ABBREVIATIONS

I have used the abbreviations listed below for the titles of works that I cite frequently. The editions used are those given in the bibliography.

Simone de Beauvoir
ASD   *All Said and Done*
FC   *Force of Circumstance*
Mem   *Memoirs of a Dutiful Daughter*
PL   *The Prime of Life*
SS   *The Second Sex*

Maryse Condé
H   *Heremakhonon*

Marguerite Duras
L   *The Lover*

Nathalie Sarraute
AS   *The Age of Suspicion*
C   *Childhood*

Monique Wittig
AA   *Across the Acheron*

Introduction

At a conference session on Marguerite Duras a few years ago, I was struck by various speakers' nervous insistence that one should not think of Duras's book, *The Lover*, as "just" an autobiographical work, that in effect it was "really" literary fiction. Their modernist position, concentrating on literature's self-reflexive or internal operations, as distinct from issues of literary *representation*, was understandable: none of the speakers wished to reduce *The Lover* to a "transparent" revelation of the author's life or a simplistic, illusory explanation of her other works. As proponents of textual criticism, the speakers carefully distinguished between "life" and the text.[1] A certain tradition of autobiography was implicitly being contested, as an outmoded genre that still supported a belief in the work's realistic, mimetic roles. What was intriguing, however, was that one speaker selectively used Duras's remarks in interviews to substantiate claims that *The Lover*'s fictive features took precedence over its referential value. Recourse to the author as origin or proprietor of the text's meaning—as authority—was used as part of a strategy to diminish the import of an *autobiographical* subject, to loosen the ties between "personal experience" and "referential writing" on the one hand, and a self-generating text on the other. What surfaces in this paradox is autobiography's slippery relation to distinct conceptual models—traditional and modern—as it stirs its mixtures of literature in life and life in literature, making it difficult to keep the "purely" literary and the "purely" referential in their "proper" (opposed) places. Autobiography, particularly in the postmodern era, balances precariously on the mobile borderline between opposing conceptions of literature.[2]

1

In the literary history of the West, autobiography has alternately been read as a mainstream literary genre (what is more canonical than Rousseau's *Confessions?*) and as a marginal or inferior form that always seems to look, as Paul de Man says, "slightly disreputable and self-indulgent," compared to other literary genres.[3] For women writers, both of these evaluations have rendered the genre particularly difficult to tackle, despite its strong attraction as a mode of writing/exploring themselves. Sidonie Smith has recently shown that critical readings of the history of autobiography have tended to ignore the crucial "interdependencies of the ideology of gender and the ideology of individualism."[4] Smith argues that from the Middle Ages through the nineteenth century, autobiography was an androcentric literary form that consecrated male scenarios of selfhood, and she faults twentieth-century critics of autobiography for perpetuating the exclusion of women's autobiographical writings by consecrating rigid (male-centered) definitions and canons.[5] In the history of autobiography, an interesting confusion arises between legitimating the individual self *and* the formal genre of autobiography.

Although modern autobiographers (both men and women) have delighted in challenging the strictures of fixed generic characterizations, women are no doubt more attuned to potential connections between generic marginality and gender. Nancy K. Miller has aptly pointed out that women autobiographers are aware that their work is always subject to tacitly genderized readings:

While for all autobiographers already figures of public fiction there is a strong sense of responsibility about speaking out, because being known, they expect their words to have an impact within a clearly defined reader's circle, the female autobiographers know that they are being read as women.[6]

A female name attached to an autobiography particularizes the text in ways that a male name does not. Whatever position a contemporary woman autobiographer takes vis-à-vis the autobiographical tradition, she is aware that gender affects the reading of her position, whether she likes it or not.

The autobiographical risk of appearing self-indulgent has

been all the greater for a woman writer because to write in the public eye is to "make a spectacle of herself,"[7] to transgress the boundaries that have historically confined women to traditional roles in the private sectors of home and family. Freud's claims that women are more naturally inclined to narcissism than men—a moral shortcoming of sorts—do not make it any easier for contemporary women to construct or question the possibilities of female subjecthood in writing.[8] None of these obstacles has ever completely stopped women from turning to autobiographical forms of writing, but the cultural discourses shaping men's and women's gendered social roles have certainly inflected their writings, as well as the ways they are read.

The traditional view of autobiography—through and against which the autobiographical texts studied here articulate themselves—grounds itself in the metaphysics of the conscious, coherent, individual subject. Language in this perspective is a tool to represent faithfully the already extant self and the past life. In the second half of the twentieth century, this conception of autobiography has, of course, radically changed (and was, no doubt, always already being challenged in practice): the "individual's" autonomy, with its concomitant social and linguistic authority, has been seriously eroded. The text now creates the fictions of a "self" rather than the reverse. Jacques Derrida's philosophical critiques of presence, of origins and the "full subject," meticulously deconstruct many of the premises of conventional autobiographical forms, as do Jacques Lacan's psychoanalytic writings on the predominant role of intersubjectivity in the constitution of the subject. With the Cartesian subject put "on trial/in process," as Julia Kristeva puts it,[9] and Roland Barthes's well-known proclamation of the "death of the author" as supreme controller of the text,[10] the possibilities for the formation of an autobiographical "I" (or its very desirability) have to be rethought. For some, these radical alterations in our understanding of the subject in language have turned autobiography into a model for writing in general, a self-reflexive mode with its subject dispossessed, if not eliminated. The subjective agency of the personal "I" is overridden in indeterminate textual processes. Michael Sprinker even speaks of "the end of autobiography," when "concepts of subject, self, and author collapse into the act of producing a text."[11]

In the chapters that follow, I explore the ways women's modern autobiographical texts respond to the frictions between traditional and modern perspectives on autobiography. I will be reading "autobiography" as both an intertextual negotiation with traditional and avant-garde notions of the formal genre, and a personal, life-writing whose referential effects remain persistent if problematic. Although my own readings of autobiography take into account the possibility of the subject's textual disappearance (as described by Sprinker), I think it will be readily clear that this self-effacement never completes itself and that issues of gender play a role in the persistence of the autobiographical subject.

The five modern French women writers I consider—Simone de Beauvoir, Nathalie Sarraute, Marguerite Duras, Monique Wittig, and Maryse Condé—have been, and are, some of the most interesting and important fiction writers in French in the second half of the twentieth century. All have taken feminist stances in their lives, and all respond more or less explicitly in their works to the issue of gendered identity, whether as theme, style, cultural and linguistic deviation, or unconscious process. They have not, however, with perhaps the exception of Duras, espoused the French (neo)feminist theories of the seventies that proclaim the specificity of feminine writing (*écriture féminine*). Suspicious of any theory that appears to essentialize sexual difference, de Beauvoir, Sarraute, and Wittig have been particularly resolute in their anti-essentialist positions. In all five writers' works, however, the idea of a gender-marked writing comes into play.

My own interest does not lie in redefining the genre in order to prove the specificity of feminine autobiography; rather, I wish to study how the internal tensions stemming from autobiography's marginality vis-à-vis literature and life affirm, displace, or put into question the creation of a feminine subject. And if autobiography is the "dark continent of literature,"[12] one may ask in turn how that other dark continent—woman—brings to light this obscurity. How does the woman writer respond to the internal contradictions of autobiography while she is already pondering the possibility of being a "subject" of/in discourse? How does the narration of the past constitute the narrating subject? The way each writer responds will be linked to her associations with the literary movements of the period, and to the way she conceives of a social and historical female subject. Through an analysis of the adherence to, and deviations from, formal definitions, I examine the peculiar difficulties and creative possibilities that autobiography presents to these women writers as they (re)invent the genre. Of the works I will be reading, none are "pure" autobiography in a narrow or conventional sense: "memoirs" is what de Beauvoir calls her four-volume work (*Memoirs of a Dutiful Daughter*, *The Prime of Life*, *Force of Circumstance*, and *All Said and Done*); Sarraute's *Childhood* makes no effort to provide the total, synthesized image of herself or her life that traditional autobiography requires; Duras's *Lover* grows out of her fiction as much as from her biographical data; Wittig's *Across the Acheron* and Condé's *Heremakhonon* are first-person novels that do not explicitly identify narrator with author. In each instance (particularly in the latter four), the formal genre is twisted and contorted as the texts play out their linguistic experiments, precariously balancing upon the mobile line between reference and text, author and subject (narrating or narrated). In Wittig's and Condé's works, autobiography most clearly metamorphoses into an exploration of collective possibilities for identity rather than remaining an individual enterprise.

Instead of ensuring a snug fit between a formal definition of autobiography and the works considered here, I provide autobiographical readings that allow for the crisscrossing of fiction and factual account within a general domain of personal writing. It is certainly true that one could argue, in the instance of a work like Sarraute's *Childhood*, that because it is composed of loosely connected fragments, it corresponds less to "autobiography" and more to Michel Beaujour's conception of the *self-portrait*, which "distinguishes itself from autobiography by the *absence* of a continuous narrative," and organizes itself around a thematic or logical principle.[13] But rather than debating what category such a work as Sarraute's belongs to, I have chosen to consider how the texts in question connect their own strategies to a general tradition of autobiography (which could include problems relating to the rhetoric of self-portraits). In this way, I hope to bring into play formal concerns without confining myself—or the texts—to a definitional standard.

Because these writers span overlapping literary generations and in many instances have written or spoken of one another's work, I sketch out, at the beginnings of chapters, some of the literary/historical connections and controversies that link and separate them. Rather than studying the autobiographical texts in isolation, I have tried to give the reader some sense of the multiple contexts with which they interact, including the writers' other works, their definitions of literature in relation to feminism and political action, as well as their ties to one another. De Beauvoir's name, as the founding figure of French feminism, or the proponent of existentialist, socioliterary commitment, turns up in the writings or interviews of all the others. Both de Beauvoir and Sarraute have commented on each other's work, often in ways that mark critical differences between how they conceive of literature in relation to society. These differences—confirmed by their respective associations with existentialism and the French New Novel—create very distinct contours for the female autobiographical "I." Sarraute's and Duras's conflicting positions on the specificity of a feminine writing (with Duras tending to favor it and Sarraute steadfastly refusing it) have often set them in opposition. Nevertheless, both have been associated with the creative experimentation of the New Novel from the fifties onward; they have been supportive of each others' literary achievements; and, in important ways, they bear many literary goals in common that overshadow their differences on the inscription of gender in writing. Wittig, for her part, has written on de Beauvoir and Sarraute, and has acknowledged her literary debt to the latter. Wittig's writing, which dreams concurrently of lesbian utopias and literary universals, often seems marked by an unusual confluence of concerns common to de Beauvoir and Sarraute. Finally, Condé, the youngest of the five, occupies an oblique position with respect to the others. As a black writer, for whom being French is secondary to being Guadeloupean, Condé's concerns for the connections between (self) representation and literary form have not been filtered through the debates on existentialist commitment and New Novel experimentation, or through the various French feminisms and neofeminisms of the seventies and eighties. She has focused, rather, on the ways the colonized woman creates images of herself. She is not alone, however, in problematizing the "fact" of being French and a woman: the autobiographical texts of de Beauvoir, Sarraute, Duras, and Wittig all raise this issue more or less explicitly. Condé's work recasts the subject of feminine autobiography through the issues of national origin and race, while also questioning feminism's role in the process.

*

The autobiographical readings in the five chapters presented here may be mapped out as follows: in the first, Simone de Beauvoir's adherence to a classical form of autobiography is shown to coincide with an anxious move to prove the logical necessity and ordering of her life. Through the study of the ironic narrator in de Beauvoir's memoirs, we will examine the moments when this order or integrity breaks down, when the trace of a "feminine" process ruptures her ("masculine") autobiographical project. Her ambivalence toward the bourgeoisie will be read not only as a class issue but as a displacement of gender questions.

After concentrating on formal textual properties in de Beauvoir's autobiography, I turn to the examination of a certain psychic content in my reading of Nathalie Sarraute's recent work, *Childhood*. The different approaches allow me to work through each writer's specific resistances and tactics in positing an autobiographical subject. Concerning *Childhood*, I argue that the author's problematic identifications with her parents provide a psychical structure that recurs as a feature of all her writing. Although she refuses any notion of "feminine writing," Sarraute's complex ties to her mother are transposed in her work as the return of a repressed feminine.

In chapter 3, I consider Marguerite Duras's rewriting of her early novel, *The Sea Wall*, in the recent autobiographical text, *The Lover*, as it transforms the earlier heroine into an active player in her sexual initiation. In the recounting of the event in the *The Lover*, Duras gives voice to a female subject through the willful assumption of the role of (sexual) object. She underlines traditional gender roles, traditional generic functions, while standing them on their heads. My essay traces how Duras affirms *and* criticizes the personal tones of scandalous confession and romantic love. Playing upon autobiography's contradictory functions (as it refers to life *and* literature), Duras performs the genre as the double affirmation of both the individual woman's particular story, and the anonymous tale of desire's circulation in writing.

Monique Wittig's recent novel, *Across the Acheron*, playfully courts autobiography by focusing on a character named "Wittig" in this tragicomic, modern variation of Dante's travels from hell to heaven. My reading of "Wittig"'s utopian quest explores the ways in which *Across the Acheron* is not only an intertextual, feminist reworking of a (male) literary tradition, but also a personal fable recounting the difficult rapports between the lesbian separatist and heterosexual women.

Maryse Condé's autobiographical novel, *Heremakhonon*, draws the reader into an anxious although whimsical identity quest, stressing the multicultural mediations that shape the heroine's (lack of a) sense of self. My analysis focuses on the way Condé makes the personal voice emblematic of the collective dilemma of Antillean identity, and on Condé's own ambivalence toward her heroine which repeats the heroine's oscillating opinions of herself. Again, autobiographical fiction enables the intertwining of problematic personal and collective identities.

In all the works studied, I have paid particular attention to the contradictions and tensions that autobiographical writing poses to these modern women writers in its double appeals to creation and representation, to textual performance and self-affirmation. I am not proposing these texts—or my critical readings of them—as idealized "solutions" to the issue of gendered identity in autobiography, for I do not think that one ever "solves" such questions. At the margins of *écriture féminine*'s theories, de Beauvoir, Sarraute, Duras, Wittig, and Condé have not taken the "collapse" of subject and author into textual production to signify the triumph of the feminine in discourse. I do believe, however, that their strategies in working through/against the genre of autobiography do provide us with new possibilities for imagining the genre and modern women's relationship to it, as well as to writing in general.

*

Because I wished to make the French writers I am considering accessible to those who do not read French, I have referred to published translations of the autobiographical texts. Whenever possible, however, I have also tried to point out ways specific properties of the French language (gender markings, idiomatic expressions, clichés . . .) play a part in the writers' autobiographical strategies or resistances. When I cite French sources that have not appeared in published translations, I give my own translation and then cite the original French in a note. Because ellipses are often an important, integral feature of the texts considered (especially Sarraute's), I differentiate my own ellipses in direct quotations from the authors' by placing mine in brackets.

Literary Contingencies and Necessities: Simone de Beauvoir's Memoirs

"The writer of originality [. . .]
is always shocking, scandalous;
novelty disturbs and repels."

Simone de Beauvoir, *The Second Sex*

The literary works of Simone de Beauvoir often encourage the illusion of pure referentiality even as they position themselves within a conservative literary tradition of characters, plots, and finite stories. Her autobiography proceeds along this path, making the double claim of being literature and factual document.[1] It has understandably triggered strong reactions, because the slippage between author, narrator, and character is a tempting (con)fusion that has beckoned the reader to forget fundamental differences among them and to enter into a polemic with the author via her text. De Beauvoir in fact often welcomed the confusion for it engaged her in a dialogue (sometimes combative, sometimes empathic) with her readers.

Geneviève Idt's insightful account of critics' responses to *Adieux: A Farewell to Sartre*, de Beauvoir's narrative of Sartre's death, is exemplary of the effects of all her autobiographical writings: "[*Adieux: A Farewell to Sartre*] is discordant because of its ambiguous status, the ambivalence of its motivations, the insignificance of its writing. [. . .] almost all the critics express discomfort and uncertainty about the meaning and value of a work that is both ordinary and surprising."[2] *Adieux* is a first-person narrative in which de Beauvoir, as personal witness to the death of her companion, tells it "all," that is to say, too much for her readers' taste. Her mixing of genres, from the public tribute to a famous man, to the detailed descriptions of his body in decline, confound the readers' expectations, their sense of decorum. The transgression of the boundaries between ceremonial testimony and intimate revelation leaves the work hovering in no-man's-land. It is ironic that de Beauvoir, who relied so heavily on intention and on straightforward clarity to justify the value of her work (and herself), is precisely the one whose intentions are so problematic and resist communication. The wavering position of autobiography with respect to literature and life invites just such uncertainties and surprises in meaning, motivation, and value.

As an "impossible genre" for which rules or laws tend to arise as they are broken, autobiography is "impure" because it is neither entirely literature nor factual document. De Beauvoir's autobiographical texts are illustrative of this tension in the way they move in and out of "literature" and "experience," continually transgressing the neat boundaries between genres, and confusing the distinctions between remembering and creating. Her autobiographical corpus disconcerts, delights, or disappoints because it doesn't meet expectations, whether one's attitudes toward the author are positive or negative. These expectations draw upon conceptions of literature, what it ought to be and do, as well as on the way one reads a *woman* autobiographer. Just as value alternately resides in autobiography's literary or factual attributes for de Beauvoir, her role as a *female* autobiographer is by turns a position to which she lays claim, and one that frustrates her attempt to proclaim an ungendered (individual) success in writing.

At issue, then, in the study of de Beauvoir's autobiography are the kinds of readings performed on a body of texts whose status is doubly in question: first, because autobiography is a marginal literary genre; second, because its gender markings differentiate it from the general (although potentially chimerical) category of autobiography. With the growing interest over the past decade in the way women's writings are read as *women's* writings, a curious effect has occasionally arisen: books written by the "opposite" sex have become off limits. Several of the critical works on de Beauvoir published since 1979 have mentioned or quoted Konrad Bieber's evaluation of the male critic's right to interpret de Beauvoir:

The handicap for any man writing about a woman writer is very real. [. . .] Whatever qualms the male critic might have, Simone de Beauvoir puts his mind at rest: she speaks and writes in such a way that one might forget about the sex of the novelist or the essayist were it not for the constant concern she voices for the cause of women.[3]

De Beauvoir writes like a man (equated by Bieber with standard narrative conventions) who delves into thematic considerations about the place of women. Bieber's discomfort and his ensuing eradication of de Beauvoir's femininity via her own texts are indicative of both the general difficulties involved in talking about women's writing and the specific problems in reading de Beauvoir's work. In her writing, de Beauvoir does strive toward a "neutral, transparent" no-nonsense style that acknowledges its indebtedness to a male discourse of logic and reason, because de Beauvoir can envision no other legitimate form of expression; there is no "feminine writing" as such.

Bieber's appropriation of de Beauvoir in terms of her traditional understanding of language's operations contrasts with her appropriation by a generation of feminists (many of them from the U.S. and Great Britain) who responded to her autobiography in terms of experiential identification. Judith Okely writes: "Hers [de Beauvoir's] was a female voice. Too often, women readers, faced with a male writer and his heroines, have had to suppress their own difference of gender and imagine themselves as male in relation to the text. But that identification can never be authentic."[4] It is no wonder that Bieber should hesitate to write on de Beauvoir; both he and Okely see gender as that which potentially closes off the text to the "opposite" sex, makes it unreadable.

For contemporary critics interested in the way writing ("écriture") plays havoc with identity, puts into question the subject of/in language and disrupts oppositional thought, de Beauvoir's work is perhaps too readable, that is, naive. To begin with, it does not respond to the contemporary imperative to break away from Cartesian thought. De Beauvoir assumes with conviction the existence of the coherent ego that attributes meaning and occupies an unassailable position over language. For this powerful subject, unconscious desire has no place. Her work is far from the generalized possibility of thinking of all writing as a "feminine operation," which Alice Jardine has defined as "that which disturbs the Subject, the Dialectic, and Truth."[5] One may well give de Beauvoir due credit for having persistently put on trial the belief in a feminine nature (or woman *as* nature.) This critique, in itself, is a powerful contribution to the study of gender. But ultimately, because she never acknowledges the correlation between certain classical conventions of writing and a humanist, universal ("male") tradition of thought, she is often relegated to the back shelves of literary and philosophical history. And yet, Jardine's "feminine operation" bears a resemblance to the way de Beauvoir once described literature: "Literature is born when something in life goes adrift. In order to write [. . .] the first essential condition is that reality can no longer be *taken for granted*" [PL, 290]. How can this unhinging of reality function in a work such as de Beauvoir's autobiography which flouts linguistic experimentation and retains its faith in representing the real? In what ways does literature interfere with her autobiography in the way the "feminine operation" confounds the full subject and its truth? What happens to the male/ female dichotomy that has celebrated (criticized) her as a "masculine" or "feminine" writer?

My reading of her autobiography does not attempt to turn de Beauvoir into a proponent of radical writing. Rather, I wish to consider, within the shifting contexts of autobiography, how the genre's "improprieties" open up involuntary gaps in de Beauvoir's text, so that both the woman and the tradition are put into question. On one level, de Beauvoir's autobiography fits comfortably into the genre's literary tradition. But on another level, both her theories of literature and her break with certain generic requisites cause an internal collapse of the established genre. At stake is the process by which de Beauvoir's traditional ("masculine") conception of writing as power, the affirmation of truth, logic, and value in representation, is displaced or destabilized by her own ambivalence to literature and by the gaps in her autobiography's causal structure. Concurrently, I am arguing that the unsettled and unsettling point of view in her memoirs reveals how the rifts in authorial intention, in origins, and in the coherent subject of the life story undermine the active, intentional effort to explain that life. The vulnerability of the text, the way its intentions are misread and its subject divided, create the space where the contingent, to use the existentialist term, becomes the sign of the ironic, literary, feminine workings of a text that weaves and unravels its own necessary constructions. Feminine is to be read here as the trace of a problematic interference in the text, as de Beauvoir's scandalous undoing of her own masculine vision.

NON-LITERARY LITERATURE?

De Beauvoir's autobiography provides an expansive, fascinating account of the intelligentsia of her time, including its ideas, its lifestyles, its celebrities . . . . More often than not, her work has been read as a way of understanding the history of existentialism from the forties and fifties in its relationship to politics, philosophy, feminism, and society. But few critics have questioned how the prized values of facts and truth interact with de Beauvoir's definitions of literature and autobiography. What is most problematic—and interesting—about the way de Beauvoir positions her autobiography with respect to notions of literature, truth, and women's writing, is that her varied pronouncements are always calling one another into question. At times, she resides comfortably within a tradition of autobiography as a faithful portrayal of lived experience, with the author in full control of the textual representation. But at other times, she envisions autobiographical writing as a creative fiction whose "truth" eludes preconceived designs of the author. Through a careful selection of quotations from her massive autobiography and numerous interviews, it is always possible to provide a coherent view of de Beauvoir's "place" in the literary history and theory of autobiography, but not without sacrificing the seesaw movement of her texts. Before discussing the narrative tensions that this movement puts into play in her memoirs, it may be useful to examine some of de Beauvoir's shifting attitudes concerning the relationships between women's writing, literature, and autobiography.

De Beauvoir defines as her formal autobiography four volumes—*Memoirs of a Dutiful Daughter*, *The Prime of Life*, *Force of Circumstance*, and *All Said and Done*—although she and others have often pointed out that all her work is more or less autobiographical.[6] Her novels rely heavily on autobiographical material, providing at times more information than her autobiography about certain events of her life. In addition, her theoretical essays, travel books, and the accounts of her mother's and Sartre's deaths all bear the mark of personal concerns.[7] It could be said that *The Second Sex* is an attempt at a generalized autobiography of women, with de Beauvoir supplying the voice of her own particular preoccupations. The genesis of *The Second Sex* is in fact described in *Force of Circumstance* as a temporary substitution for her initial project, the writing of her life: "[. . .] I abandoned my project for a personal confession in order to give all my attention to finding out about the condition of woman in its broadest terms" [FC, 94–95].

At the margins (in prefaces, introductions, epilogues, interviews . . .) and inside her autobiography, de Beauvoir unveils the profound heterogeneity of the genre as it strives to capture/create a life through time. The multiplicity of de Beauvoir's autobiography lies in its vast array of tones (lyrical, matter-of-fact, impassioned, sarcastic . . .) and in its appropriation of other genres (diaries, journals, speeches, letters from and to her, newspaper accounts, criticisms and summaries of her own works and others', descriptions of films, travelogs, and dreams). Although such diversity stresses the genre's hybrid quality—its impurity— and its reliance on other texts in its construction, it also bears witness to de Beauvoir's concern for the relationship between the "individual" and her milieu and on the factual character of autobiography, as an authenticated document. De Beauvoir's emphasis on the interconnectedness of the individual and society is signaled by a generic blurring: the terms "memoirs" and "autobiography" are interchangeable for her because her personal history and her role as historical subject become inseparable.

The mobile borderlines between de Beauvoir's fiction and nonfiction, between internal and external concerns, are not particularly surprising and can be traced in nearly any writer's work, but they do have the potential to contest the specificity of the autobiographical genre. For women writers, this unlimited interaction between "outsides" and "insides" tends to carry with it the danger of being accused of solipsism or narcissism. "The woman writer will still be speaking of herself even when she is speaking about general topics," says de Beauvoir, as if to confirm the sex-linked bias.[8] The same could, of course, be said of male writers.

But because the public/private dichotomy in Western society tends to create fundamental distinctions between men's and women's lives—the public and private spheres being more clearly defined and separate for men than for women—the odds of being read this way are greater for women. Near the end of *The Second Sex*, de Beauvoir traces the risks for the female autobiographer, but from the point of view of a (male) judge or critic, rather than as a woman writer herself:

They [women] always regard themselves as given; they believe that their merits derive from an immanent grace and do not imagine that worth can be acquired by conquest. In order to seduce, they know only the method of showing themselves [. . .] instead of elaborating their work with reflective effort, they rely on spontaneity [ss, 784–85].

A little later, she adds:

Few books are more thrilling than certain confessions, but they must be honest, and the author must have something to confess. Woman's narcissism impoverishes her instead of enriching her; by dint of doing nothing but contemplate herself, she annihilates herself [. . .] there are sincere and engaging feminine autobiographies; but none can compare with Rousseau's *Confessions* and Stendhal's *Souvenirs d'égotisme*. [. . .] We [women] are still too preoccupied with clearly seeing the facts to try to penetrate the shadows beyond that illuminated circle. [. . .] Where they [women] sometimes excel is in the observation of facts, what is given. They make remarkable reporters [. . .] [ss, 786–90].

Writing, and autobiography in particular, are described here as forms of textual seduction, *conquests* requiring hard work on the text—and on the reader. The paradox of the female autobiographer lies in the conflict between author's and reader's desires: it would appear that a woman cannot love herself if others are to love her in the textual realm. But contrary to what one might expect from de Beauvoir, this does not mean that a successful feminine autobiography is simply a matter of women "imitat[ing] male rigor and vigor" [ss, 788]. By using "masculine techniques," the woman writer is "forced to repudiate whatever she has in her that is 'different'" [ss, 788]. Such borrowings of style and reasoning falsify the feminine autobiography just as much as a passive narcissism. Her "difference," however, is precisely what is inexpressible, unnameable: "Not that these independent women lack originality in behavior or feelings; on the contrary, some are so singular that they should be locked up [!!] [. . .] if they undertake to write, they feel overwhelmed by the universe of culture, because it is a universe of men, and so they can only stammer" [s s, 787]. De Beauvoir's evaluations of female writers' difficulties are later echoed in her accounts of critics' responses to her own autobiography: she is accused of being mad, eccentric, of trying to be a man . . . . "In France," she says, "if you are a writer, to be a woman is simply to provide a stick to be beaten with" [fc, 645].

Caught in a web of alienating and/or alienated voices (passive, masculine, and mad), women writers seem bereft of a choice that would allow them a measure of literary or personal success without some kind of fundamental sacrifice. In de Beauvoir's own construction of auto-bio-graphy, the life ("bio") between the self ("auto") and writing ("graphy") is the central figure to which the other two must pay homage. Wary of the narcissistic potential of women's writing in general, not to mention the even greater dangers of autobiography, de Beauvoir tends to turn away from the problematic construction of the *self* in *writing* and banks instead on an intentional project that focuses on the *life* and is legitimated through the "observation of facts." The "history [story] of one's personality," which Philippe Lejeune deems the focal point of autobiography, tends to be played down in de Beauvoir.[9] The price of her "right to speak" on her own behalf is alienation. But she does not view this alienation as a sacrifice: she willingly becomes her own biographer, writing about another, a public figure whose private history will be a function of the public image of success. The account of personal struggles, defeats, and victories will make the public image intelligible. By virtue of the inevitable disjunction between narrating voice and narrated object, autobiography is, no doubt, always already an alienated structure, supporting a self split in two. In de Beauvoir's thought, this structure is confirmed by the problematic nature of truth for women. In *The Second Sex*, she provides a compelling account of woman's relationship to truth and identity:

Woman does not entertain the positive belief that the truth is something *other* than men claim; she recognizes, rather, that there is *not* any fixed truth. It is not only the changing nature of life that makes her suspicious of the principle of constant identity, nor is it the magic phenomena with which she is surrounded that destroy the notion of causality. It is at the heart of the masculine world itself, it is in herself as belonging to this world that she comes upon the ambiguity of all principle, of all value, of everything that exists [ss, 681].

Elaborating on this denial of constants, one could say that the "difference" in de Beauvoir's writing emerges as a silent battle between an affirmation of success in the "masculine world," where she asserts her independence, and a continual portrayal of her freedom from that world's presuppositions and foundations as illusory. In the foregoing quotation, de Beauvoir unwittingly traces the tensions in her own autobiography. By assuming the authoritative, authorial voice of truth, she inscribes her work in a masculine tradition in which her gender is not an issue, because the implicit goal is a "neutral" truth, independent of her sex: "my feminine status [*ma féminité*] has been for me neither an embarrassment nor an alibi. In any case, it is a condition of my life, not an explanation of it" [PL, 292]. It is not obvious here whether the "feminine status" refers to *sex* or *gender*. If it means the biological given of being female, the reader—and the writer—are still confronted with the issue of how cultural constructions of gender inflect the autobiographical text, disrupting the "neutral" truth. Lurking in the interstices of de Beauvoir's texts is the unresolved (and perhaps unresolvable) question of how the feminine subject chooses (creates) her gender, becomes a woman, within the framework of received social constructs that traverse all subjects. As Judith Butler has eloquently pointed out, "choosing one's gender" is "an impulsive yet mindful process of interpreting a cultural reality laden with sanctions, taboos and prescriptions [. . .] rather than a radical act of creation, gender is a tacit project to renew one's cultural history in one's own terms."[10] But to say that gender formation is an ongoing dynamic in de Beauvoir's autobiography, "a personal way of taking up and reinterpreting received social norms," is not to eliminate a certain battle between insides and outsides, or between an authoritative narration and its own undoing.[11] In de Beauvoir's case, these tensions are often enacted through her ambivalence toward the bourgeoisie and its values, rather than through a generalized conflict between masculine and feminine principles. What remains to be seen is the way certain conceptions of autobiography articulate the implicit relationship between gender and de Beauvoir's attacks on the bourgeoisie.

*

De Beauvoir's bouts with readers and critics who question the literary value of her autobiography also articulate her uncomfortable position regarding truth and facts. Although she never explicitly denies the literary quality of autobiography, she often seems uneasy about the connections between the two. In a 1982 interview with Deirdre Bair, she remarked that, of all her works, she was most fond of her memoirs, not because she necessarily thought them her best, but because they allowed her to go over the details of her life, particularly her past with Sartre. De Beauvoir legitimates her memoirs as autobiography by stressing their completeness rather than any literary quality:

I know that sometimes people compare my *Memoirs* with Colette's autobiographical writings, but it's not right to do so. Once in a while, she wrote about her memories, but they were very carefully chosen memories, very literary, very much arranged [. . .] There really isn't a work where she tried to recapture her entire existence as a whole. Whereas I really think mine can be called autobiography because my *Memoirs* are so total and complete, at least in the sense that they recount my entire life.[12]

Leaving aside the impossibility of telling all (elsewhere she recognizes this impossibility), one can note in this quotation that literature appears to be what gets in the way of a direct relationship between life and words. Although in both cases (de Beauvoir's and Colette's) the writer is portrayed as being in full control of her language, too much literary arranging places undue attention on the words. A little later in the interview she adds: "The autobiographer has to be like a policeman writing his report: accuracy is paramount."[13] In contrast to the novel, which de Beauvoir describes as a form of cheating and lying,[14] the laws of autobiography do not tolerate embellishment or trickery and they seem to respond to the feminine talent for observing facts, as stated in *The Second Sex*. One may also infer that the autobiographer's role as objective reporter presupposes that the "facts" (and hence the self) precede their linguistic formulation. The free play of language must give way to the author's control because she is responsible for delivering the truth.

In the introduction to *Force of Circumstance*, the third volume of her autobiography, de Beauvoir refuses to call her autobiography (or those of others) a "work of art," because the term serves too easily as a pretext for "elegance," thus it usurps the primary position of what one could call the main text, that is to say, the life "with its enthusiasms and disappointments, its convulsions [...]" [FC, vi]. The notion of the "work of art" is also unacceptable to de Beauvoir because it is "a collector's term, a consumer's term, not a creator's" [FC, vi]. De Beauvoir chastises the (bourgeois) reader who mistakes art for an object to be valued in and of itself, rather than a mirror of the self and the world. One is reminded of Sartre's distinction between poetry and prose in *What is Literature?*, for de Beauvoir seems to be marking an essential difference between the self-referential work of art (Literature with a lofty capital "L," or poetry for Sartre) whose primary goal would be an esthetic play of words, in contrast to a literature of representation that creates a view of the world. Clearly, autobiography belongs to the second category for de Beauvoir.

In the last volume, *All Said and Done*, she complains about the critics' evaluation of *Force of Circumstance*:

Some critics alleged that in writing the book I had abandoned all aesthetic considerations and that I had chosen to offer the public a raw, untreated document. That is completely untrue. It is not for me to determine the worth of my book on the literary plane; but I did not deliberately intend that it should not be on that plane. I did refuse to have the notion of 'a work of art' attached to my autobiography [...]. But why should the intention of bearing witness prohibit verbal discoveries? [ASD, 114].

The passage suggests that the literary markings of a work are envisioned in terms of an esthetic, but in autobiography, this becomes an incidental beauty ("verbal discoveries") at an almost unconscious level. Literature-as-style is not so much choice, intention, or goal as a fortuitous discovery. It is not, however, a gratuitous element external to the content, as in the case of the work of art's "elegance," but rather a sort of unavoidable second signature intrinsic to the work. De Beauvoir's distinction between her "verbal discoveries"—a (necessary) equivalence between thought and language—and superfluous beauty is also prompted by the need to disengage herself from typically "feminine" textual charms. In *The Second Sex*, the woman writer who beguiles with "a few well chosen graces, affectations, and preciosities" [787], is doomed to conformity. She transforms her textual/sexual self into an object of display to be admired, like the "work of art" on its pedestal, or the beautiful woman on hers. Technical "grace" is just as much a threat to de Beauvoir as is the "raw, untreated document." Significantly enough, both are typically "feminine" faults when read through the grid of *The Second Sex*.

Textual seduction in de Beauvoir's autobiography is a game of hide-and-seek (I am not where you judge me negatively or where you take away my authority). Her definitions of literature alternately provide ammunition for her critics and the strategic means to unsettle that critical judgment. In *All Said and Done*, de Beauvoir defends her autobiography as literature by maintaining that the self created in a written work is necessarily a fictive construction that can never correspond to the person in the flesh. In a 1966 interview with Francis Jeanson she maintains that "there is no truth anterior to the one that language expresses."[15] Clearly aware of the literary experimentation in the 1960s (in particular by the French New Novelists) that questions and reappraises the relationship between language and representation, de Beauvoir adeptly uses the new conceptions of writing to fend off critical attacks. But her remark *also* echoes her own famous dictum that "one is not born a woman," suggesting that one becomes a woman through writing. Her comment to Jeanson challenges any preexistant self or reality and is de Beauvoir's attempt to escape being pinned down by her text or her readers, that is, reduced to an image of herself. On the last page of her autobiography, however, she seems to revert back to a definition of autobiography that again underscores its representational function:

I haven't been a stylistic virtuoso. I have not, as did Virginia Woolf, Proust, Joyce, resurrected the shimmer of sensations or captured the outside world in words. But that was not my aim. I wanted to make myself exist for others by conveying, in the most direct manner, the flavor of my own life.[16]

De Beauvoir's project, as the "direct" writing of the personal life, curiously does not fall within the framework of great literature because it is not dealing with sensations and "the outside world." The suggestion that the outside world is not part of her endeavor is very curious. Coming from the autobiographer who devotes hundreds of pages to her place in the political and social events of her time, this new definition (that excludes her work, or at least places it in the margins of literature) cannot fail to surprise. And yet, in an odd way, the "flavor" of her textual life is well served by these paradoxical, if not contradictory, assertions. Neither a revelation of the self ("Building up a picture of myself: I am not interested by this pointless and in any case impossible undertaking" [ASD, 38]), nor an account of the outside world, her autobiography vacillates between the two. It is perhaps the very hybrid quality of her autobiography that brings to light the specificity of her literary act, one that confuses "high" and "low" literature, as well as the oppositions between private and public, significance and insignificance, masculine and feminine, control (mastery) and facility (weakness) . . . .

De Beauvoir both acknowledges and sidesteps her (inferior) "place" in the tradition of great literature by emphasizing that her intention makes the question of technical talent irrelevant in autobiography. Although it is not stated explicitly, one can also infer that it is the merits of the life recounted that confer value on the work rather than the reverse. Her right to speak is predicated upon the importance of her accomplishments. In the quotation above, literary virtuosity begins to look like the "feminine charms" that are outside the authentic autobiographical project. The reader is also reminded of de Beauvoir's remark about Colette. It is probably not by chance that in the 1982 interview, de Beauvoir chooses to distinguish herself from another *woman* writer because of the latter's selective arranging. Autobiography, for de Beauvoir, cannot be "merely" literature, but neither can it dispense with it. Literature is alternately defined as necessary (structure, order, personal signature, strategy creating meaning) and gratuitous (supplemental charm, virtuosity, elegance . . .). But how do these shifting evaluations of autobiography vis-à-vis truth and literature measure up to de Beauvoir's legitimating mainstay—

intention? One already senses that the latter, as the source or origin of autobiography, will prove incapable of stabilizing the positions of self and text, because intention—like truth—fails to remain identical to itself.

In the interplay between intentions and autobiography-as-literature, I have chosen to consider all four volumes of de Beauvoir's memoirs. I will, however give special attention to the first volume, *Memoirs of a Dutiful Daughter*, because it is the most formally arranged—thereby pressing the issue of its literary status in de Beauvoir's terms—and because the question of intention in this text proves so elusive. The French title, which refers to a "jeune fille *rangée*" (an obedient daughter, orderly, well-behaved, in her place), echoes the careful ordering of the narrative, as if to confirm the necessary equivalence between the two. But recalling de Beauvoir's definition of the origin of literature as the moment when reality ceases to be self-evident, a matter of course or natural necessity, one may well ask how this orderly girl in an orderly text measures up to a fractured reality as origin. What is the connection between autobiographical intention—a conscious, motivated source—and a figure of literature as rupture or loss of direction?

FRAMES AND CONTEXTS: THE MULTIPLE
ABSENT "ORIGINS" OF THE LIFE-TEXT

If autobiography is considered the work of the mature writer, then de Beauvoir's memoirs fit the image. She began to compose them when she was approaching the age of fifty and had already published the majority of her fictive works as well as many of her essays. When *Memoirs of a Dutiful Daughter* was published in French in 1958, Sartre and de Beauvoir had already reached the height of their fame as writers and as the leading proponents of existentialism in the intellectual circles of France and abroad. However, her decision to write about herself is never made clear at the outset: the narrator makes no effort to introduce the work with an explanation of its genesis. Simone is duly (dutifully) born into the text in the first sentence, following the injunctions of the tradition; the work, however, seems to surface out of the blue for its readers. The omission in the *Memoirs* is an interesting one for de Beauvoir, because at the time she was writing in the fifties, de Beauvoir was convinced that, according to Sartre's idea, the writer must *situate* his or her work. Within the *Memoirs*, she does delineate an ample social and historical context for the narrative of her youth, but the present of the narrator remains in the shadows.

Such a reference to the act of narrating and to the work's genesis is part of the ritual autobiographical pact which, according to Philippe Lejeune, is a structural component of autobiography. Lejeune's pact is a sort of contract or promise made by the author for the benefit of the reader: it attests to the authenticity and veracity of the work. The author pledges (implicitly or explicitly) to the reader that the author, the narrator, and the object narrated *refer* to the same person. This contract determines the mode of reading one would engage in. Its legal character recalls de Beauvoir's own metaphor of the policeman. As Paul de Man writes: "Writers *of* autobiographies as well as writers *on* autobiography are obsessed by the need to move from cognition to resolution and to action, from speculative to political and legal authority."[17] In this instance, however, de Beauvoir turns out to be the criminal who has broken the law. In *L'Autobiographie en France*, Lejeune mentions her *Memoirs of a Dutiful Daughter* as an exception to the rule (that nevertheless stands):

It is rare for autobiographies to confine themselves to a pure narrative and to abstain from any autobiographical discourse. For example, Simone de Beauvoir, in the *Memoirs of a Dutiful Daughter*, far from displaying the subjectivity linked to the autobiographical narrative, seems to tell things "the way they were": there is no autobiographical pact at the beginning of the book, and the *avowed* interventions of the narrator can be counted on one hand. It is up to the reader to decide if this feigned objectivity is inspired by discretion or by ruse. But in the following volumes, S. de Beauvoir returns to a more natural attitude: each volume is preceded by a pact in good and due form that develops the traditional autobiographical discourse.[18]

A peculiar confusion can be traced in Lejeune's analysis. The autobiographical pact is alternately a *literary, cultural* convention and a *natural* attitude. It is as if the genre could never quite choose a side in the perennial nature/culture controversy. Interestingly enough, Lejeune's criticism is articulated by the same structure as the sex/gender dichotomy. Sex and autobiographical pacts are "natural" phenomena, but gender and cultural codes are respectively grafted onto the former, in such a way as to cloud the differences between nature and culture, between truth and fiction. Without the pact, the *Memoirs* distress because they look too much like pure (nonreferential) literature, while they paradoxically appear to "tell things the way they were." Paul de Man compares this undecidable character of autobiography (of fact versus fiction) to the discomfort of being caught in a revolving door.[19] For Lejeune, autobiography should consciously point out its own uncertainty and subjectivity, while *also* stressing its veracity.

De Beauvoir makes up for the omission of the pact in the *Memoirs* by speaking about her project in subsequent volumes of the autobiography. There are indeed numerous pacts in the following volumes that provide multiple explanations for the *Memoirs*. And yet, there is already, in fact, a sort of preautobiographical pact in the *Memoirs* that announces the desire and goals of autobiography, although it remains equivocal because it is recounted from the child's point of view. The model of a life story is found in the young Simone's adolescent readings: identifying with Maggie Tulliver, the heroine of George Eliot's *The Mill on the Floss*, the child unites reader, heroine, and author in a fantasy of self-recognition, uniqueness, and superiority. What is significant about this prepact is the way gender identification is not at issue:

The others condemned her [Maggie] because she was superior to them; I resembled her, and henceforward I saw my isolation not as a proof of infamy but as a sign of my uniqueness. [. . .] Through the heroine, I identified myself with the author: one day another adolescent girl, another me, would bathe with her tears a novel in which I would tell my own story [*Mem*, 142].

Although it is not stressed as such, Simone's identification is primarily feminine, moving from girl character to woman writer and to a future female reader. But George Eliot's male pseudonym tends, in fact, to undercut a specifically feminine identification. Beneath the unassuming exterior lies the unrecognized value of the individual: because the girl feels exceptional, her belonging to the female sex is irrelevant. Without a brother, says the narrator, there was no point of comparison [*Mem*, 55]. The character's gender is not denied—de Beauvoir says that as a child she willingly assumed feminine identifications, accommodating her feminine roles to suit her own desires. Nevertheless, gender is not portrayed as a decisive factor in the way her life evolves: "Being a child filled me with passionate resentment; my feminine gender, never" [*Mem*, 56]. The deproblematization of gender in the *Memoirs* is, to a great extent, a function of the distance between the adult narrator and the child character: because the adult rarely intervenes with an explicit commentary in the present, the reader is never sure if the narrator reads the importance of gender differently from her character. It is also not clear to what extent the child's preautobiographical pact, itself rooted in another's romanced story, is a "*mise en abyme*" of the narrator's project. Is the narrator mocking the child's wish to prove her uniqueness or enacting it through writing?

The distance between the narrator of the *Memoirs* and the story narrated has been amply pointed out by many of de Beauvoir's critics who have convincingly argued that its rigorous composition adheres to novelistic convention. The self-effacing narrative "I" often resembles an omniscient third person narrator overseeing the scenario. (This is what bothered Lejeune.) In addition, the narrative is chronological; its characters are presented, situated, and their stories and personalities are developed in relationship to the main character, Simone. There is even a dramatic double denouement at the end: Zaza, Simone's best friend, dies at the moment Simone has freed herself from the bourgeois milieu of her childhood and has established ties with Sartre. There seem to be no cracks in this "pure narrative," written by the eminently successful writer at the zenith of her career who meticulously maps out her story from beginning to end, punctuating it along the way with dialogues, letters, and diary entries. Is this art imitating life or the reverse? In *Force of Circumstance*, the childhood desire for autobiography and the adult's decision to write her *Memoirs* appear to go hand in hand:

I have always had the secret fantasy that my life was being recorded, down to the tiniest detail, on some giant tape recorder, and that the day would come when I would play back the whole of my past. [. . .] When I was fifteen I wanted people to read my biography and find it touching and strange; all my ambitions to become "a well-known author" were directed to this end. Since then I have often thought of writing it myself. I have long been a stranger to the exaltation this dream once aroused in me; but the desire to make it a reality has always remained in my heart . . . [FC, 371].

The adult narrator of the *Memoirs*, as portrayed in volume 3, *Force of Circumstance*, thus responds to the imperative of the child character to be recognized and loved through her writing. She has finally become the "well-known writer"—adult and child mirror each other's self-creation in a dream of fulfillment. The success of the writer in the 1950s would appear directly attributable to the child's choices, in a progressive movement toward freedom and self-affirmation.

The self-assurance of the narrator appears so overwhelming that the reader of the *Memoirs* easily becomes skeptical of the narrator's claim to know all. To a great extent, all autobiography makes more or less this same demand: to have the last word, in a position of power over the reader.[20] The readers' resistance to their submissive role is also reminiscent of Nathalie Sarraute's "age of suspicion," that is, our twentieth-century wariness of traditional literary forms that not only characterizes our reading of novels, but of autobiography as well. Even the reader who is interested only in the facts—which *are* engrossing—becomes suspicious of the narrator's ability to remember, with such an amazing degree of detail and authority, events having occurred more than forty years earlier. But put another way, the narrator's assurance provides a means to speculate on autobiography's contradictions.[21] The complacent relationship between narrator and character raises questions about the (dis)continuity between the two. Is this a success story of how I got to be the independent narrator who has the right to tell my story of success? Or is the distance between subject-narrator and object-child indicative of an effort by the former to disengage herself from the latter? De Beauvoir's narrator retains a fundamental ambivalence toward her character.[22]

As a story of continuity, the *Memoirs* offer significant, if implicit, parallels between narrator and narrated. What strikes the reader most, perhaps, is the assertive energy in the narrator's constructions as they overlap with the young Simone's engaging drive in her projects toward self-realization, autonomy, and independence. In both instances the reader is propelled forward; de Beauvoir is particularly gifted at developing suspense in her narrative, stressing that the "past" is a function of a future. The young character's desires and goals are oriented by a system of necessity and of justification, and the narrative adheres to the same system, emphasizing its own progression. In the last volume, *All Said and Done*, when looking back on the *Memoirs*, de Beauvoir confirms this coincidence between structure and content: "All through my childhood and my young days, my life had a distinct meaning: its goal and its motive was to reach the adult age. [. . .] That is why *Memoirs of a Dutiful Daughter* has a fiction-like unity lacking in the later volumes" [ASD, 14].

At almost every turn of the page, the *Memoirs* read like a female *Bildungsroman*. The reader witnesses a battle in which the young girl Simone attempts (and eventually succeeds) in disengaging herself from a system of constraints. In breaking away from her Catholic upbringing and the bourgeois milieu (including its nationalism, as well as her parent's rigid gender models), she seeks to assert the logical, reasoned necessity of her being and becoming in the world. Her early identifications with her parents and her love for them—intimate, physical affection with her mother and (later on) intellectual sharing with her father (a common gender division of filial attention in the bourgeois family)—are gradually overridden by her rejection of them as role models, both as individuals and as a model for relationships between the sexes.

Near the book's beginning we read of Simone's early frustrations in confronting the lack of an absolute in her world: "The arbitrary nature of orders and prohibitions against which I beat unavailing fists was to my mind proof of their inconsistency; yesterday I peeled a peach: then why shouldn't I peel a plum. [. . .] I seemed to be confronted everywhere by force, never by necessity" [*Mem*, 14]. Concerning her early readings, she declares that she was sensitive to necessary "constructions having a beginning, a development and an end [. . .]" [*Mem*, 52]. As for most children—and adults—there is fulfillment in this finite logic, and it corresponds to the structure of the book that the adult is composing. For awhile, God exists for Simone because she "felt [. . .] necessary [. . .] to His glory" [*Mem*, 74]. Later, as an adolescent, she remains faithful to the dictates of necessity: "I always carried my emotions, my ideas, my enterprises to the bitter end; I didn't take anything lightly; and now, as in my earliest childhood, I wanted everything in my life to be justified by a kind of absolute necessity" [*Mem*, 218]. Her studies and formal education in general respond to an ordering of the world: to learn, to know, is to transcend one's old self in a perpetual becoming, the progress of the self out of immanence.

De Beauvoir makes no attempt to provide an origin for this belief in and need for an absolute necessity. For the existentialist, the struggle to justify one's existence through the project and transcendence, to assume one's freedom, is the authentic path for affirmation of the individual subject. The lack of necessity, or origin, is merely the point of departure for the active creation of one's self, as an "essential and sovereign" consciousness [ss, xxxiv]. De Beauvoir thus *situates* her self-affirming struggle in the familial and school milieus without always providing an etiology. The absence of a certain causality is a characteristic trait of the *Memoirs* and one in which Elaine Marks aptly locates de Beauvoir's originality:

[. . .] within the apparently coherent universe of the *Memoirs* expected causal relations do not always operate. If a narrator traces the development of a protagonist from infancy to childhood and adolescence, we generally assume the presence of determining factors which provide a rational explanation of the protagonist's behavior and personality. [. . .] Simone de Beauvoir's originality is that within the traditional fictional framework she has placed a protagonist whose drama is the struggle of a human consciousness attempting to relate to events and to discover some point of coincidence with these events.[23]

In a curious twist, de Beauvoir's literary seduction of the reader relies on what had been in *The Second Sex* a characteristic inability of women writers to provide definitive causal relations, those "shadows" beyond the illuminated circle of facts. The textual gaps in the *Memoirs*, both in terms of the motivating origins of the character and those of the narrator, leave the text open to interpretation. On the other hand, the later volumes, by multiplying the contexts for the unresolved tensions in the first one, tend to provide an excessive number of origins and intentions. Too much, or not enough, explanation propels the reader into the labyrinth of superimposed texts, in search of the connections between the woman writer and her childhood. Who is this shadowy narrator of the *Memoirs*?

We read in *Force of Circumstance*, which relates the period when de Beauvoir is writing the *Memoirs* and *The Prime of Life*, that their narrator, now turned character, is living one of the most difficult times of her life. Although well known, she and Sartre find themselves in a small minority in France opposing the Algerian War and feel isolated from most of the French population. "Our convictions [. . .] cut us off from the rest of the nation and isolated us even among the rest of the Left" [FC, 341].[24] Ostracized and estranged in her own country in 1956, as a French woman de Beauvoir feels complicitous with the war, and particularly guilty for not fighting more actively against France's position toward Algeria. She does not speak at meetings or write articles on the issue because, she says, "I would only have been saying the same things as Sartre less well than he was saying them" [FC, 369]. For fear of becoming Sartre's shadow, a somewhat ridiculous female puppet, de Beauvoir thus finds herself deprived of any means to voice her protest against France's treatment of Algeria. In addition, she and Sartre oppose the violent actions of the Algerian FLN (the National Liberation Front), because they deem it possible to promote Algerian independence through legal, peaceful means. This distances them from the Algerian freedom fighters and from some of their close friends like Francis Jeanson who support the violence in the name of independence.

In *Force of Circumstance*, the break in the text between her remarks about the war and about her "attack" on the narrative of her childhood marks the rift between her involvement in the world crisis and the personal project she tells us she was about to undertake. The autobiographical enterprise assumes in this context a decidedly literary flavor when we recall de Beauvoir's statement that literature arises when reality falls apart. But in the case of the *Memoirs*, it is precisely what she can hardly bear to look at (the horrible present) that disappears under the veil of protective writing about the past.

Alienated in the present, unable to control the events around her, de Beauvoir takes refuge in the creation of a past over which she has supreme authority. Her voice will be her own, and neither her male companion nor the political events of the time can take it away from her. The command of the writer displaces the feelings of powerlessness in the world. The past is a (literary) creation: "I kept at this work of resurrection: of creation, for it made as many demands on my powers of imagination and reflection as it did on my memory" [FC, 372], and a faithful representation of a "past already fixed" [FC, 272], something that will not careen out of control. Rejected by the sociohistorical milieu, the autobiographer seeks to create a vision of herself for others to love. In the context of *Force of Circumstance*, the *Memoirs* are a flight into the imaginary, recalling the fascination and alienation that structures Lacan's mirror stage during the psychic formation of the child. The distance between the narrator and the child character is an ambivalent one, since the narrator still clings to a good number of the same values, such as necessity, control, and stability. Autobiography becomes the space where the narrator can continue to justify her own necessity and freedom in the act of writing, while temporarily avoiding the prickly problems in the present: her relationship to the Algerian War and the ability to voice her protest independently of Sartre. De Beauvoir's feelings of guilt ultimately problematize the nature of ironic distance in the *Memoirs*.[25]

AUTOBIOGRAPHY AS DEBT

The sociopolitical guilt inscribed in *Force of Circumstance* is an echo of the end of the *Memoirs* which affords another origin for the book. The last few pages trace a compelling account of the death of her best friend, Zaza (Elizabeth Mabille), who had been struggling in her own way to resolve the contradictions between self-affirmation and her attachment to family and milieu. Since Zaza's death (at age twenty) coincided with the period when Simone felt she had finally achieved her own independence, the narrator, in the last lines, collapses the events into one, and establishes a causal relationship between its two parts: "We had fought together against the revolting fate that had lain ahead of us, and for a long time I believed that I had paid for my own freedom with her death" [*Mem*, 362]. The "cost" of freedom is the death of her best friend. The debt repaid in the form of a written tribute resembles Montaigne's acknowledgment of his dead friend, La Boétie, as the absent origin of his *Essays*.[26] Unlike the Romantic origin of autobiography in which the author starts out as the "full" or whole subject waiting to be revealed (the fantasy instilled in Simone by her reading of Eliot), this origin of de Beauvoir's *Memoirs*, as in the historical framework we have noted, turns out to be rooted in loss, alienation, and guilt.

De Beauvoir's debt to Zaza is all the greater in that when they first met as children, Zaza was much more independent than Simone and constituted a model of unconventionality that destroyed the latter's belief in her own uniqueness and set her on the path toward a concerted revolt: before meeting Zaza, Simone affirmed "that I would be, that I was already, one in a million" [*Mem*, 90], but after their encounter, she realizes that Zaza "was endowed with a host of talents to which I could lay no claim" [*Mem*, 92]; and finally: "I was completely won over by Zaza's vivacity and independence of spirit" [*Mem*, 93]. This is Zaza's "gift" to Simone, the "dutiful daughter" of the title, just as La Boétie's library was his bequeathal to Montaigne. At its inception, Simone's desire for independence not only mirrors Zaza's, it is also actively fostered by her friend's actions and attitudes. As the narrative of the *Memoirs* progresses, however, the two girls gradually exchange roles in the sense that Simone becomes more openly rebellious whereas Zaza embodies "the dutiful daughter" caught in a series of contradicting desires: to be free while still adhering to the values of family, faith, and society. Although gender issues seem relatively unimportant in Simone's development, Zaza's situation forcefully embodies the problems of growing up female in the French middle class. By the end of the *Memoirs*, Simone has usurped Zaza's role as the independent spirit. And since Simone can never "repay" Zaza, her only recourse for restitution of the "gift" is to enshrine Zaza's image in words. The book's title suggests a fundamental confusion: is "the dutiful daughter" Zaza or Simone? Zaza's dilemma, in structural terms, seems in fact closer to that of the narrator during the Algerian crisis. Both are caught in a tug-of-war between opposing desires and values.

The displacement of a typically feminine dilemma—that of the dutiful daughter—from Simone to Zaza is crucial in the *Memoirs*. In the analysis of her 1954 novel, *The Mandarins* [FC, 262–72], de Beauvoir responds to critics who complain that her novelistic heroines are negative characters who do not display the strength and drive of her male protagonists. De Beauvoir acknowledges this, saying that woman is typically a divided creature. Similar to Zaza and the autobiographer of the late fifties, woman is described as torn because she is able neither "to accept her femininity, nor to transcend it" [FC, 266]. The narrator of the *Memoirs* exteriorizes the difficulty of becoming a woman through Zaza.

The effect of the *Memoirs'* ending is to raise questions about the relationship of contingency to necessity. What allows the leap, from a chance coincidence between Zaza's death and Simone's liberation, to an inevitable connection, is the indeterminacy of Zaza's death: "The doctors called it meningitis; no one was quite sure. Had it been a contagious disease, or an accident? Or had Zaza succumbed to exhaustion and anxiety?" [*Mem*, 362]. Thwarted in her desire to marry the young student Pradelle whom she loves, Zaza dies mysteriously, and de Beauvoir does not rule out the possibility that Zaza died of a broken heart. The broken heart theory tends, in fact, to equal if not outweigh the medical explanations, however debatable the theory might be. Simone could not be responsible for Zaza's death if it were a matter of a purely physiological illness, but if it is a question of an inability to contend with personal and social frustrations, there is room for doubt. The narrator transforms this doubt into the character's certainty in the last sentence (hence, the "debt"). Carrying the logic one step further, one might speculate that if Zaza's death remained indeterminate, useless, and unexplainable, it would seriously contaminate its correlate, that is to say, the logical necessity of Simone's self-styled liberation. It is as if Simone owed it to Zaza—and to herself—to prove that there was a reason for Zaza's demise, for nothing could be more horrible in a life constructed by necessity than to witness the gratuitous end of a loved one. As in a classical case of mourning, it is easier for Simone to take on the responsibility for the death than to deprive it of some psychological or social origin. But at the same time, the text's causal chain is too sketchy for the reader to readily accept the self-accusation in the last lines.

De Beauvoir's very first writings included many attempts to tell Zaza's story in fictional form: the budding writer is haunted by the death of her friend. But each time de Beauvoir and her friends had to acknowledge that she had failed to do it justice. Critics have concurred in this evaluation, preferring the autobiographical account to the fictionalized ones. One of the greatest advantages of the *Memoirs* version resides in the way the narrator relinquishes control of the interpretations surrounding Zaza's death. Entire letters from Zaza (spanning several pages) trace the character's desperation and courage, with very little commentary from the narrator. The causes of the death remain open to conjecture. Again, de Beauvoir's "talent," the strength of her account, lies, at least partly, in what was described in *The Second Sex* as a female writer's faulty sense of causality and in the narrator's willingness to relinquish absolute control of the account.

Although I have indicated that the genesis of de Beauvoir's autobiography stems from a sense of loss and alienation (both in the distant past and at the time of the writing), I hasten to add that the ambivalent connections between the narrator and the character Simone in the *Memoirs* seriously vitiate the very possibility of pinpointing origins, even when they are in the plural. In the last sentence, the narrator of the *Memoirs* distances herself from the culpability toward Zaza by the marking of a temporal limit: "for *a long time* I believed that I had paid for my own freedom with her death" (my emphasis), thereby implying that she no longer feels this way. There is, however, no explicit break with these feelings of guilt in the next volume, *The Prime of Life*. In the latter's preface, she states that the *Memoirs* were not written to advance a moral lesson, but rather "to discharge a debt" [PL, 10]. In the experience of reading the first two volumes, the remarks about the debt appear within a couple of pages of each other (at the very end of the first volume and at the beginning of the second), so that the debt mentioned in the preface would seem to coincide with the obligation at the end of the *Memoirs*. The "discharging of a debt" (*s'acquitter d'une dette*, literally, to acquit oneself of a debt) evokes both the juridical exoneration from guilt and the release or freeing of oneself. According to this schema, Simone the character has managed to gain her freedom, and de Beauvoir the narrator appears to have acquitted herself through the telling of her guilt. Both these meanings coalesce in the ending of the *Memoirs* and implicitly put in question the narrator's detachment from the text, particularly when one takes note of de Beauvoir's reasons in the preface of volume 2 for continuing her autobiography: "Beneath the final line of that book [the *Memoirs*] an invisible question mark was inscribed, and I could not get my mind off it. Freedom I had—but freedom to do what?" [PL, 9]. The preface states that freedom has been achieved; the narrator seems to be identifying with the character. But in effect the stress on freedom is just as much a *textual* mandate to continue the story left *in medias res*, since *The Prime of Life* relentlessly points out de Beauvoir's erroneous assumptions about freedom. "We were wrong about almost everything" [PL, 18], she says of herself and Sartre in the early pages of volume 2.

De Beauvoir writes in *Force of Circumstance* that the equation between the *Memoirs* and the repayment of a debt is not fully accomplished until after the first volume is published and read. As this time Zaza no longer haunts de Beauvoir's dreams: the debt *appears*, finally, to be written away and the past laid to rest— before the public: "since it has been published and read, the story of my childhood and youth has detached itself from me entirely" [FC, 463]. De Beauvoir's remark also implies that the narrator of the *Memoirs* had not yet thrown off that past or the debt at the time of the work's composition, so that the "long time" of its last sentence is not locatable in any chronology. The public's reading of the debt cannot occur simultaneously with its writing. De Beauvoir keeps trying to write away a debt that crops up again in the next work because it is literally nonrepayable. The comfortable distance that the "long time" seemed to create between narrator and character in the *Memoirs* ("for a long time I believed I had paid for my own freedom with her death") is again rendered problematic through the subsequent volumes.

It is not until *All Said and Done*, the last volume published much later (in 1972), that the reader comes to appreciate fully how the debt was eventually *displaced* from the personal to the social realm: "it was through Zaza that I discovered how odious the bourgeoisie really was. [. . .] For me, Zaza's murder by her environment, her milieu, was an overwhelming, unforgettable experience" [ASD, 10]. What had perhaps been a nagging fear of complicity with the bourgeois milieu—an internalized social value in Simone—is now externalized in the last volume. Zaza's death becomes the fault of the bourgeoisie and de Beauvoir's debt to her is transformed into a social responsibility to acknowledge and attack the bourgeoisie's power. Whether or not the narrator of the *Memoirs* had consciously effectuated this displacement at the time of the writing is uncertain. What does seem likely, however, is that the narrator felt it imperative to distance herself from the social milieu she was describing, just as the character is portrayed as disengaging herself from it.

Because Zaza's name is not mentioned in the preface to *The Prime of Life*, it is already possible in the second volume to infer that the discharging of the debt in the *Memoirs* could exceed the confines of that particular obligation. In *The Prime of Life*, Zaza's important role in de Beauvoir's life is assumed by Sartre, on whom de Beauvoir relies for her happiness. Given her upbringing in a bourgeois environment that de Beauvoir gradually repudiated, much of the *Memoirs'* energy is channeled into liquidating a debt to the bourgeoisie via a demonstration of the ways Simone freed herself from its prejudices and constraints. This liquidation remains incomplete for the narrator because she later acknowledges [PL, 27] that her reliance on Sartre fits into a chain—God, her father, Zaza, Sartre—thereby connecting her bourgeois childhood to her adult life.

Critics have pointed out (particularly in examples from de Beauvoir's early childhood in the *Memoirs*) that her positive, sometimes hyperbolic statements about her self-worth, independence, and superiority are in fact ironic. Robert Cottrell sees the use of irony as a strategy for attacking the bourgeoisie:

When Beauvoir describes herself as having been insufferably smug and complacent, as having reveled in her "glorious singularity," [the words are de Beauvoir's] she is not confessing. Her strategy is to damn the bourgeoisie by ridiculing the young bourgeois girl she once was. Irony informs nearly every page of *Memoirs d'une jeune fille rangée*.[27]

Cottrell aptly notes that the child's desire to dominate the world, and the concurrent fiction of a budding superiority, are an echo or repetition of the bourgeoisie's own self-importance. As narrator, the demystified adult pokes fun at the child's assumptions. De Man, in "The Rhetoric of Temporality," defines ironic language as one that "divides the subject into an empirical self immersed in the world, and a self that becomes like a sign in its attempt at differentiation and self-definition."[28] The fictions of and by the child Simone in her surroundings would thus be the reversed mirror image of the narrator, what the self is not.

Within the context of de Man's conception of irony, certain complications arise in Cottrell's interpretation of the *Memoirs*. De Man states that irony is *not* an intersubjective relationship "with all the implications of will to power [. . .] including the will to educate and to improve."[29] We already noted that de Beauvoir stated in the preface to *The Prime of Life* that she was not concerned with giving a moral lesson in the *Memoirs*. Whether one chooses to believe this statement is another issue. If the reader does accept it, irony becomes not so much a question of affecting others, of establishing a superiority over them, as the mark of an internal awareness of difference between a previously deluded self and one that understands the error and laughs at it. But Cottrell makes the relationship intersubjective by refusing the *confessional* quality of the text, thereby implying that the primary target of irony is not so much the child as bourgeois society. If the narrator is not confessing, then the internal relationship (between narrator and child) is lost. This may not be entirely wrong (indeed, I think that it is not), but its effects are most interesting. On one level, Cottrell's interpretation paradoxically makes the text *not* ironic and frees the child-character of guilt or responsibility because it is the milieu that forms her choices. She is only the means by which the critique of the bourgeoisie is effectuated, a sort of mediator for the narrator's attacks. The child's relationship to the world is inauthentic, deluded, whereas the narrator's, in Cottrell's schema, is one of power and wisdom. But if the narrator shows us not only the illusions of the dutiful daughter, but also of the daughter who extricates herself from the social web of obligations, then the irony (in Cottrell's sense) that "informs nearly every page" applies to the free will of the child to act "independently," and in the process contaminates the narrator's attack on the bourgeoisie.

When Cottrell conflates narrator and author (in the quotation above he refers to de Beauvoir rather than to the narrator), irony becomes a question of authorial intention and of an empirical being as opposed to a linguistic trope. Autobiography—especially when it is taken seriously as it is by de Beauvoir—invites us to make this switch from linguistic construction to a reality outside the text. But what meanings are being advanced in de Beauvoir's *Memoirs* if irony takes over both the indictment of the bourgeoisie *and* the struggle to get out of it? A provocative tension arises as the narrator both acknowledges and refutes her debt to the bourgeois milieu of her childhood and adolescence. De Beauvoir sacrifices the past images, criticizes them in the name of the present of narration (a future for the character), but at the same time the pleasure involved in erecting the statue of herself resists the critical obliteration. The ironic narrator, although wary of identification with the child's misconceptions, is still attached to the nostalgic image of successful self-creation, especially at a time in de Beauvoir's adult life (during the Algerian War) when she feels incapable of coming to terms with society's values. One senses that the adult narrator continues to be involved in the double movement of attachment to, and separation from, her past, that is characteristic of the way the child internalizes *her* milieu.[30]

De Beauvoir's attachment to the bourgeoisie is made all the clearer to her via her readers: in *Force of Circumstance* she bemoans the fact that her public is precisely the social group that she contests:

Since the publication of the *Memoirs of a Dutiful Daughter*, and even more so since that of *The Prime of Life*, my relationship to the public has become ambiguous because the horror my class inspires in me has been brought to white heat by the Algerian war. There is no hope of reaching the wider reading public if one's books are not the sort they like; one is only printed in a cheap edition if the normal first-run edition has sold well. So, willy-nilly, it is the middle classes one is writing for. [. . .] But I feel ill at ease if the middle class as a whole gives me a good reception. There were too many women who read the *Memoirs of a Dutiful Daughter* because they enjoyed the accuracy with which I had depicted a milieu they recognized, but without being at all interested in the effort I had made to escape it [FC, 649].

For de Beauvoir gender does not become a *personal* issue (rather than a theoretical one, or someone else's problem) until she faces her readers' reactions: she is particularly concerned with the way her *female* readers do not identify with the character Simone. One suspects that the intersubjective irony Cottrell delineates is in fact confirmed by an unavowed wish on de Beauvoir's part to help other young women (perhaps like Zaza) to escape from an environment that stifles women's potential. De Beauvoir's authorial intention has been misread by the female bourgeois readers who have not appreciated the emphasis on liberation or on the social critique and have identified with the wrong sections of the book. They have taken the work to be an authentic, straightforward representation of reality rather than a literary reworking of the life material: in *Force of Circumstance*, de Beauvoir scoffs at her female readers who exclaimed after reading the *Memoirs*: "There's not much to that. I could've done as much myself" [FC, 273].[31] The model of the female autobiographer's accomplishment (including the character's liberation, as well as the writer's unique literary act) is devalued if it can be easily copied by other women *without hard work* in the writing and the living. Carrying out her public endeavor in a male-centered value system, de Beauvoir asserts herself as an ungendered writer criticizing the bourgeoisie, but she knows that she cannot avoid being read as a *female* of that class. In such a framework, her work vacillates between a position of solidarity with other women (they read it as an example of how to break out of oppressive gender molds), and a position of competitiveness with them (their life-style and accomplishments are challenged).

De Beauvoir is caught in her own trap if she insists that her autobiography is not literature, for the ironic distance necessary to provide a social critique is too easily erased in a "faithful" reading where one believes what the "author" says instead of its (ironic) opposite. The bourgeois women have missed the point of the narrator's social commentary, perhaps because they have taken the adolescent rebellion as an integral component of the bourgeois childhood scenario and have thus been unable to see where the irony starts and stops. It is not a farfetched supposition, since we have already noted that de Beauvoir attacks her own self-deceptions regarding her freedom and independence in the volumes after the *Memoirs*.

The slippage between sincerity and irony is facilitated by another conflation that Cottrell points out:

[. . .] de Beauvoir covertly equates the metaphysically privileged state of childhood with the economically privileged state of the bourgeoisie. The two are not commensurate, and if they are artfully equated (an unacceptable procedure, I believe, because it blurs crucial distinctions), it is for ideological purposes.[32]

The "metaphysically privileged state of childhood" is explained by the child's belief in the necessity of the world as it is, as a natural phenomenon with preestablished meaning. De Beauvoir turns the misconceptions of childhood in general into a specific class question. One can note, as an example, how the narrator associates the bourgeois values concerning order, hierarchy, and property with the young girl's sense of self-worth, rigor, and justification. Both are anchored in an absolute sense of necessity. But the "artful equation" proves in fact to be too artful, because de Beauvoir's bourgeois readers seem to apprehend only the child's errors as they accept the class values as natural rather than arbitrary. The literary "deception" hides the author's "message." In this case, the artifice of literature is what prevents autobiography from communicating. But if autobiography is situated outside of literature (in a pure, faithful representation), the difference between the child's false necessities (her belief that the "world is regulated by unwritten laws that [. . .] seem natural and indisputable,"[33] the bourgeoisie's confirmation of its own superior values) and the adolescent's escape from those necessities in favor of her own, is also problematic. Both kinds of necessity—the child's and the adolescent's—flow together in a continuum. In the intersubjective relationship between reader and autobiographer, the literary trope (irony) risks disappearing as the work becomes naturalized and homogenized. The *Memoirs'* critical force becomes dependent upon the book's artistic configuration.

The irony of irony in the *Memoirs* resides in its impossible relationship to literature within the context of its female bourgeois readers. On the one hand, the narrator's ironic intervention seems to be recognizable (and critically effective) only if the work is considered literature, that is, as a careful arrangement involving critical strategies. On the other, the narrator's artful combining of childhood and bourgeois illusions—another literary strategy—works against itself precisely by making the two indistinguishable. In this instance, the bourgeois female readers do not read the work as a specific critique of their social class. Ironic distance is perceived by these readers as they identify with the superior position of the narrator over the child ("we used to be that way too, but are not so any longer") and then neglect the social commentary.

The narrator's control of the dual reading (faithful and ironic) concerning the individual's relationship to society proves to be just as illusory as the child's control of her environment. This is not to say that the person de Beauvoir did not manage to reject certain bourgeois beliefs and modes of behavior: she did come to disavow traditional marriage, God and religion, her class's ultranationalism, political conservatism, its emphasis on material possessions and status, as well as many of its prejudices against women. Nor is it a question of claiming that the text is entirely unreadable: de Beauvoir welcomed a limited public of young readers and intellectuals in the fifties and sixties who shared her dislike for the political and social precepts of the bourgeoisie and who identified with the narrator's superior position over her class (as well as the character's struggle against it). But this group's reading tends to immobilize the ambivalent irony in the text by assuming that the subject-narrator could be constituted over and above the text and the milieu. Such an interpretation is contingent upon *not* reading the following volumes that reopen the question of control and the escape from the milieu's values.

When irony is at work in the *Memoirs*, authenticity becomes precarious at the very least. True irony, says de Man, does not stop one from falling again into inauthenticity, because "to know inauthenticity is not the same as to be authentic."[34] The balancing act repeatedly performed on the line between the two produces what de Man calls "unrelieved *vertige*,"[35] a dizziness that in de Beauvoir's text blurs the firm border between child and adult. On a conscious level, de Beauvoir envisions freedom (and authenticity) as a state of being that is never fulfilled, a subject-project in process. But the difference between de Man's *vertige* and de Beauvoir's *conscious* project is significant: whereas de Man's irony plays upon the simultaneity or confusion of present and past, of subject and object in a dizzying spin, de Beauvoir's intentional project presupposes a faith in a linear, chronological progression and in the subject's control. But as I have suggested, irony as control inadvertently gives way in the *Memoirs* to an irony playing havoc with that control.

BROKEN PROMISES

Although the temporal limit of "the long time" at the end of the *Memoirs* was not locatable between it and the description of the work's composition in *Force of Circumstance*, the latter's controversial ending reopens the question of distance between the narrator and her text. The first critics, de Beauvoir tells us in *All Said and Done*, thought that her concluding statement in the third volume, "I was swindled," [FC, 658], referred to the disappointments of old age, but she reads it instead as a generalized indictment of a bourgeois ideal she had been trying to live:

["I was swindled"] was not the outcome of seeing my own reflection in the glass but of my very deep distress, my revolt at the horror of the world. When I compared this state of mind with my adolescent dreams, I saw how those dreams had led me astray. "We were promised nothing," says Alain. That is untrue. Bourgeois culture is a promise: it is the promise of a world that makes sense; a world whose good things may be enjoyed with clear conscience; a world that guarantees sure and certain values forming an essential part of our lives and giving them the magnificence of an Idea. [. . .] The discovery of mankind's unhappiness and the existential failure that cheated me of the absolute I had hoped for when I was young—those were the reasons that caused me to write the words "I have been swindled" [ASD, 117].

What seems crucial to me here is the way the autobiographer's disappointment is *not* a function of a difference *within* the self. Rather than stressing the way the social promise is lived and incorporated into the self-construction, as it is shown in the *Memoirs* and described in *The Second Sex* (see de Beauvoir's remarks about the masculine world inside woman), the preceding quotation externalizes both the promise of happiness and harmony and its destruction ("the horror of the world"). But was she ever "free" to choose or reject the promise? Again, it is unclear as to whether the child's and the bourgeoisie's desires could ever be distinct.

Although de Beauvoir admitted in her interview with Francis Jeanson in 1966 that the ending of *Force of Circumstance* was a "literary dramatization,"[36] that is, an overstatement or exaggeration of her disillusionment, its textual equivalents in *Force of Circumstance* and in the last volume, *All Said and Done*, are quite striking. The realization that the bourgeois promise is a deception parallels de Beauvoir's recognition that the chronological structure of the first three volumes fails to provide the synthetic, totalizing view of the life or self that the structure seemed to promise:

In the earlier books I followed a chronological sequence; and this has its drawbacks, as I know. The reader has the feeling that he is never being given anything but the non-essential, the side-issues—a series of forewords: the heart of the matter always seems to lie somewhere farther on. Page after page he hopes to reach it; but he hopes in vain, and at last the book ends without ever having come to a full close [ASD, Prologue].

Sheer chronology does not link past and present, and therefore does not supply an all-encompassing logic, replete with a dialectic of causes and effects, origins, determining factors . . . . *It cannot deliver what it promises.* Lejeune accuses de Beauvoir of hopeless naïveté and conformism for using a chronological framework (that assumes a past-in-itself) and then for complaining about its insufficiencies.[37] He also suggests that she should have confined herself to the diary format because she is incapable of organizing her material with an overriding, creative principle. Underlying this criticism is the notion that the diary is a form considered inferior to autobiography, because it does not master the material; it is supposedly more spontaneous, immediate, thereby suitable to the stereotypical feminine penchant for pouring out raw emotion. One thinks of Sartre's character in *Nausea*, Roquentin, who refers to diary-writing as a little girl's activity.[38] Thus, autobiography is restricted to the "literary master" and is inappropriate for a woman like de Beauvoir who, although belonging to the literary, intellectual (male) establishment of her time, doesn't have what it takes to dominate the genre. Such control supposes a unitary subject remaining identical to himself.

And yet, in a contorted or even perverse way, the traditional, chronological autobiography is precisely what "works" for de Beauvoir, not because she controls it, but because it reveals its own impossible underpinnings and responds to the structure of the broken promise. Given that chronology is *conventional* and *arbitrary*, it is particularly apt for portraying the breakdown in a *necessity* or *absolute* through the writing and the life. The form is "adequate" to what it describes. Although de Beauvoir is not intending such an outcome, and seems to ignore it by the end of her autobiography, the collapse of the chronological structure of the first three books successfully registers the broken promise. The "failed" structure enacts both her continuing belief that a totality can be revealed and its textual impossibility through time.

Significantly, this same structure of the unfulfilled promise marks de Beauvoir's conversion to feminism in the early seventies. At the end of *All Said and Done*, de Beauvoir explains that she had previously banked on the socialist class struggle to bring about the liberation of women. But with the realization that the utopian future of an egalitarian society is a promise that never seems to materialize, she turns to an active feminism that can work on women's problems in the present. Ideologically, of course, the bourgeoisie's broken promise and the unfulfilled socialist ideal are quite different, and de Beauvoir never eschews her belief in socialism. What they have in common, however, is that in each instance, de Beauvoir ultimately envisions herself outside the issues: she judges the bourgeoisie as an outsider; she participates in the women's movement in order to help *other* women accede to her own status. Again, it is as if her appurtenance to a class and to a sex were resolvable problems or not issues at all. In the case of her sex, this would mean that gender questions involving personal and collective identities, the interactions among women, among men, between the sexes could be established once and for all, rather than fluctuating in a continually changing dynamic. Some of the strength of her memoirs lies in the way they stage internal, shifting tensions involving class, gender, and autobiography, rather than objectifying them.

*

Having thus come to reject the notion of chronological progression at the end of *Force of Circumstance*, de Beauvoir tries to remedy the structural defect of the preceding volumes in the final one, *All Said and Done*. She chooses a thematic treatment of her material, still within the general confines of chronology, but with the hope that she will be able to provide an overview of her (textual) past as well as the factors that determined who she is. Thus she starts over, but from the point of view of the narrating present. She sets up the framework in a Proustian opening where she describes the moment of awakening, when one wonders who and why one is:

[. . .] if I go to sleep after lunch in the room where I work, sometimes I wake up with a feeling of childish amazement—why am I myself? What astonishes me, just as it astonishes a child when he becomes aware of his own identity, is the fact of finding myself here, and at this moment, deep in this life and not in any other. What stroke of chance has brought this about? [ASD,1].

De Beauvoir then proceeds to reread her autobiography, beginning once again with her birth, but this time with the explicit metanarrative that was absent in the *Memoirs*. In a sense, this new reading constitutes an attempt to resolve once and for all the inherent tensions in the first volume between external pressures and internal drives in the formation of character and life choices. But rather than working under the sign of individual necessity or conscious, free design ("I did it my way"), the narrator concentrates instead on the role of the social and familial demands, the contingencies of situation, that shape her course.

"Luck" is Simone's new star: the narrator deems herself fortunate to have been born into a bourgeois family that meets her physical and affective needs because of its relative wealth and its favorable attitudes toward children, education, culture, reading . . . . Because Simone is the eldest child with no brothers to make her feel inferior as a girl, and because she has a younger sister over whom she affectionately dominates, Simone is able to thrive on the attention given to her by her family. The divergences in her parents' moral beliefs (with her mother devoutly Catholic and her father a nonbeliever) push her to question organized religion and eventually God. Her chance meetings with Zaza and later with Sartre encourage her to break away from bourgeois conformism, in particular the traditional gender roles her parents fill. Even her parents' economic misfortune, when she is about eleven years old, turns into an asset because, as a girl with no dowry, she must learn a profession to support herself: formal education, already a delight for her, becomes, by chance, an external necessity.

The examples go on and on. But the causal chain I have been describing does not tell the whole story. What begins as chance or luck turns into a demonstration of the character's free will to choose within the context of historical and social circumstance. By chance she is born a girl and a bourgeoise; but being a girl is not much of an issue, she says, because she has no brother and is the oldest child. Being a member of the bourgeoisie gives her material advantages, but this in no way stops her from rebelling against it.[39] Without the financial difficulties of her family in 1919, the narrator feels confident she would have continued her studies anyway. She owes her break with religion to her ability to think: "[. . .] I had learnt to think, and faith had lost its pristine simplicity: it had become that dubious compromise which satisfies many people and which amounts to believing that one believes: I was too direct to put up with it" [ASD, 11].

Practically every example of a contingency is thus countered with an already established inclination on the part of the character, so that there is never a clear-cut origin or cause for each turn in de Beauvoir's life. Each time the narrator envisions another possible scenario, "what if I had had a brother, what if my family's financial situation had been better . . . ," she concludes either that she doesn't know the answer or that the change would have not made a great deal of difference in the long run. One of the more amusing instances of her flip-flop explanations concerns her choice of profession. On one page she states: "It took me a year to realize that I did not want to specialize in mathematics, nor letters, but in philosophy: I convinced Mademoiselle Lambert [her teacher] that my idea was sound, and through her my parents" [ASD, 12]. But a few pages earlier she had described it somewhat differently: "Mademoiselle Lambert encouraged me to read philosophy, and that determined my way of life. But I should certainly have taken that course in any event, for it was my fundamental vocation" [ASD, 9]. Who is making the decisions? Who is influencing and convincing whom? The narrator's aggressive insistence on her own active choices ("I was never inert" [ASD, 12]) is rendered suspect—and rather comical—by that very aggressivity. This is not to say that de Beauvoir does not scrupulously point out the typicality of her situation and her choices. In terms of age, for example, she suggests that her difficulties with her parents during her adolescence (when she was rebelling against them) were in part due to the nature of the "awkward age" [ASD, 16]. In the attempt to pinpoint origins de Beauvoir's autobiography continually bears witness to the fact that, like fiction, life is a messy affair that undoes tidy oppositions and limpid causalities.

As if to confirm (perhaps unwittingly) the impossibility of explaining causality or of providing an unequivocal meaning, in the subsequent sections of *All Said and Done* the narrator lists many of her themes without taking the trouble to interpret them. Dreams, for example, are recounted in detail without any particular interpretation. But the apparent nonsignificance *is* justified in the introduction to *Force of Circumstance*:

Not only do [these so-called trivial details] allow us to apprehend a period and a person in flesh and blood, but by their non-significance they are the very touch of truth in a true story. They indicate nothing other than themselves, and the only reason to include them is that they were there: that is enough [FC, vi].

Truth as triviality, insignificant detail, unassimilated fact—de Beauvoir dismantles her own efforts to provide an intelligible totality of her life by undermining causality, and by casting doubt on the narrator's conscious ability to point out what is significant and to render conclusions. The autobiographical project explodes its own premises, even as it continues to affirm them. By the end of her autobiography, de Beauvoir dispenses with the idea of concluding. She will have delivered the "whole" of her life, but without knowing its meaning.

*

Like the woman in *The Second Sex* at the "heart of the masculine world," the de Beauvoir of the memoirs incorporates into her work the values and goals of a tradition of autobiography dating back to Rousseau that is predominantly male and bourgeois (and, of course, white). But while de Beauvoir implicitly and explicitly attacks the French middle class—including many of the ways it discriminates against women—her fear of being marginalized as a *woman* autobiographer (interpreted in terms of a feminine nature) causes her to shy away from a construction of identity involving gender and from forms of writing that would overtly question the (autobiographical) subject's autonomy, the faithful representation, the notions of progress, free will . . . . These concepts are not confined to the bourgeoisie, although they are certainly a part of its value system. Because the feminine is the Other of the masculine for de Beauvoir, in a clear-cut *opposition* that devalues one side in favor of the other, femininity, as we have seen, is understandably played down, if not erased. But the differences within the woman successfully "assimilated" into a male-centered culture bring to light the disruptions in an autobiographical economy calling for truth, control, mastery, unswerving intention, causality . . . . De Beauvoir's autobiography, at times unwittingly, chips away at these absolutes from the inside. For ultimately, she knows that there aren't any absolutes and her autobiography ambivalently struggles with that recognition. Working within this framework, she always runs the risk of being accused of being a woman who can't play the game or understand the rules. And yet, the unresolved tensions in her autobiography, its paradoxes and irony, as well as its triviality and broken promises, can also be viewed as a powerful enactment of the way those rules prove their own inadequacy. If we agree with Lejeune that what is most interesting about autobiography as a genre is the way it challenges its own norms, then the "dutiful daughter" who keeps inadvertently breaking things is bound to seduce. In this context, de Beauvoir's "feminine operation," to use Jardine's term, consists in revealing the strength of her own impasse.

Family Scenarios: Transcriptions of Gender and Transgressions of Genre: Nathalie Sarraute's *Childhood*

2.

Before the war, an unknown woman had sent Sartre a copy of her little book *Tropisms*, which had gone unnoticed and whose quality struck us both; this was Nathalie Sarraute [. . .]. In '41 she had worked in a Resistance group with Alfred Péron; Sartre had seen her again recently, and I had made her acquaintance. That winter I went out with her a lot. She was the daughter of Russian Jews exiled by the czarist persecutions at the beginning of the century, and it was to these circumstances, I suppose, that she owed her restless subtlety. Her vision of the world spontaneously accorded with Sartre's own ideas: she was hostile to all essentialism, she did not believe in clearly defined characters or emotions, or, indeed, in any ready-made notions. In the book she was writing at the time, *Portrait of a Man Unknown*, she was determined to recapture, beneath its commonplaces, life's ambiguous truth. She was very reticent and talked mostly about literature, but with passion [de Beauvoir, FC, 19].

Nathalie Sarraute's name crops up several times in de Beauvoir's *Force of Circumstance*, first as a friend, as in the description above, and then, increasingly, as de Beauvoir's literary antagonist. In itself, the antagonism is not surprising, since Sarraute-the-New-Novelist represents for de Beauvoir the next literary generation that challenges many of her own assumptions about literature. As an existentialist, de Beauvoir concentrates on a sociopolitical content in traditional narrative forms, and shows a strong penchant for personal evocations that involve the author in her texts. Sarraute, on the other hand, directs her attention to New Novelistic forms, creating multifaceted realities that do not explicitly represent sociopolitical positions or personal revelations of the author.

In many ways, de Beauvoir's succinct portrait of their first encounters is quite accurate, and provides a good deal of interesting factual information about Sarraute in the forties. But it is also precisely the kind of "objective" description that Sarraute's own writing persistently puts in question. De Beauvoir deftly reduces Sarraute's identity to her (political) actions, social origins, personality, and ideas. She even establishes a highly dubious causal relationship between Sarraute's Russian Jewish background and her personality.[1] In short, Sarraute is a "character" viewed from the outside, as a set of appearances. For her own part, Sarraute has avoided this type of personal reminiscence about herself and others nearly as much as de Beauvoir has reveled in hers. Often curt with interviewers who try to ferret out details about her life, Sarraute has continually maintained that the data of her biography have little direct bearing on her creative work.[2]

It thus came as a surprise to many of her readers when, in 1983, Sarraute published *Childhood*, a series of childhood evocations that immediately became a tremendous success.[3] The switch in genres is less startling when one realizes that autobiography is not for Sarraute so much a faithful representation of her life or personality as another *literary* genre, involving selective arranging, a literary articulation of life material. Thus, turning to autobiography does not represent a fundamental change in Sarraute's attitudes about the relationship between life and literature. In contrast to de Beauvoir, for whom autobiography's status in literature remains problematic because the "real" life takes precedence over the writing, Sarraute emphasizes the continuity between her fiction and her autobiographical narrative. We will see later how crucial this continuity is for Sarraute when discussing her relationship to feminist issues. What *is* problematic for Sarraute is the question of gender: if literature is defined as a gender-free sphere, how can autobiography account for a subject's specificity?

Given the consistency of Sarraute's theoretical positions on literature, authorship, and women's writing throughout her career, I would like to take a detour back to her rocky friendship with de Beauvoir and her career as a novelist and essayist. The digression will pave the way for the discussion of *Childhood* by charting the author's literary stances, particularly in reference to feminist issues, and the various hurdles that autobiographical writing will present to her.

Although Sarraute has long been associated with the younger generation of New Novelists (Robbe-Grillet, Butor, Simon, Pinget, Ricardou . . .) rather than with the existentialists, her entry into the literary world predates the celebration of both groups and was actually first promoted by the existentialists. Six years de Beauvoir's senior, Sarraute published her first work, *Tropisms*, in 1939, three years before de Beauvoir's first published novel, *She Came to Stay*. As seen in the foregoing portrait, during Sarraute's early career in the forties, when she was still virtually unknown, she became friends with Sartre and de Beauvoir who actively encouraged her work.

In the late forties, Sarraute wrote three essays for the existentialist journal, *Les Temps Modernes*, two of which appeared later in *The Age of Suspicion*, her collection of theoretical essays on the novel.[4] Sarraute's existentialist connection is also confirmed by Sartre's complimentary preface to her first full-fledged novel, *Portrait of a Man Unknown*, first published in French in 1949. Calling the work an antinovel, Sartre credits Sarraute with the lucid undoing of the novelistic conventions that would make us believe that characters are irreplaceable, unique individuals. He also praises her effective portrayals of the swampy terrain of ill-defined feelings and sensations, what he calls the "indistinguishableness of the universal," that simmer beneath the reassuring, inauthentic façades of our commonplaces, clichés, and standardized marks of identity.[5] Her novels also bear certain affinities with some of Sartre's philosophical theories. His description in *Being and Nothingness* of the "look of the other,"[6] that is, a violent struggle between individuals to assert their identities over/ through one another, resembles the confrontations in Sarraute's novels between solid external identities created by others in the social contract, and the fluctuations, changes, and oscillations actually experienced by individuals as they engage in that social contract.

But if Sarraute and the existentialist group of *Les Temps Mo-dernes* believed that literature should apprehend "the truth about the world and about ourselves," there seems to have been a misunderstanding about how such a project should be carried out, and what the shape of that truth might be.[7] In a 1976 interview, Sarraute says that Sartre was wrong about her work. She refuses the designation antinovel, stressing that such a term assumes that there is only one kind of novel that merits the name. And although they importantly agree that solid personalities are created by the "look of the Other," from the outside, Sarraute does not consider, as Sartre does, the commonplaces of everyday life to be inauthentic modes of being that should be denounced:

Clichés, commonplaces, that's all there is in everyday life, why pounce upon them? One doesn't even need to be suspicious of them: if the weather's fine, the weather's fine. What is interesting is to know why I am going to say that to my neighbor, in what tone, etc.[8]

By the fifties, when Sarraute was beginning to receive some recognition, the gap between her views of literature and those of de Beauvoir and Sartre was ever widening. Sarraute's attention to the effects of language seemed less and less compatible with a committed literature that was concerned more with describing a (preextant) reality than with creating untold ones.

Sarraute's *Age of Suspicion* and de Beauvoir's *Force of Circumstance* provide a contrapuntal dialogue about the direction that literature should take in order to remain viable. And although both are ostensibly talking about the novel, as partisans of committed literature and the New Novel respectively, the arguments spill over to autobiographical issues as well.

In the last two essays of *The Age of Suspicion*, entitled "Conversation and Subconversation" and "What Birds See," Sarraute maps out her new literary credo in contrast to novelistic tradition. They are eloquent pieces of rhetorical strategy whose issues have remained surprisingly contemporary. Initially, Sarraute seems to side with those writers who, like de Beauvoir, would deem the psychological novel a thing of the past. But then, positing a fictitious male writer who, while recognizing and admiring people and characters of important actions, those who experience "deep suffering, deep, simple joys, powerful, very evident needs"

[AS, 100], cannot help seeing what lies in the interstices of these solidly constructed beings and their sharply outlined adventures. Although she never names de Beauvoir or existentialism, the polemic, particularly in "What Birds See," about what is revolutionary in literature includes an implicit indictment of the traditional approaches to literary form and content that de Beauvoir uses.

Sarraute's solitary, male writer, an "unfortunate die-hard" [AS, 99], is haunted by the barely visible existence of ill-defined sensations and feelings, a new psychological matter that Sarraute says has always existed, but that traditional character analysis has left untouched or has been unable to enact dramatically. Her humble writer strives to make his readers undergo the same sorts of minute reactions, so that they understand, through the experience of reading, these "'darker sides'" [AS, 99] of human interaction, beyond clear-cut identities, unambiguous situations, and conventional dialogues. His task does not consist of copying or imitating reality. Rather, he invents new novelistic forms that allow us to perceive the barely detectable responses woven into our transactions with the world. This new writer's efforts continue the literary explorations of Proust, Dostoevski, Joyce, Virginia Woolf. . . .

Elsewhere Sarraute has defined the tropism, the hallmark of her writing, in much the same terms: "these movements glide quickly round the border of our consciousness, they compose the small, rapid, and sometimes very complex dramas concealed beneath our actions, our gestures, the words we speak, our avowed and clear feelings."[9] Although she does not name the tropism in the two essays, it is not difficult to figure out that the new forms her male writer is working on pertain to the tropism. Nor is it hard to surmise that her anonymous male writer is a third-person description of her own preoccupations, experiences, and struggles in writing. In the preface she added to the 1964 French edition, Sarraute acknowledges as much. The initial displacement of her own concerns onto a fictive male writer would appear to be a protective measure to ward off personal attacks and a means to make her arguments more compelling, untroubled by the particularities of the female author, especially at a time when her works remained unread. In a 1983 interview, she adds that writing *The Age of Suspicion* was a way of convincing herself that what she was doing in literature was a valid enterprise.[10] Despite these justifications, however, it is hard not to read the imposition of a male figure in the place of a female author as a fundamental negativity, the denial of the female gender.

Several dangers thus seem to lurk in the use of the first person for Sarraute. If she writes in her own voice, she risks being accused of translating private quirks into a generalized phenomenon. Because the tropism often enacts the discomfort and anguish of interpersonal struggles beneath seemingly innocuous or rational dialogues and actions, it is all the more imperative that Sarraute *not* link them exclusively to herself. By using a hypothetical male writer, she detaches the obsessive quality of his search for new forms and his lived experience of the tropism from her own identity. The male author becomes any modern writer genuinely interested in uncovering new ways of investigating unexplored territory in literature, beyond the realm of individualized characters, plots, and conventional dialogue.[11] His work runs counter to neoclassicism (and this implicitly includes the existentialist literature of commitment), which uses traditional, conventional forms of narrative, as if they were "necessary" and "eternal" [AS, 104].

In *Force of Circumstance*, de Beauvoir brings Sarraute's claims directly back to the author's "personality" and to a specific social configuration, the bourgeois family, despite Sarraute's precautions. For de Beauvoir, Sarraute's tropisms are, no doubt, a product of what de Beauvoir interprets as her "restless subtlety," and have no bearing on history or sociopolitical concerns.[12] In defending the (traditional) style of her own novel, *The Mandarins*, for which she received the Goncourt Prize in 1954, de Beauvoir names Sarraute as her principal detractor, and then mounts a counterattack against her and New Novelists Alain Robbe-Grillet and Michel Butor. For de Beauvoir, the tropistic reactions of Sarraute's often-anonymous characters inevitably reveal the paranoid, schizophrenic character of no one but their author. "Robbe-Grillet, Sarraute, Butor interest us insofar as they are unable to keep themselves, their schizophrenia, their obsession, their mania, their personal relations to things, people and the age out of their writing" [FC, 622]. But at the same time, she criticizes the New Novelists (and Sarraute in particular) for divorcing themselves from their works. "[. . .] the man in them becomes dissociated from the writer; they vote, they sign manifestos, they take sides—usually against exploitation, the privileged classes and injustice. Then they go back into their old ivory tower" [FC, 622]. The New Novelists are not faulted in their actions and they are even "present" in their works, but not in the "right" way, that is, not as conscious writers of their personal commitments in the political and social arenas. The argument is not about whether reality should be represented, but rather which realities merit the writer's scrutiny.[13] Were it not for de Beauvoir's reference to the generic New Novelist as a *man*, one might have been tempted to read her reproach as particularly directed toward Sarraute and her rejection of her gender.

De Beauvoir also reacts strongly to the family milieu that Sarraute often uses as a backdrop for her novels. The paranoia de Beauvoir sees in Sarraute's novels becomes class specific in her commentary, and it is the class that she most abhors, the bourgeoisie. Unlike de Beauvoir's novels, Sarraute's novels acknowledge her own bourgeois background as the social group to explore, because it is the one she knows best.[14] Because de Beauvoir stresses in her own autobiography the way she frees herself from the grips of the bourgeois family, Sarraute's hothouse portrayal of the latter must have been particularly unsavory to de Beauvoir. She forcefully takes her distance from Sarraute's characters, their milieu, and from Sarraute herself, as if de Beauvoir were undergoing her own version of a tropistic reaction, one that might identify her with something distasteful, murky, and vaguely menacing.

Sarraute's discursive strategies are bound to disorient and dismay a traditional reader like de Beauvoir who is obliged to slide through multiple layers of consciousness (between characters and within a single character) without the support of a reassuring intent or stable point of view. Situating such moves within the bourgeois milieu makes de Beauvoir all the more ill at ease. The de Beauvoir/Sarraute hostilities are rather like a "serious" version of Sarraute's humorous and highly entertaining portrayal in the novel, *The Golden Fruits*, of literary debates on the value of a fictitious novel. The latter is a pretext for power struggles among the discussants as they vie for authoritative control of the "truth" about the work. But no position ultimately triumphs; what is portrayed is the way power is exercised in social groupings. Through the use of satire, irony, and a humor triggered by the clash between "serious" discussions and the strange phenomena transpiring underneath them, Sarraute constantly puts on trial all shapes and forms of social terrorism, the practice of those who would silence others in the name of some abstraction: truth, beauty, good taste . . . . Working within the dominant bourgeois ideology, Sarraute slashes into its smooth surfaces. Her textual politics recall Barthes's enjoinder that modern literature become a theft: "fragment the old text of culture, science, literature, and change its features according to formulae of disguise, as one disguises stolen goods."[15]

For all these differences and antagonisms, de Beauvoir and Sarraute have significant points in common. Both view literature as the portrayal of, to use de Beauvoir's words, "the equivocal, separate, contradictory truths that no one moment represents in their totality [. . .]" [FC, 263]. And as women writers, both are leery of identifying with a specifically feminine point of view. They refuse the notion of a feminine nature or essence, as well as any idea of a feminine writing. This is, no doubt, another major reason for Sarraute's choice of a hypothetical *male* writer in *The Age of Suspicion*, for she knows that her own identity as author is susceptible to being read as a function of her gender, something she insistently denies. Speaking for herself as a social being rather than as an author, Sarraute stressed in an interview with Bettina Knapp that she is no more sensitive or subject to tropistic reactions than anyone else, nor is she more adept at detecting them in others.[16] And like de Beauvoir, Sarraute has consistently supported women's rights. In 1935 (well before de Beauvoir's feminist consciousness was raised), Sarraute fought for women's right to vote in France.[17] Nevertheless, she is not concerned with women's issues in her writing: "the feminine condition is the last thing I think about in writing."[18]

Both she and de Beauvoir have written novels about writers, but in each instance the principal character or consciousness is male. In *The Mandarins* de Beauvoir avoids representing the "exceptional" character, that is, a woman writer like herself, preferring instead to channel her writerly concerns through a male protagonist. In Sarraute's *The Planetarium*, a woman writer, Germaine Lemaire, appears in the plot as the idol of one of the main characters, Alain Guimier. But for much of the novel, she is viewed from the "outside" as a construction of others' opinions, with few references to her actual writing. When Sarraute does focus on literary creation in her novel *Between Life and Death*, she chooses to portray a male writer who is less a character in the conventional sense of a personality or specific identity, than a set of problems besieging any writer.

The disembodied voices in many of Sarraute's novels and plays—nameless figures in interaction—seem to constitute attempts to circumvent gender issues altogether. In looking for the means to convey the junctures between external dialogue and internal, almost automatic responses, a phenomenon that anyone and everyone experiences, she seeks a "neutral voice" that belongs neither to a particular individual nor gender. But in practice, she says, the closest she can come is the masculine, because French has no neuter. For Sarraute, the female protagonist cannot, given the persistent clichés about gender, unequivocally represent both sexes. Sarraute does not eliminate female characters or voices from her works, but their gender is never a decisive factor. There are no "heroines" to speak of in her works. Sarraute's search for the neuter is another stunning denial of gender.

Also like de Beauvoir, Sarraute has stirred up her share of controversy and has understandably found herself going against the grain, not just of traditional literary theory, but of various feminist and postfeminist positions on women's writing. During the seventies when women's movements in France were advocating a search for the specificity of feminine voice (connoting a certain writing style of/with the female body) and in the U.S. were identifying a female experience in writing (concerning a gender-specific content as well as a literary tradition of women writers), Sarraute repeatedly refused any association with their causes.[19]

Because she strives to undermine notions of uniqueness, fixed identity, and unequivocal truth, the specificity of gender constitutes for Sarraute another firm categorization that the tropism unravels. Her wariness of the notion of feminine writing goes in tandem with her desire to avoid making women writers marginal, and her interest in the tropism transcends the content of gendered experience. Thus she resists connections between the experimental, revolutionary aspects of her writing and both kinds of feminist propositions. Sarraute has dismayed many a student and teacher on American college campuses by maintaining that there are no masculine and feminine writers, no black or white writers, only writers *tout court*.

Sarraute's frequent choice of the masculine over the feminine can, nevertheless, and perhaps paradoxically, be read as a maneuver that sidesteps stereotypes of women, at the same time that it gives voice and credence to what has historically been linked to "feminine" aspects of life and of literary affinities. These "feminine" aspects include the following: first of all, she situates her works in the close-knit arenas of family or friends who engage in conversations full of the commonplaces of daily life. Whereas de Beauvoir carefully places the personal experiences of her characters (and herself as autobiographical character) in public life, the legitimated "masculine" context of important historical actions and ideas, Sarraute concentrates on microcosms in the private domain, or where public/private distinctions tend to blur.

Second, the tropism emphasizes the *fluidity* of interpersonal experience against the solidity of appearance, including personality traits, proper names, autonomous individuals, and unambiguous meanings. It characterizes an involuntary, prerational reaction to words, objects, and people, one that "hasn't yet been caught up in standard forms."[20] Boundaries between individuals become mobile through the elimination of words that attribute discourse to a particular voice: phrases like "she said" or "George exclaimed" disappear from Sarraute's work. And the "subconversation," that renders verbally "what is hidden beneath the interior monologue: an immense profusion of sensations, of images, sentiments, memories, impulses, little larval actions [. . .]" [AS, 105] flows into dialogue, so that insides and outsides are coterminous.

Her images of oozing fluids, viscosity, secretions, rhythmic waves . . . are designed to suggest a hesitant, vacillating, and unnameable experience that underlies and betrays "objective" reality. These metaphorical dichotomies of solid versus fluid not only belong to our Western cultural mythologies distinguishing masculine and feminine, they also continue to play a role for psychoanalytic theorists of the feminine such as Luce Irigaray, Julia Kristeva, and Nancy Chodorow.[21]

In "The 'Mechanics' of Fluids," Irigaray argues that a phallocratic complicity between the concept of solids in science (physics, metaphysics, psychoanalysis) and reasoned discourse has systematically excluded (or reappropriated) the properties of fluids that she associates with woman. With playful punning and a dose of sarcasm, she traces the dangers that women's fluid modalities present to men's solid discourse:

[. . .] women diffuse themselves according to modalities scarcely compatible with the framework of the ruling symbolics. Which doesn't happen without causing some turbulence, we might even say some whirlwinds, that ought to be reconfined within solid walls of principle, to keep them from spreading to infinity. Otherwise they might even go so far as to disturb that third agency designated as the real—a transgression and confusion of boundaries that it is important to restore to their proper order.[22]

The "proper order" refers to the Lacanian psychoanalytic model that labels the material real the impossible because we can never grasp or articulate the real in language. Outside of language, this order relies on firm distinctions that (feminine) fluidity blurs, and thus threatens. Fluidity characterizes that which resists/exceeds normative (rationalist) discourse, stable identity, and meaning; it is both a metaphor for the "continuous, compressible, dilatable, viscous, conductible, diffusable"[23] moves of the feminine, in particular feminine sexual pleasure, as well as a set of physical properties of fluids. For Irigaray, feminine pleasure (which she calls a "self-affection" that does not follow a masculine model) is kept silent because it menaces phallocratic power structures. "Feminine pleasure has to remain inarticulate in language, in its own language, if it is not to threaten the underpinnings of logical operations. And so what is most strictly forbidden to women

today is that they should attempt to express their own pleasure."[24] Seeking strategies for a *parler femme*, that is, woman
speaking (from/through) her body, Irigaray refers to a "feminine
syntax" in which

> there would no longer be either subject or object, "oneness" would no
> longer be privileged, there would no longer be proper meanings, proper
> names, "proper" attributes . . . . Instead, that "syntax" would involve
> nearness, proximity, but in such an extreme form that it would preclude
> any distinction of identities [. . .].[25]

Irigaray emphasizes in "The Power of Discourse and the Subordination of the Feminine" this need for another way of speaking,
one that would "disconcert the staging of representation according to *exclusively* 'masculine' parameters, that is, according to a
phallocratic order."[26] Women's fluidity provides the means to
disrupt and modify the dominant discourse that has excluded
women as well as a theory of fluids.

Kristeva's theory of "the semiotic" plays off against the paternal order of language and the symbolic.[27] The semiotic emphasizes color, tone, rhythm, and (unconscious) drives that puncture
the logic of linguistic representation (the realm of the symbolic),
but it is also "a psychosomatic modality of the signifying process"
and is "necessary to the acquisition of language."[28] Finding support for her theory in Mallarmé's texts, Kristeva describes the
semiotic as "enigmatic and feminine, this space underlying the
written is rhythmic, unfettered, irreducible to its intelligible verbal translation; it is musical, anterior to judgment [. . .]."[29]
According to Kristeva, the semiotic originates in the preverbal,
pre-Oedipal fusion between infant and mother. She associates
it with avant-garde literary practice (Mallarmé, Lautréamont,
Bataille, Joyce . . .), qualifying it as a disruptive and revolutionary
force challenging the systematized, closed codes of the (phallocentric) symbolic. Both Irigaray and Kristeva link their theories
of the feminine to breaks with traditional modes of discursive
writing and concepts of autonomous identity.[30]

Sarraute's tropisms have much in common with Irigaray's fluids and Kristeva's semiotic in the way they afford a stylistic breakdown in conventional forms of representation. Their vocabular-
ies to describe all three phenomena are strikingly similar in many

respects and all three writers devise strategies to suggest something that exceeds the boundaries of rational discourse. Like Irigaray and Kristeva, Sarraute forces her readers to reassess their relationship to the text, never letting them rest comfortably in one position from which to determine meaning once and for all. The textual resistances—which require that the reader work on and in their texts—undo attempts at mastery, of possessing an objective truth.[31] Kristeva's analytic focus on nonlinear, poetic modes of writing recalls the way Sarraute uses poetic imagery, rhythm, and ellipses to convey the intrusion of the tropism upon conversation. In addition, Kristeva's insistence that the semiotic in art is not limited to female writers brings her closer to Sarraute's position.

But whereas Kristeva and Irigaray anchor their theories and practice in (an unchanging, although multiple) female sexuality (in the mother, in female sexual pleasure), and thereby run the risk of essentializing woman through biological determinations, Sarraute conspicuously avoids explicit references to the body and to sexuality.[32] Although the vocabulary used to evoke the tropism draws upon characteristics that Western culture associates with femininity, the terms apply, in Sarraute's work, to anyone, male or female.

Sarraute portrays a commonality of experience that breaks down inherent distinctions instead of affirming them. But she does not sacrifice female characters in making male narrators or characters more prevalent in her works, because her characterizations of humans veer away from androcentric conceptions of human representation. The privileged status of the unitary voice, of unique identity, is undermined. Her male characters, just as much as her female ones, are prey to the invisible, diffuse workings of the tropism. If the tropism can be said to align its vocabulary and structures with the typically feminine, the masculine subject becomes "feminized," and no longer holds sway over the language he uses or the truth of the situations he lives through. Instead of assuming a marginal status for female characters (as Kristeva does for women, madmen, the culturally oppressed . . .), Sarraute decentralizes all discourses.

This is not to say that all social differences disappear in Sarraute's works. Gender allows the reader to separate one voice from another: it is a conventional linguistic and social marker rather than a sign of inherent difference. The social markers distinguishing male and female characters are often positions within a family structure of daughters, fathers, mothers, nephews, and so on. Although these relationships adhere to conventional social (and gender) codes, this is a concession, says Sarraute, to novelistic verisimilitude and it sets up the façades that the tropistic reactions will unglue.[33] She feels most successful when her readers cross the conventional gender lines of identification (reading beyond verisimilitude): for example, she is thrilled when a young male reader tells her that he identifies with an old aunt's obsession with doorknobs in *The Planetarium*.[34] In this instance she measures the success of her work by its ability to allow the reader to transcend its own façade of gender verisimilitude.

Although Sarraute's tropisms are resistant to modern gender theory at the level of individual characters, they do seem to respond to the insights of feminist psychoanalytic theory at the level of textual creation and reception, that is, the way the text stresses relational configurations, rather than individualized identity. The theories of Nancy Chodorow on the dissymmetries between girls' and boys' early development and Judith Kegan Gardiner's use of those theories in speaking about women's writing are useful here. They stress that masculine identity is based on successful separation and individuation from the mother: to be a male is not to be female like the mother; the boy's sense of self is rooted in the need for autonomy and independence. Women's identity, on the other hand, is traced more along relational lines. A girl's early attachment to the same sex (her mother) is never fully broken and her ego boundaries tend to be more permeable, emphasizing contact and fusion with the other rather than differences. Boys tend to deal with the world in contractual, often aggressive, terms between separate individuals, and find it difficult to express the affective needs (for the mother) that they have had to repress during the Oedipal phase of their development. Girls' development is said to be more complex because the highly seductive (and unchallenged) union with the mother also entails absolute dependence and a loss of self. Repeating these scenarios in adulthood, women vacillate between a desire for fusion and contact with the other and a need to separate themselves in relation to others. Chodorow explains this dissymmetry between gendered identity concepts by the fact that women are the sole or primary caretakers of infants in our society. She also persuasively argues that the dissymmetry creates constitutive difficulties in relationships between men and women.[35] Gardiner describes female identity as "a process, and primary identity for women is more flexible and relational than for men."[36] In writing, this translates as a breakdown in traditional generic boundaries (autobiographies are novelistic, novels are autobiographical) and a blurring of the public and private.

Sarraute has said that "if there is an absolute that [her] characters are seeking, it is always the need for *fusion* and *contact* with others" (my emphasis).[37] It is almost uncanny how Sarraute chooses the same kinds of words as Chodorow (in reference to female identity formation) to articulate one of the most fundamental moves in her works. At the origin of Sarraute's creations lies a desire for harmony, a possible merging with others, that likens it to Chodorow's and Gardiner's descriptions of female identity formation and feminine writing.

And yet, despite these resemblances, there remains one crucial aspect of the tropism that sets it apart from Irigaray's fluids, Kristeva's semiotic, and Chodorow's concept of female identity. Whereas the latter are positive forces advocated by the authors, the tropism appears openly confrontational in nature.[38] Sarraute's readers rarely fail to recognize the negativity of the tropism: it involves them most often in the pain and anguish of *missed* contacts, of failed attempts at communication, or of violent forms of interaction. In Sarraute's world, the possible fusion between people is always threatened. In *The Age of Suspicion*, Sarraute characterizes the subterranean movements that interest her hypothetical male writer in fundamentally (although not exclusively) combative terms, through a series of fierce metaphors that suggest the intensity of split-second reactions: "[. . .] inner dramas made up of attacks, triumphs, recoils, defeats, caresses, bites, rapes, murders, generous abandons or humble submissions

[. . .]" [AS, 117–18]. In an important sense, the erasure of gender differences wards off negative definitions of women. If female characters were the unique or even primary filters of tropisms, the sensitivity necessary to undergo the experience, coupled with its negativity, could too easily be read as a specifically female character trait. The common misogynous tendency to view women as weak and emotional and men as strong and rational would be reaffirmed. What remains unexplained, however, is why the tropism is negative in the first place.[39] I shall be addressing this issue later in the discussion of *Childhood*.

    *

Among Sarraute's many talents as essayist, novelist, playwright, and autobiographer, one of the most striking and successful is her ability to weave together conflicting views *in dialogue*, whether between characters or within one voice that is divided in two (as in the "subconversation"). The univocal, personal point of view in traditional autobiography thus appears particularly incommensurate with her writing. It is true that her first two novels, *Portrait of a Man Unknown* and *Martereau*, are narrated in the first person, but each time it is via the consciousness of one of the male characters, so that an authorial, controlling voice is never present. In her later novels, up to *"fools say,"* the narration moves in and out of various characters or voices, with no single one being predominant. *The Age of Suspicion* even raises potential objections that readers may have to first-person narrative: it looks too egotistical, like a "youthful malady" [AS, 85]. Sarraute judges first-person narration an acceptable form only because several great novelists have effectively used it with "very evident mastery and rare forcefulness" [AS, 85].[40]

In *The Use of Speech*, her last work before *Childhood*, Sarraute seems to be preparing the way for autobiography, since it is in this work that she comes closest to creating a narrator whose position she might occupy. Composed of a series of short texts that demonstrate the multiple, fleeting resonances underlying such abstract notions as "Love," "Friendship," or a stifling phrase like "don't talk to me about that," Sarraute connects the episodes via a narrating "I" who speaks to potential readers as "you" in a collaborative effort, and sometimes combines the two in a "we."

Contrary to the conception of the "masterful" first-person novel (as mentioned in *The Age of Suspicion*), this new kind of narrator is quite vulnerable to readers' possible criticisms and objections, and acknowledges as much in a fictive dialogue with them. In the midst of exploring a one-sided conversation between two friends, for example, the narrator interrupts:

But you are already becoming impatient, you're already preparing to jettison the whole thing, to throw it in the dustbin, wrapped in one of those specially-made bags; a torrent of words issuing from "an interminable windbag" [. . .] But don't you imagine that if it had been anything so out-worn I would myself have thrown it on the scrap-heap? [. . .] Have confidence in me for a little longer [. . .].[41]

The readers fill an active position, and are encouraged to pull out of their own stock of linguistic and social experiences material analogous to what the narrator has chosen: "You could easily, if you agree, add to them or substitute others [examples, words] you may find amongst those in your possession . . . ."[42] *The Use of Speech* is an overture to autobiography, in that the narrator's personal choices and interpretations of speech usage, while still personal, can be replaced by the readers'. The transition to formal autobiography will thus be a smooth one for Sarraute.[43]

CHILDHOOD

In the preface to *The Age of Suspicion*, Sarraute tells the reader that her attention had first been directed to the tropism during her childhood, and it is precisely to these memories that she returns in her autobiography. Because the principles of feminine identity and individualized voice appear incompatible with the nature of the tropism, the autobiographical genre presents special problems to the novelist suspicious of the gender-specific, personalized "I." Who will be speaking? Will the singular content of her early experiences be sacrificed in the name of the generalized phenomenon? Will parents and family members be deindividualized? How does one tells one's "story" without reverting back to outmoded literary forms that codify experience into neat categories, or conversely, without having new forms undo any possible portrayal of identity? My reading of the tensions between the genre and Sarraute's pronouncements about gender and writing will explore connections between the structure of the child's parental identifications and the adult writer's narrative choices, in *Childhood* as well as in her other works. Without setting out to prove a causal relationship, I suggest that Sarraute's complex, difficult rapport with her mother and stepmother is articulated in her tropisms and theoretical pronouncements as a sign of the repressed, forbidden feminine. Sarraute's identification with her father and her desire for her mother become inscribed in her writing, both as themes and as style. Thus the content of her early family experiences will be linked to her writing strategies.

*

Although Sarraute legitimates the use of the first person in *The Age of Suspicion* by turning to "masterful" precedents, they too can be irksome in their own right. It is with some reluctance that Sarraute yields to the desire to "'evoke [her] childhood memories'" in *Childhood* [c, 1] because it sounds so clichéd. One is not only going over old experiences, the form itself is also worn. The quotation marks around the expression stress the intertexual resonances of the project and its lack of originality.[44] Sarraute even fears that this desire might be a sign of declining talent, thereby implying that one writes of oneself when there is nothing better to say, the senile equivalent of the juvenile malady mentioned in *The Age of Suspicion*. Sarraute also worries that she may well be "abandoning [her] element" [c, 2]. Whereas many (or perhaps most) writers would find a personal investigation of one's memories to be precisely their element (de Beauvoir even warns women against succumbing to it too freely or facilely), Sarraute feels estranged from hers. Her "element" is not defined—naming, defining, labeling . . . are precisely the kinds of operations that destroy it—but it is evoked as something alive, not yet put into words, that the staid form of autobiography risks obliterating. Can the tropism rise from such rock-solid ground?

In order to make the genre her own, Sarraute wastes no time in violating certain generic conventions, or at least in rendering them more supple and suitable to her writing needs. On the very first page of *Childhood* the reader discovers *two* voices in conversation, two "I"s that dramatize the split inherent in the autobiographical subject.[45] Perhaps in the "true spirit" of the autobiographical genre, Sarraute's deviation from the rule of univocal narrative traces all the more strongly the mark of modern autobiography as a "mixed and transgressive genre."[46] The authority of the unique, autobiographical "I" is undermined by the doubling, but at the same time the subject's authenticity is strengthened: while one narrating voice's primary function is to recount the memories of the past, the other's consists in questioning, encouraging, and probing the interpretations involved in the writing of those memories. The autobiographical "I" becomes a "you" in the words of this second, regulating voice who checks for factual as well as emotional accuracy. This voice is much like a skeptical reader, suspicious of such a dubious project as autobiography. To dare to "evoke one's childhood memories" is an uphill battle, with one's readers, one's (reading) self and a generic tradition that has a bad reputation. But these resistances, obstacles, and challenges are precisely what make the genre most irresistible to Sarraute.

As is often the case in the tropistic movements of her fictive characters, the autobiographical voices of *Childhood* take part in a double gesture of advancing into the material of the past and then withdrawing from it in a self-conscious move. Quoting Gide in an interview, Sarraute affirms that " 'I compose in madness and reread in reason.' "[47] But the judgmental voice never completely erases the storyteller's viewpoint. The vacillating point of view destabilizes attitudes toward the past and casts doubt on evaluations of people and events that the voices remember. The meanings of any given episode always hover in the interstices of dialogue. The doubled voice thus precludes any attempt to unify the fragments of memory into a finished image of the unified subject.[48]

The constitution of the autobiographical subject becomes all the more complex when one realizes that neither of the initiating voices on the first page of *Childhood* is identical to that of the child Nathalie.[49] When Nathalie's point of view does appear, it is also in the first person, and in a dramatic present that suggests the vividness and intensity of lived experience. Thus there are three voices, distinct but overlapping. The adult storytelling voice is, in fact, quite close to the child's, and only becomes distinguishable from the latter when the two adult voices appear in dialogue, primarily when the censuring voice doubts an interpretation by the storyteller. This is also the point at which past tenses are used, as a relational device to distinguish between storyteller and child character.

The third differentiating element among the three voices—and perhaps the most intriguing—involves the voices' gender marks: while, as would be expected, the adjectives referring to the storytelling voice and the child are in the feminine, those referring to the more distant, critical voice are in the masculine. If the reader is not careful, however, the difference can easily go unnoticed, because the masculine identity of the critical adult voice is visible only in two masculine adjectives of the opening passage [c, 2], when the female storyteller calls "him" grandiloquent and presumptuous: "*Oui, ça te rend grandiloquent. Je dirai même outrecuidant.*"[50] In the English translation, the gender difference is nonexistent.

But why this deliberate inscription of two genders in reference to the autobiographical subject? It is as if the distinction were quickly made in order to get rid of the issue of gender while simultaneously complicating it. What is the correlation between the characterizations of the voices, their functions, and the gender assignations? Since the storyteller labels the other voice grandiloquent and presumptuous, it is clear that either voice is capable of assuming a critical stance toward the other. Although interlocutors involved in a collaborative effort, the different voices arise primarily when the two disagree. On the whole, their roles are relatively stable: the feminine voice dramatically recreates the past and identifies with the child while the masculine one evaluates the interpretations in more distant terms. Like Virginia Woolf, Sarraute has said that a writer must be androgynous.[51] The androgynous subject is not defined here as a homogeneous or neutralized unity, but rather as heterogeneous discourses in movement and exchange.

In *Childhood*, the androgynous narrative entails a dividing up of gendered elements that are then woven together in dialogue.

Many of the traits that characterize the voices coincide with standard gender coding: affective identification with the child prevails in the feminine voice; reason, accuracy, and critical distance triumph in the masculine voice. For example, when describing a picture in the child's favorite book, the feminine narrator is interrupted by the critical masculine voice: "Is it certain that that picture is in *Max and Moritz*? Wouldn't it be better to check?" [c, 38]. To which the feminine narrator responds: "No, what's the point? What *is* certain is that that picture is still associated with this book and that the feeling it gave me has remained intact [. . .]" [c, 38]. The masculine voice is concerned with verifying factual precision and is the one who abruptly breaks into the narrative in order to challenge it. The feminine voice, on the other hand, insists that what is important is the feeling that has endured over time. Together, the voices are ultimately the sign of the autobiographical subject that is never quite identical to itself. The division is ingenious from a formal point of view because it facilitates a moving, thoughtful portrayal of Sarraute's early memories that allows the reader both proximity to and distance from the text. What remains to be explored is the relationship between these gendered narrative forms and gender patterns of the past.

Sarraute's stylistic splitting of the subject is played out several times in the *content* of her memories. Her early experiences of exile—continually moving back and forth between Russia and France, between languages, and finally between divorced parents whom she never saw together—provide a physical counterpart (linguistic, cultural, and familial) to a narration attuned to its own fragmentation and dividedness. And although the child's experience of exile as a wrenching split is passive, in that it is not of her own choosing, we will see that the author recalling the past first turns to a willful rupture, a transgression that brings together stylistic deviation and unruly self-affirmation.

The parallel between psychical and physical splits is heralded in the two opening passages of *Childhood*: first, the disapproving, censuring masculine "I" produces in the feminine voice a perverse desire to talk about herself, that is, a desire to be contradictory or rebellious:

[. . .] we know very well that when something starts haunting you . . . .
—Yes, and this time, it's hardly believable, but it was you who prompted me, for some time now you have been inciting me . . . .
—I?
—Yes, you, by your admonitions, your warnings . . . you conjure it up, you immerse me in it . . . [c, 3].

If it is "inappropriate" or "improper" to speak of oneself, then, in a defiant pose, that is precisely what the feminine narrator will do. The storyteller is "immersed" in the memories the way a character or reader plunges/is plunged into a tropism: "He [the reader] is immersed and held under the surface until the end, in a substance as anonymous as blood, a magma without name or contours" [AS, 93–94].

In the very next sequence of *Childhood*, Sarraute stages what one might call a primal scene that again launches the thematics of laws and transgressions. Although it originates in the author's remote memories, when Nathalie is living with her father, it is told in a dramatic present that gives it an energy equal to the narrators' present. The passage opens with a quotation in German from her governess: *"Nein, das tust du nicht"* ("No, you're not to do that"), followed by the child's quick response (also in German): "Yes, I will." The foreign words echo clearly in Sarraute's memory, and the linguistic apprenticeship (learning German) is accompanied by an affirmation of the child's will. Braving the governess's interdiction, Nathalie announces in German: "I am going to slash it" and then gleefully stabs a settee with a pair of scissors. Unafraid of any serious reprimand by her father, Nathalie responds to the governess's "no" as if it were a dare. The images of rupture coincide with an exhilarating liberation in the child: "these words surround me, constrain me, shackle me, I struggle . . . 'Yes, I'm going to do it' . . . There now, I'm freeing myself, excitement and exaltation impel my arm, I plunge the point of the scissors in with all my strength [. . .]" [c, 6]. The violent act creates a gaping wound in the fabric.

The force of Nathalie's action, its brashness, is brought on by the governess's negative reaction: the prohibition transforms an otherwise childish, idle threat into a real desire. The little girl's liberation stems from a new linguistic prowess (she has mastered

German now in addition to Russian and French), and from the action that delivers her from the governess's constraining words. Physical action and speech act are woven together metonymically and have equal force here. A perverse pleasure involving power, mastery, and the transgression of rules has enabled the confirmation of the individual. But the episode does not stop with the self's coronation. There is something else that seems to defy identity posed exclusively in these terms. Sarraute's description of the stuffing protruding from the gash in the back of the settee is reminiscent of the way she has portrayed the oozing cracks in language's smooth surface: "something soft, greyish, is escaping from the slit" [c, 6]. The settee stuffing provides a metaphor for language's indefinable, "messy" spaces, where identities shift, where insides and outsides meet, clash, mix . . . .[52] The nonverbal image (rendered, of course, verbally) exceeds, overflows the neat contours of (self) definition. Sarraute's fictional tropisms portray this kind of multiform matrix that is in excess of solidifiable sense. It recalls the "place" where anonymous voices seek one another out—in order to establish identity through contact and exchange with the other, or to assert selfhood over the other through hierarchical struggle.

The violent imagery of the short passage in *Childhood* sets in motion a network of obvious, if ambivalent, sexual symbols: the phallic scissors that brutally stab and penetrate the settee coincide with a model of language as power, or inscription of selfhood. This version stresses the process of successful individuation, of making one's mark, and is reminiscent of what by now has become a clichéd version of *male* self-conceptualization. But female sexual imagery, while not developed so extensively, is also suggested in the passage: the oozing crack in the silk fabric is the fascinating end point toward which the passage heads. If we focus on this opening in the back of the settee as a metaphor for the unleashing of a desire that has been constrained by a certain kind of decent, ordered, prohibitive language, then the little girl's verbal scissors—she repeats "I am going to do it" after the governess's prohibition—release her from the binding words of the taboo. Her bold riposte rises up within her, breaks through the tension in a quasi-orgasmic explosion:

"No, you're not to do that" . . . these words flow in a heavy, massive tide, what it carries with it sinks into me in order to crush what is stirring in me, what is trying to rise . . . and under this pressure, it braces itself, rises more vigorously, rises higher, grows, and violently projects out of me the words . . . "Yes, I'm going to do it" [c, 5–6].

In this context, the scissors are merely a projection of an internal phenomenon, a (sexual) pleasure whose trace is tangible in its extensions: the protruding stuffing, the scissors, and language belong to a continuum of desire. The sexual symbolism of the passage implies that, although sexual identifications in the text are by no means simple or even stable, a series of associations between desire, power, and language can be traced.

In considering this sexual imagery, it is important to keep in mind that Sarraute does not thematize sexual or gender differences in *Childhood*, nor does she even acknowledge their importance in identity formation. She does remark once, however, that men and women were treated as moral and intellectual equals in the social gatherings of Russian friends at the home of her father and her stepmother, Vera [c, 177–78]. It is one of the rare instances when the narrator even raises an issue of gender difference. What is odd about it is that Sarraute's narrator also states in the same episode that her stepmother conspicuously did not participate in discussion; instead, she was busy attending to her guests' needs, serving them more tea or food . . . . Somehow the question of equality does not pertain to the stepmother, who is portrayed as filling a feminine social role that makes it difficult for her to take full part in the conversations. Both narrators appear blind to the oversight—for them, Vera's role is played according to Vera's peculiar quirks, not as a function of social demands. Nathalie's own rapport with her families will be based on their specific properties, but we will see that her ties to them are informed by gender differences.

One is struck in reading *Childhood* at how drastically Sarraute's relationships to her natural mother and stepmother differ from her relationship to her father. Although Sarraute makes every attempt to show her mothers' qualities and to balance her judgments of them by using the alternating voices, one cannot help but note the number of rejections and betrayals Sarraute remembers from the two. The close, communal moments between mother and daughter are overshadowed by the remembrances of anguished experiences of estrangement which heighten the desire for union. This is not at all the case in the way Sarraute remembers her father who, although not very affectionate, seems a pillar of stability and support, and who never presents any enigma for the daughter. Let us compare male and female figures.

Concerning Sarraute's natural mother, the masculine voice asks early in the book: "How long did it take you to realize that she never tried—unless very absent-mindedly and clumsily—to put herself in your place? . . ." [c, 19] to which the feminine voice responds: "Yes [. . .] that indifference, that casualness were part of her charm [. . .] No word, however powerfully uttered, has ever sunk into me with the same percussive force as some of hers" [c, 19]. Whereas the masculine voice depicts an "objective" critical portrait of the mother, one in which she is faulted for her lack of empathy, the feminine voice focuses on the effects of the mother on the child and turns the "faults" into her charms—that is, the powerful magic she exerts on the child.

The scene immediately following the scissors episode sharply contrasts Nathalie's paternal and maternal links: after witnessing the ease and assurance with which the child breaks the paternal law, we turn to a scene of *absolute* faithfulness to the absent mother [c, 7–10]. Having been told by her mother (before going to stay with her father) that she must remember to chew her food until it is "as liquid as soup," the little girl endures ridicule and her father's irritation in order to obey her mother, to chew her food to the bitter end. This amusing, touching scene is indicative of the extent to which the child internalizes her mother's law. Not to follow instructions would be tantamount to treachery. The cliché, "as liquid as soup," seems particularly apt: it is as if the connections between mother and daughter must become "as liquid as soup," with the child asserting herself through the mother's identity, particularly when they are no longer physically together. The figure of liquidity that is associated with eating and with the mother even suggests their early nurturing bonds.

Any frontal attack from Nathalie's father appears feeble compared to her mother's power over her. For example, the narrators quote the father's extremely sarcastic comments about Nathalie's choice of reading material (the adventure novel, *Rocambole*, is not up to his literary standards), but his verbal assaults are without effect on her [c, 235–36]. Undaunted, Nathalie immerses herself in the novel's escapades with great relish. On the other hand, numerous instances are given when her mother's words resonate strongly and negatively in the child's mind, regardless of any intent on the mother's part. The memories of separation are not just those imposed by the physical distance between mother and father; the mother is remembered as the one who pushes the child away, with whom the child's idealized union is shattered. Nathalie's difficult relationship with her mother, involving care and torment, identification and distance, is reminiscent of the family relationships in her novel *Do You Hear Them?*, in which the tensions between a father's love for an art object (a small pre-Columbian statue) and his love for his children (who do not care for the statue) involve conflict and caring at the same time. Sarraute describes it as an "an interaction between consciousnesses which are extremely close to one another to the extent that they almost fuse and communicate by a kind of continuous osmosis."[53] What likens this osmosis to Nathalie's situation is the way confrontation and struggle are entwined in profound attachments.

In an early episode of *Childhood*, Nathalie joins in with her mother and her stepfather Kolya who playfully wrestle on the floor, but she is gently pushed aside by her mother, with the latter saying: "Husband and wife are on the same side." The masculine narrator forces the feminine one to admit that the remark has made Nathalie feel like a bothersome "foreign body" [c, 64], although the feminine narrator questions whether this interpretation did not come later, long after the experience. The feminine voice also finds positive ways to explain the remark:

—It seemed to me at that moment that Mama had thought that I was trying to defend her in earnest, that I believed she was being threatened and she wanted to reassure me . . . Let go . . . don't be frightened, nothing can happen to me . . . "Husband and wife are on the same side" [c, 63].

She consistently finds it more difficult to accuse the mother and seems closer to her than her male counterpart. But in one particularly poignant example of rejection, not even the feminine narrator defends the mother because the daughter is utterly devastated right at the time (and not just in a subsequent analysis). Through their correspondence, Nathalie's mother learns that her daughter is unhappy living at her father's. It is a secret which Nathalie has shared with her mother via their private code, writing "I am happy" in her letter instead of "I am *very* happy" [c, 100] in order to reveal her discontent. Worried about her daughter's care, the mother complains to the father. Nathalie is disconsolate about this "betrayal" and it brings her closer to her father who, uncharacteristically, shows a fair amount of tenderness toward his daughter. The drama is described as a crucial turning point in Nathalie's life:

> At that moment, and forever after, despite all appearances, an invisible bond, which nothing was ever able to destroy, united us [Nathalie and her father] .... [...] I perceived at that moment, at a stroke, en bloc ... all my relations with my father, with my mother, with Vera, their own relationships, were only the unravelling of what was then enravelled [c, 102].

Although Sarraute almost always manifests a certain torment in accusing her mother, in the example above the "crime" is so great that no excuses are given. She "chooses" her father and gradually distances herself from her mother. And yet, it seems quite plausible that Nathalie's mother reacts out of concern for her daughter's well-being even if the daughter perceives herself to be a victim.

By the process of accumulation, the episodes of *Childhood* dramatically sketch the interaction between mother and daughter. The memories of maternal rejection and the desperate moves to maintain the bond with the mother create a pattern that is consistent despite a variety of contexts and the persistent interpretive questioning by the masculine narrator. In fact, the latter's dialogues with the feminine voice enhance the clarity of the lines: he insists on uncovering the hurt that distances the mother, while she emphasizes the desire for contact. In accordance with Chodorow's theories, Nathalie's development adheres to the dual needs of fusion with the other on the one hand, and self-individuation on the other. The language of the mother is the fascinating space where Nathalie alternately bathes in security or becomes lost. Conflict with the mother becomes a threat to identity, a loss of self, but so does unity with her. As she grows older, it is as much Nathalie who distances herself from her mother as the opposite.

Nathalie's stepmother, Vera, who favors her own child over Nathalie, seems less ambivalent than the natural mother, to the point that the narrators worry that Vera is becoming the "wicked stepmother type" in the text [c,115], a two-dimensional fictive being. When Vera says to her stepdaughter "It isn't your home" [c, 115], the feminine narrator manages to draw out a positive interpretation of the remark, and the male narrator finds a plausible (if negative) explanation for Vera's comment. Nathalie repeats her attempts to bond with a mother, but Vera's plainly negative attitude toward Nathalie ultimately pushes the latter to look elsewhere for recognition and to develop a stronger self-concept.

The one wholly positive female figure in the book is Vera's Russian mother who reads and laughs with Nathalie, helps her study her lessons, and whose accent in French is impeccable. Significantly enough, this adoptive grandmother, whom Nathalie meets when she is about nine years old, resembles Nathalie's father in the most important ways. With both, Nathalie finds order, stability, an interest in the precision of linguistic performance, and in the learning of formal knowledge. Nathalie shares with both adoptive grandmother and father a love of book-learning which she sees as a means to become responsible for oneself. Sarraute shares this trait with de Beauvoir: access to formal education is a delight and a challenge to both of them. It affords a sense of independence and self-worth through its rigor, and facilitates a break with the family milieu. Nathalie finds in school exactly what she needs: "a world whose boundaries have been drawn with great precision, a solid world, visible all over . . . just made to my measure" [c, 214].

The opinions of Nathalie's mother on schooling offer a marked contrast: "I remember that Mama doesn't attach much importance to schoolwork . . . she even rather despises it . . .—She had often told you that she herself had been a bad pupil, always daydreaming . . . she seemed to be proud of it" [c, 223]. And Nathalie's stepmother is perceived as stupid because her natural mother has indicated as much. In the framework of the father's and grandmother's values, language and knowledge equal power and are a positive confirmation of the autonomous self. Nathalie willingly makes these values her own.

Another notable difference in the child's perception of her natural mother and her father lies in their use of language. Her mother's discourse is effusive, capricious, and playful. She writes letters to Nathalie which abound in tenderness, whereas Nathalie's father uses words sparingly and has difficulty showing his affection for her. The father also possesses a great wariness for clichés and "big words," that is, melodramatic or oppressive words, as well as intimate ones. At one point the child teasingly forces her father to say "I love you" [c, 48] to her, not because she is unsure of his love, but because she wishes to be recognized by him and to assert her power. Her father's silences eventually "speak" to the child: although words of affection do not flow between them, there remains an unspoken bond. Nathalie comes to understand her father's inability to express sentiment, the danger of "lay[ing] yourself bare, to disclose what you are filled with, what you only ever allow to escape in dribs and drabs [. . .]" [c, 48]. For both, naming can be a dangerous business because it makes one vulnerable, exposed, reveals tender insides that could be attacked. But it *also* risks destroying the lived, living experience that it is designed to show. Early in *Childhood*, for example, Sarraute refuses to describe an experience with the word "happiness" because it is too pat:

I was looking at the blossom on the espaliers along the little pink brick wall, the trees in bloom, the sparkling green lawn strewn with pink and white petaled daisies, the sky, of course, was blue, and the air seemed to be gently vibrating . . . and at that moment, it happened . . . something unique [. . .] but what? what word can pin it down? not the all-encompassing word: "happiness," which is the first that comes to mind, no, not that . . . "felicity," "exaltation," are too ugly, they mustn't touch it [. . .]. "Joy," yes, perhaps . . . this modest, very simple little word may alight on it with no great danger . . . but it cannot gather up what fills me, brims over in me, disperses, dissolves, melts into the pink bricks [. . .] [c, 56–57].

Like her father, Sarraute comes to distrust "big words"; the name easily crushes the imponderables of experience. And even at its best, like the word "joy" in the foregoing passage, it appears inadequate to what it designates. Sarraute's novels abound in two sorts of squirming characters who resemble her father (and herself): those who cannot stand the inflexibility of pronouncements that immobilize and impoverish experience ("Language," says Sarraute, "is a rigid and very stifling instrument. Terms and definitions can kill"); and those who shiver in dismay when complex, fluid insides are scandalously revealed.

But naming is also *essential* to the child: Sarraute remembers the painful difficulties involved in deciding whom to call "maman." Her natural mother tells her that she cannot call Vera "maman": although mothers might be substitutable for the daughter, they are not so for the mother. When her father calls her "my daughter," she feels something special: "like the assurance of his constant support, and also a little like a challenge . . ." [C, 240]. This is not necessarily an idyllic rapport, but its solidity does confirm Nathalie's sense of self because she is recognized. It is as if the father provided the frame of the mirror in which Nathalie's self-image could be constituted. Of equal importance for the construction of a point of view is the fact that the reader is allowed to see the father (as an object) undergoing the movement of a tropism (in the "I love you" episode), whereas the mother is more a *catalyst* of tropistic (re)actions and therefore remains an enigmatic subject, too opaque to provide a satisfying framework for identification. Nathalie plays the man to Freud's narcissistic woman who, in this instance, is Sarraute's own mother.[54] That is to say, the mother is portrayed as wrapped up in her own concerns, a form of self-love, that fascinates the child but which she cannot penetrate. And in another twist, one can add that Nathalie plays mother to her father since she protects him from the strife between her stepmother and herself.

Now what is interesting to me in this schema is not the "truth" of the good father/bad mother characterization. In many instances her natural mother's very caring prompts Nathalie's perception of treachery and her adopted grandmother could easily function as a "good mother." Nathalie mourns her grandmother's departure in much the same way as she had her mother's. What is striking, however, is the way the movement of Sarraute's familial identifications interacts with her writing. Her fictive characters and anonymous voices repeat her intense childhood need to fuse with others—especially with her mother. The fear of rupture, which Sarraute describes as the motivating force for the characters in her works,[55] recalls the agony she undergoes at feeling shunned by her mother. The recurrent image of the mother's rejection in *Childhood* provides a dramatic content that is embodied in the structure of the tropism with its constant shifts and myriad reversals.[56] The act of betrayal—of an idea, a position, a person—intervenes in practically all Sarraute's creative works as a primary form of reversal.[57] Stylistically, it is a useful strategy to avoid a singular point of view.

The association between Sarraute's writing style and the rapport with her mother and father is certainly not a connection that Sarraute would readily acknowledge. Nevertheless, the parents are, in an important sense, intricate figures of particular conceptions of reality and writing that work their way through Sarraute's creative endeavors and theoretical positions.[58]

We already noted that during Nathalie's adolescence, when she is living with her father, she finds security in the formal, controlled education that her father encourages: "I liked things that were fixed, determinable, immutable. . ." [c, 190]. After the wrenching experiences with her mother (and the ongoing ones with Vera), she enthusiastically welcomes this new security, like the solidity of plane geometry or inorganic chemistry [see c, 190]. In accordance with the system, Nathalie never seeks to go beyond the limits of what is expected of her. She thrives on dictation assignments because of their precision, their lack of ambiguity. In her essays she derives pleasure in using the formal elements at her disposal and experiences a feeling of power and domination vis-à-vis her readers (in particular her father), who in turn recognize her worth. To be first in classwork, says the female narrator, is not so much to be better than others as to be beyond comparison, unique [c, 192].

It is significant that in the writing assignment Sarraute remembers best, "My First Sorrow," the young author is completely uninterested in telling something from her own experience! It never occurs to her to write something personal. She chooses instead a "sorrow" that will please her readers—the death of a pet dog. Both narrators agree that in the early school years creation adheres to a set of formulas in order to produce a clean, tidy story: "You needed that clarity, that smooth roundness, you didn't want anything to stand out . . . . [. . .] 'My First Sorrow' is as fixed and rounded as one could wish, not the slightest asperity, no abrupt, disconcerting movement . . ." [C, 189–90]. One is reminded of certain voices in Sarraute's *The Golden Fruits* or *Do You Hear Them?* who seek perfection in art. In the autobiography, the child's depersonalized version of writing is like an amusing echo of critics in the sixties who attacked the New Novel for its supposedly dehumanized quality. The young Nathalie also embodies Simone de Beauvoir's description of the female writer who seeks to please rather than to surprise or shock.[59] As an adolescent, she does not even dream of being a writer; to become a teacher is what attracts her most. It is not until Sarraute begins to contest this training that a measure of the personal marks her writing.[60]

It is imperative to note that *Childhood* does *not* develop a series of positive identifications between mother and daughter, as it does between father and daughter. Understandably so: in her father's home, any sign of the mother's traits in the daughter is automatically viewed negatively: "And now it seems that not only does she [the maid, Adèle] know of the existence of my mother, but she never lets my mother out her sight . . . [. . .] she still sees her mark on me. Signs that I carry unwittingly . . . bad signs" [C, 141]. And Sarraute as an adult writer even seems to perpetuate the fear of resembling her mother. Although the author devotes several pages in her book to writing under the father's influence, she makes no explicit connections between her writing as an adult and the fact that *her own mother was a writer*.[61] This similarity does, nevertheless, give the reader cause for reflection about potential connections between the two. That her mother writes is only mentioned in passing in two early scenes of *Childhood*. The first scene in which the information is provided describes the mother and child in a park:

With my back close up against the warmth of her leg under the long skirt . . . I can no longer hear the sound of her voice as it was in those days, but what does come back to me is the impression that, rather than to me, it's to someone else that she is telling . . . no doubt one of the children's stories she writes at home on big pages covered in her large handwriting with its disconnected letters . . . or is she composing it in her head . . . the words addressed elsewhere flow . . . I can, if I wish, grasp them in passing [. . .] I can let myself go, I can allow myself to be immersed in that golden light, that cooing, that chirruping, the tinkling of little bells on the heads of the donkeys and the goats [. . .] [C, 12].

This is a wonderful lyrical scene, too "pretty" in fact for the masculine narrator; it suggests a comparison to the mother's expansive, affectionate language in her letters. And yet what appears clear in this warm, poetic moment is the total *lack* of verbal exchange between mother and child. The mother's voice does not seem to address Nathalie; the stories she invents are for someone else. The mother/daughter relationship is physical and the words are like the incantatory flow in a lullaby. Although the little girl appears old enough to understand the stories, it is the ties to the mother's body which are most gratifying in the adult's memory. Empathic merger prevails over a communication between individuals. We are reminded of the reader's plunge into the world of the tropism as described in *The Age of Suspicion*. It is as if a possible tie between mother and daughter as writers could only surface in its denial, in favor of the physical rapport. When that is gone, the lack of verbal rapport between mother and daughter is reconfirmed: later on, her mother's affectionate letters seem childish to Nathalie, now that she lives with her (unaffectionate) father: "She doesn't know who I am now" [C, 111]. This distance helps Nathalie to make the (necessary) move of becoming independent of her mother by rejecting her in turn. But the break is not quite complete: "I feel I don't ever want to get a letter again, I want to break these bonds forever, but every time, the tender, caressing words at the end hold me back, envelop me . . ." [C, 111]. The bonds are strong, even if they cause great pain and are repudiated.

In the second scene where her mother's profession as a writer is mentioned, we witness a "childhood trauma." The little girl has ventured to write her own romantic novel inspired by her readings. This very early creative endeavor is squelched, however, when the director of the review for which her mother writes curtly tells Nathalie that she should learn to spell first. The narrators somewhat sarcastically label this her "childhood trauma," a convenient way to explain that she did not begin to write before age thirty-two. But the narrators do agree that it corresponds to her perception of the experience. Curiously, however, what Sarraute omits from the passage, but includes in an interview, is that the daughter's novelistic initiation is a direct imitation of her mother's writing activity.[62] In the *Childhood* scene, the mother's influence on the actual desire to write goes unspoken. In fact, her participation in the scene appears rather negative: she forces Nathalie, albeit gently, to show her work, while the daughter resists. The mother becomes part of the "trauma." In the interview Sarraute scoffs at her own childhood creation, underlining its conventionality, its platitudes. If the association between mother and daughter is made, it is only to emphasize that the adult daughter's work has little to do with that early maternal influence. Such a move is understandable for a writer who refuses facile origins and causalities. Sarraute does not write because her mother wrote; but she *does* conjecture that she may not have written for a long time because her mother and stepfather were writers.[63] The narrators add that the early taboo on creative writing turns out to be an advantage, for it keeps Sarraute from blindly reproducing traditional forms of literature in her adult works. Instead of imitating the mother's writing, she will repeat her relationship to her.

Sarraute stated in a recent letter to Gretchen Besser that the current emphasis on *women's* writing makes her "regret the time when women wrote under masculine pseudonyms, and how right they were!"[64] In the interview after *Childhood* Sarraute also mentions quickly that her mother wrote under a male pseudonym that was never discovered.[65] And Sarraute preserves her mother's secret by not supplying the pseudonym in the interview. If we link her two comments, Sarraute paradoxically denies feminine writing by repeating her mother's own veiling of feminine identity. While the mother covers over her feminine signature, the daughter, in her fiction, gradually phases out fictional characters' names and chooses male narrators. Again, the rapport with the feminine in general and with the mother in particular surfaces as a disclaimer or a denial.[66] But it is the strongest link yet, since Sarraute faithfully reproduces the mother's negation of her own gender.

In considering how *Childhood* supplies a psychic content to Sarraute's tropistic phenomena, I must at least mention one fundamental element in *Childhood* (and in all her works), an element without which I risk turning her scenarios into "tragedy" in the most anti-Sarrautian way. If distance characterizes the anguishing dimension of Nathalie's rapport with her mother—both physically and emotionally—it also allows for a large dose of *humor* to diffuse the tension. It keeps the author from taking her past too seriously and allows the reader breathing room in the hothouse atmosphere of the tropism. Whether it involves the occasional squabbles of feminine and masculine narrators, a child blurting out on a whim that her mother resembles a monkey, or writing an essay called "My First Sorrow" that has nothing to do with her . . . the intensity of Sarraute's empathic-combative moves is broken up by laughter or at least a smile. And we laugh as much at ourselves as at others, because we all are implicated in the tortuous and yet commonplace interactions that her works act out. If Nathalie's separation from her mother and the subsequent desire to reunite with her inform Sarraute's most intense literary moves, it is the distance from her that affords a space in which the return of the repressed feminine identification creatively breaks through.

Sarraute's writing turns into a transgressive activity when it breaks with the modes of formal knowledge that the paternal order had instilled in her as a girl. Like her mother, she eventually becomes the rebellious student, stressing the creative deviation from the standards of an education preaching rules, reason, order. In one interpretation, at least, the slashing of the settee in the opening anecdote enacts the violent refusal to remain within the paternal rules. This early experience is, in important ways, closer to the creative process than Nathalie's writing attempts as an adolescent. The adult writer slices through the satiny surface of classical writing instead of trying to duplicate it.[67] Language will be the scissors *and* the fabric of this transgression. But Sarraute's creative work—autobiographical and fictive—also (re)-produces the impossible desire to communicate without words getting in the way, in a prelinguistic immediacy where the subject/object dichotomy is not operative.[68] The scene with her mother in the park is emblematic of an almost magical experience that exceeds words, one in which verbal betrayals are not possible.

Sarraute's texts contest the idea that language is adequate to experience or that communication could exist with little or no effort.[69] If her father's logocentric world is reassuring to Nathalie, it is not the place of her most intense experiences. It covers over, hides, and even denies the existence of the tropistic movements which are the stuff (stuffing?) of desire. The unsettling rapport with her mother is inscribed in Sarraute's work, not as a character or a type, but rather as a mode of interaction, and more specifically as a reaction to the desired other. The poetic quality of Sarraute's style—with its unexpected rhythms, repetitions, and variations on a single event, its profuse imagery (evoking tenderness, as well as combativity), its clichés and elisions—defies the classical rules that produce a solid, well-rounded composition with no holes (the kind that Nathalie created while in her father's care), and unwittingly traces the movements of attraction and repulsion felt toward her mother.[70]

*

Childhood stops, somewhat abruptly, with Nathalie's entry into a lycée, because from then on the past seems clear. The desire for autobiography is rooted in an exploration of the remote, unlit regions of the past [c, 246]. And although Sarraute's conscious autobiographical choices are based on the literary, formal qualities of the memories, their subject matter creates a family scenario very close to Chodorow's descriptions of female identity formation. We have seen that the psychic investment in the figure of the mother is both powerful and ambivalent. The father retains a characteristic distance from the daughter, while the mother figures as fascinating self (I find myself in her) and other (I lose myself in her). In terms of the literary tradition, Sarraute deftly manages to remain within its limits, while concurrently poking it full of holes, a form of creative deconstruction, but one which is not necessarily "feminine." (All avant-garde texts tend to do this.)

It is rather the interweaving of psychic processes (characteristic of women's identity formation) with the formal innovations of Sarraute's writing, that reveal a feminine trace in her work. Beyond the realm of intention, *Childhood* forcefully enacts the negativity involved in the asymmetry of mothers' and fathers' roles in child-rearing. The tropism reproduces this negativity, while manifesting our desperate human need for love in the difficult dealings with "Mother," an internalized representation of total fusion (a figure of the self's death), and complete separation (the self comes into being through an impossible desire). Sarraute creatively succeeds in making the personal struggles of the female child she was into the dramas of all subjects in language. "I" am much more than people see or say, but "I" only exist through contact with them. As a speaking subject within the social contract of language, my gender belongs to a conventional code that reifies the fluctuations and shifts of my being, but it is also the unnameable, violent response to others as "I" reach out for or withdraw from them.

Rewriting Her Story, from Passive to Active: Substitutions in Marguerite Duras's *The Lover*

3.

With an artistic production spanning over forty-five years (thus comparable to that of Sarraute), and including an impressive array of novels, plays, and films, Marguerite Duras is no doubt one of the most widely read contemporary French writers today.[1] She has become a favorite among a heterogeneous audience ranging from psychoanalytic, semiotic, and feminist critics, to the general reading public. Her autobiographical work, *The Lover*, was awarded the Goncourt Prize in 1984 (exactly thirty years after de Beauvoir received it for *The Mandarins*), and became an instant best-seller, thereby confirming Duras's appeal among a nonacademic audience. Much of the allure of her novels (particularly following *Moderato Cantabile* in 1958) stems from the sparse, hypnotic language whose unusual rhythms, repetitions, and pronominal ambiguities always appear to evoke more than the few words on the page, as if the blank spaces were made to speak the promise of something more substantial, more poetic, and more true than ordinary language or thought. Her unorthodox stories of love, madness, passion, and violence haunt the reader as they make their way through a seductive, exotic atmosphere, heavily laden with unnamed or indirectly suggested states of being, from despair to intense pleasure, sometimes underneath a character's mask of indifference. The Durasian narrative most often focuses on female characters who fascinate by virtue of their double nature as mesmerizing enigmas *and* familiar representations of women as mothers, daughters, wives, lovers . . . . Her woman-centered universe continually calls attention to the relationships of women to their desires, their bodies, to language, and to the question of female subjectivity.

Like Sarraute's *Childhood*, *The Lover* came as a surprise to many Durasian aficionados, but unlike *Childhood*, critical reactions to it were more mixed. Although—or perhaps because—*The Lover* was such an incredibly popular success, Duras's turn to autobiography was perceived by some professional critics as a "betrayal" of her talents, a turn to facility and vanity, a crossover from high to low (commercial) literature.[2] For while her early novels from the fifties, such as *The Sea Wall* and *The Sailor from Gibraltar*, had appealed to a nonacademic readership, professional critics had been most interested in her more stylized, obscure novels of the late sixties, the seventies, and the early eighties. In her 1984 televised interview with Bernard Pivot, Duras noted that the autobiographical piece had been commissioned, so that the connection between money and writing about the self is made explicit.[3]

The critical reaction to *The Lover* is in keeping with autobiography's less than respectable status vis-à-vis literature and confirms Duras's perennial tendency to straddle categories and to confound opinion. Whether in politics, literature, or feminism, Duras resists dogmatic stances and evaluations. In the introduction to her recent book, *La Vie matérielle* [Material Life], a collection of personal reflections transcribed from oral exchanges, Duras cautions readers that although the book represents what she thinks, she does not carry in her the "flagstone of totalitarian thought," meaning her thoughts are not "definitive." "I avoided that affliction [*"plaie"*]," she adds. The book thus represents what she thinks "sometimes, on some days, about some things."[4] Like de Beauvoir, she refuses to be pinned down by her statements. Duras's dodge also points up that for her, speech (and writing) do not function as an affirmation of eternal truths, and that the self can only be thought of as an inconsistent, mobile figure in discourse, rather than as a legitimized/legitimating, preordained origin.[5]

Stylistically and generically, *The Lover* is a hybrid that brings together elements of Duras's writings from other periods. Less opaque than the short stories or *récits* immediately preceding it, *The Lover* nevertheless pursues the scandalous subject matter of eroticism, violence, and sexual contact already found in the earlier works of the eighties such as *The Malady of Death* or "The Seated Man in the Passage." Its sexual violence, however, seems attenuated in comparison to a story like "The Seated Man in the Passage" (where a woman is beaten and possibly killed by her lover), but its tale of impossible love certainly carries the romantic tenor present in all her works. Rather than a pared-down short narrative or *récit* (like the works immediately preceding it), *The Lover* resembles more a full-fledged novel in its breadth, at the same time that it openly adopts the referential mode of autobiography. On one level, then, the reader encounters a captivating, even titillating, story of sexual initiation on the part of a well-known author—the sort of "true confession" subject matter reminiscent of the tabloids—while on another, the work anchors itself in the continual resumption of Durasian fiction: *The Lover* takes up, in fact, much of the autobiographical material from her early novel, *The Sea Wall*,[6] written over thirty years before, although in a very different style and with a distinct emphasis. *The Lover* also tells stories that intersect with other works, such as the long story/novella entitled "Whole Days in the Trees," and her play, *Agatha*.[7] In the "rewriting," Duras moves from third- to first-person narration and establishes coincidences between author, narrator, and character. Like de Beauvoir's rewriting of the account of Zaza's death in the *Memoirs*—moving from fiction to autobiography—Duras's *Lover* is not a foundational text of truth, but a new version or offshoot of other fictions.

This act of rewriting—selecting a new focus or frame for familiar material, developing a fragment already present in another work, bringing out what wasn't said in a previous fiction—characterizes nearly all Duras's writings. Her novels, plays, and films continually overlap and defy generic categories. And the interlocking continues with the life-text, since Duras's fictive landscapes draw upon her own biography—from her childhood in Indochina, or her experiences during World War II, to her bouts with alcoholism. Rather than as an inventor, she describes herself as an echo chamber that transforms the material of others, of her surroundings . . . as they pass through her.[8] Duras thus does not place the emphasis on a manipulating feminine "I," fictive or autobiographical, that successfully controls or reigns over the fiction. In discussing her characters, for example, she readily notes that she would be incapable of telling/knowing everything about them: "'I find the madmen of S. Thala on the beach. I don't know how they got there.' It's other people who know how it began. It's others, maybe, who have inside them the beginning of that."[9] The first-person female (and author-identified) narrative is not, in fact, characteristic of most of the narratives published before *The Lover*.[10] In earlier works (for example, in *The Sailor from Gibraltar*, *The Ravishing of Lol V. Stein*, or *The Vice-Consul*), a female character is frequently the indirect subject whose story a male character attempts to tell and (fails) to appropriate. The female character resists being reduced to the male's object, but it is unclear how her subjectivity would be defined. This is in part why *The Lover*, as an autobiographical project, is so intriguing: the female narrating voice posits the possibility of resuscitating (creating) her past from her "own" point of view. I place "own" in quotation marks because Duras continually makes us aware that a point of view is always relative to others and is itself split and mobile, rather than a fixed property of the self. *The Lover* poses the question of female subjectivity via the interaction between the narrating "I" as storyteller, and the "she" the narrator remembers having been. In her version of feminine/feminist autobiography, Duras unveils the feminine as a dynamic, perverse force that calls into question, from within the traditional system of representation, the oppositions active/passive, subject/object, that have been used to assert gender/sexual difference as hierarchy.

The Lover stresses the affirmative power of feminine desire as a disruption of a repressive social order that deprives women of the position of subject. But in Duras's autobiographical economy, the "I" also writes (reads) feminine desire as a circulating movement that poses identity in a constitutive *and* alienated self-creation. Her doubled subject (I/she) draws her strength from the myriad identifications with others' desires, rather than from the presumption of a unique, undivided self, impervious to others' demands. Instead of trying to shore up the split in the subject, Duras's feminine subject—like Duras the writer—is open to the intersubjective currents that pass through/create the subject. Like Sarraute, Duras uncovers how a certain "feminine" position in language and the social order is exemplary of all subjectivity. She takes on the (male) tradition, assumes its modes of thinking as she dismantles them. What is perhaps most provocative about Duras's sophisticated profiles of feminine subjectivity in *The Lover* is that they figure in a highly seductive, romantic love story that appeals to the reader's sense of an absolute, an image of an undying, impossible love. Duras's feat is to bridge the gap between an exotic, alluring romance and an effective reevaluation of its premises.

DURASIAN TURNS—
EXISTENTIALISM, THE NEW NOVEL, AND FEMINISM

Whereas consistent views throughout Sarraute's career allowed us to highlight certain features of her literary practice as well as her positions on feminism, Duras's writing performs chameleonlike transformations that make it impossible to connect her name with just one literary movement, one political stance, one style, or one kind of feminism. *The Lover*, moreover, bears witness to some of these multiple, often contradictory trends through its intriguing combination of traditional and avant-garde figures of literature (as representation, as nonrepresentation . . .). A brief review of some of Duras's "places" in the literary history of her time will set the stage for our reading of *The Lover*.

Duras has been an active participant on the French intellectual scene since the early forties. Like Sarraute, she was friends with de Beauvoir and Sartre during her early career in the forties, fought in the Resistance (along with François Mitterand) during World War II and published in de Beauvoir's and Sartre's *Les Temps modernes*.[11] Her political activities include her membership in the Communist Party for seven years, beginning in 1947. Forced out of the Party in the fifties, Duras has since tended to commit herself to unorthodox political viewpoints that wreak havoc with narrow party positions, whether from the left or the right. At one point in *The Lover*, Duras establishes an equivalence between some friends' collaboration with the Germans during the War and her own membership in the Communist Party: "The two things are the same, the same pity, the same call for help [. . .]."[12]

This skepticism has not stopped her, however, from providing strong ideological criticisms of oppressive social and political institutions. All her artistic endeavors implicitly (or explicitly) challenge colonialism, racism, sexism, anti-Semitism, and so on. Literature never works "at the service" of these causes for Duras, even though her position on the relation between politics and literature has wavered: she has alternately held a position proclaiming the "absolute non-commitment of the writer," and the idea that "revolutionary demands and literary demands are one and the same."[13]

Duras's early novels of the forties and fifties, such as *The Sea Wall* and *The Sailor from Gibraltar*, are stylistically her most traditional (in structure, plot, characters, point of view, syntax . . .) and have been compared to those of Hemingway and Camus. During this "existentialist period,"[14] Duras, like Sartre, seems to have been literarily influenced by American realism.[15] Her early novels feature struggling individuals in an absurd world devoid of transcendental meaning. And similar to Camus in *The Stranger*, Duras shuns psychological analyses of intimate feelings, preferring instead to trace a rugged ethos via actions, terse dialogue, and attitudes.[16] Choosing one's fate—or accepting it—is a primary issue in her early works. Although Duras (unlike Sartre, Hemingway, or Camus) always figures a major female character among her protagonists, Alain Vircondelet's early study of Duras qualifies her writing as "virile."[17] No doubt the lean style, attentive to sensations with few references to an inner emotional life, contributes to Vircondelet's impression. "Virile" writing is stereotypically simple, direct, not "flowery," and deals with "strong" (that is, unemotional) figures.[18] For Vircondelet, this virile writing of Duras is "revolutionary": the critic's description is meant to be complimentary and, in effect, to save Duras's work from being (negatively) categorized as "feminine literature." The critic justifies Duras's depiction of couples and women (traditional "feminine" topics) through her sociopolitical commitment.

Interestingly enough, Camus's style and Duras's *later* prose have both been characterized as an "*écriture blanche*," Roland Barthes's term to denote a neutral, ("white") writing that works toward eliminating any adornment, "an ideal absence of style."[19]

In the context of Duras's entire writing career, what is most striking and paradoxical about the ties to Camus and Hemingway is that, while Duras's writing has been described as "virile," her work as a whole has also come to be representative of "feminine writing" for many readers. Even if one allows for the very real differences between Durasian styles in early novels and later ones, it is nevertheless difficult to sort out the contradictory gender categorizations. What is intriguing is that Duras will eventually glean "masculine" characteristics (narrative distance to characters' emotional lives, reduced interpretative analyses, extreme economy of words) in fashioning a style that is perceived as responsive to a "feminine" experience.[20] Duras confounds essentialism even as she uses its play of gender difference. Her "feminine" style will unsettle conventional oppositions between masculine and feminine (culture/nature; active/passive; subject/object; straightforward/circuitous . . .), without, for all that, doing away with a mobile notion of difference.

In the late fifties—starting with *Moderato Cantabile*—and continuing on into the sixties and seventies, Duras's novels become markedly less realistic and break away from traditional novelistic conventions. This occurs just at the time when the New Novel is gaining in prominence. In this second period of her career, Duras's name is associated with those of the New Novelists, although she remains at the fringes of the group, declining to take part in New Novel colloquia or to explain her works through New Novel theory and criticism. In the seventies, in fact, she will qualify theory disdainfully as a masculine imbecility that smothers creativity instead of assisting it.[21] Nevertheless, Duras has never actively discouraged critics' efforts to link her works with the New Novel: in an interview with Madeleine Chapsal, she stated that it did not bother her when critics called her a New Novelist.[22] But contrary to Sarraute, for whom the New Novel phenomenon becomes a means to justify her work, to obtain recognition and an increased audience, Duras has remained largely indifferent to it, even though her name cropped up many times in the 1972 Cerisy colloquium on the New Novel, even though her works of the late fifties and onward do share many concerns with other New Novels.[23] Duras explains her own break with a traditional (realist) style of novel-writing through her personal biography:

I had a love affair and I think that's when everything changed. [. . .] It was an erotic experience that was very, very, very violent—how do you describe it?—I went through a crisis that was . . . suicidal; that is . . . what I tell in *Moderato Cantabile*, this woman who wants to be killed, I lived that . . . and from that point on, my books changed . . . [. . .] I think that the turn, the veering around toward . . . toward sincerity happened then.[24]

The autobiographical crisis that marks an important change in Duras's writing uncannily coincides with the changing winds of literary taste that welcome the transformations of the New Novel. Duras seems to provide a sort of personal confirmation that the New Novel's attention to new linguistic forms (that challenge the tradition) is intimately involved in new ways of apprehending the real, and not just a sterile formal exercise.

Duras's literary affinities with the New Novel are multiple and frequently enable us to gauge the potential links between stylistic innovations and the women's issues running through her work. Like the New Novelists, Duras is constantly undoing the traditional novel and reworking its components. For example, de Beauvoir's reproachful description of the New Novelists as the "*école du regard*," that is, "the school of the gaze," or "objective school,"[25] might aptly include Duras's and Robbe-Grillet's works, since both have considered the gaze in relation to sexuality and desire.[26] Like Robbe-Grillet and Claude Simon, she is fascinated by the politics of the gaze, an essential component in the construction of point of view, although she articulates the question more as a function of *gendered* subjectivity and its transformations than do the others.[27] Duras frequently stages the typical scene of the woman who is being looked at and does not know it, but with the emphasis on the active look's inability to capture fully or possess the object of the look. And by shifting the origin of the gaze from a male viewer to a female viewer, she stresses the circulation of the look rather than a unidirectional movement (from male subject-viewer to female object).[28] The reader is made to identify with the position of the object of the gaze, as well as with the gaze itself, so that the spectacle is no longer exclusively feminine, or the gaze exclusively masculine.

Although Sarraute and Duras belong to the same literary generation and have had ties to the New Novel, few critics have noted the features that their works hold in common. On a simple thematic level, both Duras and Sarraute locate their novelistic interrogations in the familiar social relationships of families, friends, and couples. Both are interested in the way desire invests these relationships—although its sexual character is repressed in Sarraute. Marcelle Marini has noted that Sarraute's incessant battle against stultifying abstractions that limit the force of experience in language runs parallel to Duras's indictment of theoretical discourses that deaden literary invention and stifle political action (May 1968 is Duras's example).[29] Sarraute's distaste for a language that reifies experience and its multishaded, shimmering forms is shared by Duras. With a fulminating shorthand—Hélène Cixous calls it an "art of poverty,"[30]—Duras electrifies simple, old words that have become limp from overuse. She revitalizes, complicates, and intensifies an "I love you" so that the words become thoroughly explosive. By stripping them of adornment or realistic supports, she scrapes away the cliché, frees them of any psychological banality, and restores their magical power.[31] In *The Use of Speech*, Sarraute accomplishes a similar feat when she charts all the subtle detours, the slight "nothings," that make up the "experience of love" before it has been named, before it knows itself as an identifiable phenomenon.

Both Duras and Sarraute consider their fiction to aim at what others have neglected or might well consider unworthy of treatment. In *The Age of Suspicion*, Sarraute defends her obsessed, solitary writer, hesitantly insisting that his slight discoveries are indeed significant. In an interview, Duras declares herself "suspicious" of the confident, prefabricated story: "I don't know how it's possible to write what's already been explored, inventoried, reviewed [. . .]."[32] In *Woman to Woman*, she says that for her, what is most important is what others take for leftovers or remains.[33] Both women conceive of their endeavor as a formulation of what has been silenced or elided in other forms of literature. Through their own repeated use of ellipses, they push their texts beyond themselves. In their fiction, the word "nothing" recurs persistently, as if to make present the memory or trace of what ordinarily is denied existence in literature.

In accordance with the tenets of the New Novelists, Duras

avoids traditional linear chronology and psychological causality. Her novel use of the past conditional and the future perfect sets her stories' actions adrift in a temporal mode that does not limit itself to a simple logic of sequential events. And as Michel Foucault has pointed out, her stories retain a certain opacity, as if we readers were outside the characters and their situations.[34] She creates an effect of strangeness by positioning the reader outside the characters' inner lives. Sarraute, although coming at the problem from a completely different angle, also achieves this effect of strangeness, but it is by immersing the reader in the magma of anonymous interiors (or tangential points between exteriors and interiors). Both Sarraute and Duras prevent us from identifying completely with their characters/voices in a mimetic game, but at the same time, we experience their fascination and become fully engaged in the multiple constructions of potential meaning. The reader bathes in an opaque, indeterminate language and cannot control or even, perhaps, hold on to the text. Cixous says that one can't seize or retain the Durasian text, because it resists being taken in as a knowledge or memory to possess; it slips or flows through our fingers.[35] Instead, the reader *is possessed* by the haunting atmosphere evoked, like a person possessed by a spirit. This is the passive position to which the reader must submit, but it is also a highly pleasurable part of the textual seduction.

Like Sarraute, Duras questions the autonomy and uniqueness of individual subjects by stressing the interchangeability of the positions that people occupy in language and in relationship to one another. Female character identity circulates as an autobiographical fiction: "And when I speak of these other women [Duras's characters], I think of them as containing me in them; it's as if we were porous, myself and them."[36] Although Duras's characters are not anonymous, their identities frequently become confused when a personal pronoun, "*il*," "*elle*," and so on, seems potentially applicable to more than one person or name. Given that all nouns are gendered in French, the confusion multiplies, because a gendered personal pronoun can *also* refer to an idea, a thing, or an animal, as well as a person. Here, Sarraute parts ways with Duras: the former consciously uses gender in her novels according to wholly conventional codes, whereas Duras, particularly in her later works, uses the linguistic properties of gender in French to unsettle our expectations about masculine and feminine assignations. Sarraute wishes to make us forget about gender difference since all identity traits are being questioned, whereas Duras problematizes gender in the undoing of stable or unique identities. In "The Seated Man in the Passage," for example, Duras plays with the difference between gender and sex. In a text that, on the surface, appears pornographic and misogynist (a woman is beaten during sex), the male character's penis is referred to as "*elle*," the feminine pronoun "she" (feminine nouns denoting the male sexual organ do exist in French), while the woman's sexual organs are referred to with the masculine noun, "*le sexe*." These "cross-references," entirely consistent with French gender rules, perversely interfere with any unambiguous message of sex: linguistic gender has the potential to disrupt our perceptions of biological difference.[37]

During the seventies (and eighties), Duras's writings are read more and more for their feminist attributes, so that her textual inventions (alterations of standard syntax, unusual punctuation, her play with point of view, and her generally elliptical style) are highlighted not as New Novel techniques, but as elements contributing to the feminine character of her writing. While Sarraute resolutely continues to separate her literature from the topical issues of her feminism, Duras's outlook evolves (more like de Beauvoir's) from a denial ("Do you consider yourself a woman writer?—Never")[38] to a feminist position linking her life as a woman and her art. In *Woman to Woman*, Duras even notes that her relationship to Sarraute bears a characteristically "feminine" aspect: "When Sarraute had such success with her play, with her play *Isma*, I felt a real joy. And then, telling about it to my friends, I noticed that this joy was felt by women ["*que cette joie était féminine*"] [. . .]. We aren't in competition because we're the opposition."[39] Duras celebrates the artistic success of her friend Sarraute as a shared joy that outwits the competitive (masculine) system. For Duras, women writers constitute a group of outsiders to the cultural institutions, a group supportive of one another's efforts to chip away at the literary traditions and conventions. As we shall see in *The Lover*, for Duras, the bonding of women—as outsiders—is frequently effectuated through their rapport with a man or men in general. Sarraute, while equally supportive of other women's experimental writing, tends nevertheless to repress (the female) gender as an issue in the avant-garde, because it remains a threat to the acknowledgment of literary value for her.

During the seventies, Duras openly rejects de Beauvoir's egalitarian brand of feminism. In *Woman to Woman*, she scorns the idea that women should assume typically "masculine" positions of power or adopt "masculine" values. She iterates her dislike of male theorizing and defends women's passivity and silence as effective forces against oppression.[40] "Men must learn to be silent," she says in another interview.[41] In her later fiction, these views translate as a certain passivity in her characters and the concurrent passive position of her readers (as if one were *traversed* by her words) that can be read as a position of force instead of weakness. Rather than controlling the reading of Duras's texts, one surrenders to them, gets wound up in them.[42] In the well-known footnote to her 1975 essay, "The Laugh of the Medusa," Cixous includes Duras's name among the writers she considers to be practitioners of feminine writing.[43] Although Cixous does not tie feminine writing to the sex of the writer (Jean Genet is on her list), Durasian critics since then have found it difficult to make a claim for Duras's feminine writing without at least raising the question of essentialism. Duras herself certainly does not seem to mind toying with the idea of an essential feminine that is translated in "feminine literature,"

[. . .] an organic, translated writing . . . translated from blackness, from darkness. Women have been in darkness for centuries. They don't know themselves. Or only poorly. And when women write, they translate this darkness. . . . Men don't translate. They begin from a theoretical platform that is already in place, already elaborated. The writing of women is really translated from the unknown, like a new way of communicating rather than an already formed language. [. . .] I know that when I write there is something inside me that stops functioning, something that becomes silent. I let something take over inside me that probably flows from femininity. But everything shuts off—the analytic way of thinking, thinking inculcated by college, studies, reading, experience. [. . .]

Nothing is concerted. Perhaps before everything else, before being Duras, I am—simply—a woman . . . .[44]

For antiessentialists like de Beauvoir and Sarraute, a writing that "flows from femininity" resurrects the reified notions of innate, natural characteristics in women and banishes them to the status of irrational object or immanent other. But Duras's essentialist position is more complex than this. To begin with, she too is suspicious of a stereotypical feminine writing that responds to an already established (masculine) conception of woman.[45] Her "translation from darkness" is an invention—and interrogation—of the feminine in writing, rather than a faithful representation of something clearly defined or definable.[46] The adverb "probably" in the passage denotes a certain hesitation to connect the two (feminine gender and writing) in any unequivocal way.[47] But what is most remarkable in Duras's comments is that her personal description of the scene of writing is so strongly reminiscent of Sarraute's writing scenario, as if Duras's "feminine writing" were her version of Sarraute's efforts to "translate" the tropisms. In both cases, a certain affect is tapped, while the dominant orders of logic, knowledge, and univocal truth are momentarily silenced or made to reveal what they cover over.[48] Duras's "new way of communicating" recalls Sarraute's understanding of what is revolutionary in literature: "[works that] break away from all that is prescribed, conventional and dead, to turn towards what is free, sincere and alive, will necessarily, sooner or later, become ferments of emancipation and progress."[49]

The value of silence remains ambivalent in Duras's texts, since it is both the sign of a suppression of women's voices and the sign of their power, their rebellion. Duras's works proclaim women's revolt even as they acknowledge that the forms of this revolt (madness, silence . . .) do not liberate the subject from her contradictions. From the hysteric Lol to the sensual seductress Anne-Marie Stretter, or the listless, passionate mother and housewife (Anne Desbaresdes in *Moderato Cantabile*, Elizabeth Alioune in *Destroy, She Said*), or the Indian beggar woman, Duras protrays women as anesthetized subjects coming with touch with—silently rehearsing—their own (impossible) desire, as they see it circulate in others, or as others recognize it in them.[50] Duras's images do not figure an idealized "Woman."[51] They do, however, stage certain codings of femininity, as well as their expunction or distortion. *The Lover* will bring into play these various representations (and deviations) as they interact with/construct the referential subject of autobiography. Woman as lack, dispossessed of presence, voice, self, identity . . .—woman as plenitude, narcissistic and self-sufficient . . .[52]—the Durasian "I" will adopt and pervert these images as she weaves together the stories of desire in relation to her sexuality, her sense of self in discourse, in history, in the family, in love.

THE LOVER

Unlike Sarraute, Duras seems quite unabashed about turning her attention to herself within the confines of the much-used autobiographical genre. Flaunting the pleasures of self-representation from the very first page, she coyly opens with a quotation from an admirer:

One day, I was already old, in the entrance of a public place a man came up to me. He introduced himself and said, "I've known you for years ["*depuis toujours*"]. Everyone says you were beautiful when you were young, but I want to tell you I think you're more beautiful now than then. [. . .] I prefer your face as it is now. Ravaged" [L, 3].

The quotation prompts reflections on Duras's visual attributes through time. Instead of Sarraute's ethereal voices, Duras focuses right away on her body, and her face in particular, bringing up, via a man's words, the typical question of feminine beauty and aging. Perversely, the feminist Duras begins her autobiographical portrait with her face as the object of a male gaze. It would almost seem as if she were gleefully assuming the risks that de Beauvoir feared for women's autobiography: the threat of self-indulgence, narcissism, the danger of making oneself into a spectacle: "In order to seduce, [women] know only the method of showing themselves [. . .]," de Beauvoir writes disapprovingly in *The Second Sex* [SS, 786]. But Duras raises the possibility of evaluating youth and age via the spectacle of the woman's body only to undercut the standard chronology of gradual decline, as well as the fear of aging. Even the man's distinction between Duras's youth and age is lessened:

Very early in my life it was too late. It was already too late when I was eighteen. [. . .] I grew old at eighteen. [. . .] My aging was very sudden. I saw it spread over my features one by one, changing the relationship between them, making the eyes larger, the expression sadder, the mouth more final, leaving great creases in the forehead. But instead of being dismayed I watched this process with the same sort of interest I might have taken in the reading of a book [L, 4].

Duras displaces the question of formal, codified beauty in favor of the intriguing changes the body undergoes through its own idiosyncratic time. The aging face becomes a system of signs to be actively *read*: the body is already a form of autobiography, a personal text wound up in speculation and specularization, that is to say, fiction.

Later on in *The Lover*, Duras will point out that the ability to attract, to seduce, is not contingent upon cosmetic aids or physical beauty. The beautiful women she remembers from her adolescence, those who waited to be loved, who killed themselves when they were "ditched," in effect betrayed themselves: "You didn't have to attract desire. Either it was in the woman who aroused it or it didn't exist" [L, 19]. Duras is referring here to feminine desire at the level of the (sexed) body—an active feminine desire that generates others' desire without any willful effort—but it also metaphorically describes the workings of her autobiographical seduction. One senses that Duras is conveying her own textual pleasure, her desire as she sees it represented in the image she is about to evoke. "I often think of the image only I can see now, and of which I've never spoken. [. . .] It's the only image of myself I like, the only one in which I recognize myself, in which I delight" [L, 3–4]. Instead of defensively fending off accusations of narcissism or exhibitionism—all autobiography is, after all, a form of mediated self-love—Duras acknowledges the textual pleasures of self-representation as she invites us into her hall of mirrors. What she will make clear, however, is that a third term will constantly intervene in the formulation of the narcissistic subject. Autobiography is the place or mode in which to celebrate the most pleasing, "secret" figures of the self while flouting decorum. On the surface, at least, this is a relatively traditional view of autobiography. But as Duras flirts with the genre's revelatory properties, she does not become its dupe: "The story of my life doesn't exist. Does not exist. There's never any center to it. No path, no line" [L, 8]. The secret image she focuses on will not provide a "key," because there is no unitary, static ego (or origin) to be discovered. Duras thus makes no claim for a cohesive totality to her life, nor does she orient her autobiographical text with a temporal hierarchy and a single direction of movement. *The Lover* insists rather on the episodic fragments that make up the fabric of "pasts," and on the juxtaposition and/or interweaving of life threads from many ages. Duras tells her stories in circles and leaps, passing through narrative points more than once, skipping ahead to much later periods, returning to earlier moments. Stories do get told, but it is through a series of detours, with one story cutting into another, so that none are intact. Instead of stabilizing the relationship between the narrator's present and the narrated past—as the traditional autobiographical pact tries to do—Duras's alternating images become entwined and confused. Present and past tenses are applied both to the adolescent's story and to the adult narrator's in a sort of collage. We move immediately, for example, from the image of a present: "I have a face laid waste," to the distant present of an image: "So, I'm fifteen and a half" [L, 5]. The past images already anticipate the future (present) in which that anticipation is looked on retroactively: "Now I see that when I was very young, eighteen, fifteen, I already had a face that foretold the one I acquired through drink in middle age. [. . .] I acquired that drinker's face before I drank" [L, 8–9]. In the reading of personal traits, time is a texture, not a straight line. The reciprocal mirroring of pasts and presents self-consciously deprives us of an explanation of the self that would be prior to the self's representations.

*

The image that attracts Duras in *The Lover* belongs to her adolescence in Indochina (today's Vietnam). Like Sarraute's childhood, Duras's early years straddle cultural boundaries that intensify her family scenarios and the distinctions between self and other—in social, cultural, and sexual terms. *The Lover* is both a tale of poverty, desperation, and death, and an intense, alluring story of impossible love.

Raised with her two brothers by her widowed mother, Duras

experiences at an early age French colonial life with all its cultural, economic, and political divisions and glaring social inequities. Because she is French and white, she is automatically distanced from the local population, and is aware of the racial hierarchy that operates in the colony. But she spends her childhood and adolescence speaking Vietnamese everywhere except home, takes her baccalaureate examinations in Vietnamese, and has only limited notions about a France she will not see until age seventeen. Economically, her family is not part of the colonial elite: her mother barely ekes out a meager living for the family as a teacher. By French standards, they are very poor, although they are still more privileged than the native Vietnamese population. When pondering the cause of the myriad lines in her face, Duras remarks on her family's poverty:

Children like little old men because of chronic hunger, yes. But us, no, we weren't hungry. We were white children, we were ashamed, we sold our furniture, but we weren't hungry, we had a houseboy and we ate. Sometimes, admittedly, we ate garbage—storks, baby crocodiles—but the garbage was cooked and served by a houseboy, and sometimes we refused it, too, we indulged in the luxury of declining to eat. No, something occurred when I was eighteen to make this face happen [L, 6–7].

To be poor and white in the French colony is to live a set of contradictions that keeps the child's identifications continually shifting.

When Duras focuses on her first sexual experience at age fifteen and a half with a wealthy Chinese man twelve years her senior, an "inferior" racially and a "superior" financially, the episode becomes emblematic of a willful breaking of social and sexual codes and barriers and is embodied in a narrative that erodes standard oppositions between dominator and dominated. Although romantically doomed from the start because of the social pressures that the racial and economic differences aggravate, the liaison will last one and a half years, until Duras's family moves to France.

Before telling the story of the relationship, Duras carefully builds up the image of herself at the first encounter with her future lover, before they actually speak. The *mise en scène* is drawn from an imaginary photograph, one that could have existed but was never actually taken. The status of the imaginary photo insists on autobiography's creative construction of the self-image, without, however, completely undermining the reference to a lived past. Duras thus composes an image of herself at age fifteen and a half, crossing the Mekong River on a ferry. She is returning to school in Saigon, following summer vacation with her family. Metaphorically, the river-crossing represents the ritual passage from childhood to womanhood via sexual initiation. This passage, however, is read through a grid of cultural transgression and violence to "natural" processes. Duras first stresses the willful scandalousness of the adolescent's attire: a hand-me-down silk dress (from her mother), low cut, "threadbare and almost transparent" [L, 11]; high-heeled gold lamé shoes bought on sale, doubly marked down; and, most important, "a man's flat-brimmed hat, a brownish-pink fedora with a broad black ribbon," of which Duras says: "The crucial ambiguity of the image lies in the hat" [L, 12]. Duras points out that just as the masculine hat contradicts the feminine dress and shoes, the young girl's clothing—clearly chosen (with meager means) to attract attention, to compose an image of seduction, of womanliness—contradicts a frail, adolescent body whose physical traits are not yet anchored in sexual definition. But as the girl transgresses the boundaries between female and male accoutrements, between innocence and worldliness, "nature" itself is altered:

[. . .] beneath the man's hat, the thin awkward shape, the inadequacy of childhood, has turned into something else. Has ceased to be a harsh, inescapable imposition of nature. Has become on the contrary, a provoking choice of nature, a choice of the mind. Suddenly it's deliberate. Suddenly I see myself as another, as another would be seen, outside myself, available to all, available to all eyes, in circulation for cities, journeys, desire [L, 12–13].

When it is combined with the man's hat, the indeterminate nature (gender?) of the child is transformed into a deliberate part of the "feminine" composition. Nature and culture are no longer opposed or separate entities.

This confounding of social and natural attributes produces a doubling of the subject. The narrator's gaze at/reading of the imaginary photograph is a *mise en abyme* of the adolescent's look that is in turn imagined through others. This "look" is both active and passive: the young girl sees herself/is seen by others, sees herself as others would see her, seizes that look (appearance/gaze) for her "own." Subject identity is articulated through the concomitant, inseparable processes of identification and alienation. To evidence the (already) distanced identification in the image, the narrator, using the third person, continually takes her distance from the image, looks at it as would someone else, as if it were someone else. "The girl in the felt hat is in the muddy light of the river [. . .]" [L, 21]. It is not, however, simply a matter of assigning fixed positions to the "I" and the "she." Duras constantly plays with our perspective, keeping us guessing as to whether the "I" in a given passage fills the function of narrator or character, or both. This situation recalls the play between narrator and character in de Beauvoir's memoirs, but in Duras's work the shifts are self-conscious, since there are two pronouns that can designate narrator and/or character. The mirroring of time periods through anticipation and retrospection clouds the differences between past and present. Autobiography becomes a game of hide-and-seek: "I" does not wholly coincide with the past "she," nor is "I" completely distinct from "her." The reader is positioned in the pronominal gap.

Because the story of the sexual relationship does not unfold in an uninterrupted chronicle, but is rather interspersed among other stories, about Duras's mother, her brothers, Indochina . . . , the interpretations of the love story multiply through an array of interlocking interpretative grids. Like Sarraute, Duras is leery of univocal truths. On one level, *The Lover* is a romantic, emotionally charged tale of intense desire and impossible love set in the sizzling tropics. The relationship is clearly defined by a beginning, development, and end, and holds its share of social obstacles to overcome during the course of the affair. On another level, Duras's first sexual relationship could easily be read as a female victimization scene—with the lure of the man's wealth, a poor, adolescent girl is seduced by a much older rich man. The exchange of sex for money is even inscribed in the hat the girl wears: "The link with poverty is there in the man's hat too, for money has to be brought in somehow" [L, 24]. The young girl becomes the potential breadwinner via her sexuality, assuming her dead father's role when her mother and brothers have proven incapable of supporting the family. Her family, because of its racism, automatically assumes that she sees the Chinese man only for his money, never for love.[53] The mother, whom Duras describes as a madwoman intensely loved and hated by her daughter, and as a victim herself of the corrupt colonial bureaucracy that has sold useless land to her, is complicitous with her child's actions, tacitly approves of them. Despite a vehement prohibition (and, later on, even beatings when the mother becomes suspicious), "the mother lets the girl go out dressed like a child prostitute" [L, 24].

The narrative insists upon the connection to prostitution and outrageous social transgression. Her lover calls her "a whore, a slut" [L, 42]; her mother refers to her as "this little white tart" [L, 92]. She is shunned by her aunts, ostracized by everyone in her lycée; the Chinese lover's rich slumlord father says his son would be better off dead than married to "the little white whore from Sadec" [L, 35]. But as in all Durasian fiction, the figure of the prostitute is not just that of a victim, because it is freely chosen and because the woman is not cut off from her own pleasure.[54] At their first encounter, the young white girl's self-assured demeanor contrasts with the Chinese man's nervous, intimidated advances. Despite the fact that he is the experienced one who initiates her into the lovemaking, the girl is the actual initiator in their encounter, even if she only realizes it afterward: "she suddenly knows: she was attracted to him already on the ferry. She was attracted to him. It depended on her alone" [L, 37]. In the girl's reading of her own actions, the sexual experience is turned into an affirmation of her desire and of the intense transports of pleasure and passion. She is not solely the object of the man's desire.

This autobiographical account's insistence on the girl's active, joyful participation in the sexual encounter contrasts sharply with its much-earlier fictive version in *The Sea Wall* (published in French in 1950).[55] In this conventional realist narrative in the third person, the story focuses a great deal on the plight of the mother and on the socioeconomic evils of colonial life.[56] The young heroine Suzanne appears almost secondary at times, and is much more a passive victim than her autobiographical counterpart. On the whole, Suzanne is resistant (because largely indifferent) to the advances of her wealthy suitor, Mr. Jo, and passively accepts his visits because her mother wishes to take him for whatever she can (or to make him marry her daughter). Contrary to Duras's lover, Mr. Jo is a particularly unsavory character who is depicted as a ridiculous, ugly, hypocritical, and weak man disdained not only by the family, but also by Suzanne. There is no sexual relationship between the two: the man's lascivious designs on the girl do not go beyond a little voyeurism as the girl bathes. The traditional heroine's rebellion against the feminine roles of virgin and wife is anticlimactically consummated at the end of the novel in a sexual encounter with a local (white) man who prides himself in conquering all the women of the Indochinese plain where they live. The secret that *The Lover* brings to light, in contrast, is the scandalous assumption of feminine desire and passion in a culturally and racially proscribed relationship that flirts with the idea of willful prostitution.

In *The Lover*, the prostitute is the woman who understands herself to be "in circulation," not belonging to anyone, possessing no one. When the adolescent girl and the man prepare to make love for the first time, she quickly sets some unexpected ground rules:

She says, I'd rather you didn't love me. But if you do, I'd like you to do as you usually do with women. He looks at her in horror, asks, Is that what you want? [. . .] He says he knows already she'll never love him. She lets him say it. [. . .] He says, You've come here with me as you might have gone anywhere with anyone [L, 37].

The girl escapes victimization by undoing some of the pretenses of romantic love. For Duras, the girl's power lies in part in the understanding that she is not singular, whereas others (traditionally men in the social contract, but also women) delude themselves, thinking that they are irreplaceable. Instead of presuming the uniqueness of the couple or the individuality of its participants and their desires—all of which reinforce the idea of romantic possession, particularly of the woman/ object—Duras's female voice emphasizes the way identity is structured by resemblance, mimetism, substitutability.[57] Irigaray describes the potential of mimicry, a historically "feminine" role, thus: "One must assume the feminine role deliberately. Which means already to convert a form of subordination into an affirmation, and thus to begin to thwart it."[58] Duras's autobiographical scenario posits prostitution as the objectification or victimization of the woman (using the third-person voice for this purpose), and then, through the first-person female voice, overturns this subordination by revealing the romantic illusions that subtend it and by affirming the young woman's desire (and, in effect, all desire) as a function of "alienated identifications." The latter are also shown to articulate the man's position: the young girl's lover suffers (and jealously loves her even more) as he recognizes through her words that not only is the girl exchangeable, but *so is he*: "You've come here with me as you might have gone anywhere with anyone" [L, 37]. As we enter into a circuit of interchangeability, our positions in sexual (linguistic, social . . .) systems are shown *not* to be a function of intrinsic properties of individuals. A little later in the text, the man is also cast in the role of the professional lover, which likens *him* to a prostitute: "He's used to it, this is his occupation in life, love, nothing else. His hands are expert, marvelous, perfect. I'm very lucky, obviously, it's as if it were his profession, as if unwittingly he knew exactly what to do and what to say" [L, 42].

Instead of fighting prostitution as a pernicious institutional subjection of women (obviously a common move among feminists), Duras perverts its structure from the inside by confusing "subjects" and "objects" (aggressors/victims) and their gender assignations. She extends the definition of prostitution so that it becomes an apt metaphor for all social transactions. Early in the book, Duras associates the imaginary photo of her frail adolescent body and its outlandish attire with the (future) act of writing, suggesting the tie between the prostitute and the writer:

The body is thin, undersized almost, childish breasts still, red and pale-pink make-up. And then the clothes, the clothes that might make people laugh, but don't. I can see it's all there. All there, but nothing yet done. I can see it in the eyes, all there already in the eyes. I want to write. I've already told my mother: That's what I want to do—write. No answer the first time. Then she asks, Write what? I say, Books, novels. [...] Later she said, a childish idea [L, 21–22].

Without origin, the desire to write, like the desire to love, is already inscribed on/in the unlikely body of the child. And writing—like prostitution—entails an act of seduction that submits the writer to the open-ended, indiscriminate circulation among readers, just as the girl's body and attire are openly offered to the gaze of others.[59] Just as the prostitute makes herself "available" to others, so it is for the writer who, in Duras's terms, is an echo chamber, is "passed through." Interestingly enough, Duras's texts over the years seem to strive toward "embodying" the "thin, undersized" physique of her youth, as if to recreate in writing the connection between sparseness and an ambivalence concerning sexual identity. Her novels become progressively thinner, pared down, even undersized—and her female characters are always thin.[60] Both the body and writing use their spareness in portraying a sexual ambivalence, a certain tension in the unveiling of feminine desire. Writing and the body are props or supports for each other as Duras weaves together nature and culture to produce an image of the feminine that partakes of "feminine" *and* "masculine" attributes.

Duras's seemingly prophetic writing style draws out of the purely personal or idiosyncratic image of herself certain exemplary conceptions of feminine identity formation. The adolescent girl "in circulation," as a desirable object of others' gazes, recalls Lévi-Strauss's structuralist understanding of society as organized around the exchange of women (by men).[61] Irigaray has adroitly questioned the necessity of this social structure that defines women as commodities or fetish-objects enabling relations between men.[62] What is curious about Duras's text is that Duras does not contest the alienated vision of woman, but rather takes on the view while subjecting it to her own particular twists. We have seen that Duras's major alteration in the image of the prostitute lies in the fact that the young girl derives pleasure in the sexual exchange and acquires a certain power from being "in circulation," identifying with the desire of other women, resisting man's possession.

Duras thus turns the girl's prostitution into a link among

women. The link with her mother, for example, goes beyond the latter's acceptance of the monetary benefits that the shocking attachment may bring. Forgetting momentarily the constraints of established morality, the mother "not only accepts" the child's indecency ("embodied" in the outrageous clothing), "she likes it," approves of it [L, 24]. The daughter's enjoyment of sexual pleasure appears almost as a compensation for her mother's lost youth. After the scene of the girl's first lovemaking, the narrative turns abruptly to the mother, but as a virgin child rather than as an adult or parent, as if the mother/daughter roles were reversed: "The image of the woman in darned stockings has crossed the room, and at last she emerges as a child. The sons knew it already. But not the daughter, yet. [. . .] Their mother never knew pleasure" [L, 39]. Near the end of *The Lover*, the mother confirms this last remark, saying to her daughter: "I wasn't like you, I found school much harder and I was very serious, I stayed like that too long, too late, I lost the taste for my own pleasure" [L, 93]. The imaginary photo "contains" both the intense kinship with the mother—the daughter is wearing her dress, enacting her missed pleasure, flaunting a wicked colonial system that has caused her mother so much suffering and despair—and the break with her rule: Duras's defiant pose in the image presages both the assumption of her sexuality and her will to become a writer despite her mother's wishes.

The feminine identifications in *The Lover*, and in all Duras's fiction, articulate identity through triangular desire. Remembering her friend Hélène Lagonelle, the only other white girl at the Saigon boardinghouse, Duras pays tribute to her beauty and expresses her own violent, erotic impulses toward/through Hélène:

Hélène Lagonelle's body is heavy, innocent still, her skin's as soft as that of certain fruits, you almost can't grasp her [. . .]. She makes you want to kill her [. . .]. I'd like to eat Hélène Lagonelle's breasts as he eats mine in the room in the Chinese town where I go every night [. . .].

I am worn out with desire for Hélène Lagonelle. [. . .]

I want to take Hélène Lagonelle with me to where every evening, my eyes shut, I have imparted to me the pleasure that makes you cry out. I'd like to give Hélène Lagonelle to the man who does that to me, so he may do it in turn to her. [. . .] It's via Hélène Lagonelle's body, through it, that the ultimate pleasure would pass from him to me.

A pleasure unto death [L, 73–74].

The feminine "I" multiplies the ways in which the love identifications take place. Duras first operates a reversal of the standard social configuration of two men establishing contact with each other via the exchange of a woman. She begins by insisting instead on the connection between the two women, with the man playing the go-between.[63] But it is also clear that in this fantasized trio, each person can actively play love object, desiring subject, and an intermediary for the two others. Duras defines pleasure in movement, circulating desires, creating more connections, more identifications until one loses oneself in "a pleasure unto death." In this dream of fulfillment, accomplished through a *mediated* desire, all positions can be occupied by all participants. The introduction of a third term in the love rapport—a gesture that Duras repeats several times in *The Lover* and that is characteristic of her fiction—again defines the self through the other's desire. The desiring subject, and, by extension, the autobiographical "I," are shown to be positional effects, not absolute origins. Toward the end of the book, the narrator even imagines the desire and loves of the Chinese man and his future wife, as Duras is eventually replaced by another woman. Again, the power of the feminine lies in envisioning oneself as other, of seeing someone else put in one's "place" and vice versa. What has historically been an oppression of women is turned into a strength.

At the middle of *The Lover*, interrupting the various stories of Duras's youth, are two distinct feminine portraits that do not seem to "fit" into the autobiographical account of Duras's childhood and adolescence because they are from a different period of her life and are not topically connected with the rest. And unlike the portrait of the Lady from Savanna Khet (a model for her fictive character Anne-Marie Stretter), or the madwoman of Vinh Long (the beggar woman of her novels), the descriptions of Marie-Claude Carpenter and Betty Fernandez do not appear to link up with any particular element of Duras's family story, her adolescence, or her fiction. But Duras's brief sketches of these two women, whom she knew during the Occupation, are curiously

apposite in reinforcing her own portrait of/as the female outsider, the woman on the border between cultures, and in establishing bonds with other women in this role. Marie-Claude Carpenter and Betty Fernandez are foreigners whose heterogeneous
names suggest the straddling of cultures and a social alienation—
or at least disaffection—analogous to that in Duras's own self-
portrait. The two women capture attention precisely because
they stand out against their milieus, the historical period, as well
as their context in *The Lover*. The portrait of Betty Fernandez is
particularly shocking because, bound up in Duras's fond personal
memory of her, is the fact that she and her husband were collaborators, thereby implicated in a historical "crime" (this is Duras's
word). The reader is relatively unprepared for the political revelation: "[Betty Fernandez] was always concerned with the practi-
cal details of life, she didn't go beyond that, always a good friend,
very loyal and affectionate. Collaborators, the Fernandezes were"
[L, 68]. The text stresses the incoherence of its parts, the incom-
patibility between the public and the private, the community
image and the personal one. Instead of using the political affilia-
tion to undercut the affinity between herself and Betty Fernandez
(as one might have expected), Duras uses it as another ground for
feminine analogy. As I noted earlier, Duras attenuates the judgment of the Fernandezes, not by justifying (or explaining away)
their political position during the War, but by pointing out the
strict equivalence between their crime and what she considers her
own political error: that of joining the Communist Party. "The
parallel is complete and absolute. The two things are the same,
the same lack of judgment, the same superstition if you like, that
consists in believing in a political solution to the personal problem" [L, 68]. At the end of the second portrait, just after noting
Betty Fernandez's collaborator status, Duras abruptly returns to
her personal data, uncovering her resemblance with the other
woman: "She too, Betty Fernandez, looked out at the empty
streets of the German occupation, looked at Paris, at the squares
of catalpas in flower, like the other woman, Marie-Claude Carpenter. Was 'at home' certain days, like her" [L, 68–69]. Although
Duras is extremely attentive to the way the sociohistorical moment inflects the portrait, ultimately she focuses on the way the

personal exceeds political nomenclatures. These portraits are exemplary in the way they propose common bonds among women that go beyond national origins and political definitions.

Duras's lover is also linked to the series of feminine identifications.[64] The initial distinctions between the adolescent girl (strong, decided) and her lover (fearful, weak) become blurred in their lovemaking: both partners share in all these traits. In Durasian terms, the opposition active/passive is meaningless in the experience of pleasure. In the following passage, an unexpected physical resemblance between the two lovers produces a momentary confusion. The man's body becomes peculiarly "unmasculine" as it is first explored in the text:

The skin is sumptuously soft. The body. The body is thin, lacking in strength, in muscle, he may have been ill, may be convalescent, he's hairless, nothing masculine about him but his sex, he's weak, probably a helpless prey to insult, vulnerable. She doesn't look him in the face. [. . .] She touches him. Touches the softness of his sex, his skin, caresses his goldenness, the strange novelty. He moans, weeps. In dreadful love [L, 38].

Until readers arrive at the first "he," it is not clear to which body, male or female, the text is referring. In a conventional heterosexual love scene, the object of erotic spectacle would no doubt be confined to the woman's body. The initial confusion in the above passage is reinforced when one remembers that the adolescent girl's body has already been described as puny. In two later passages, her mother and then her lover even worry about her body's thinness, as if it might be a sign of illness. The gender ambiguity is prolonged in the French text because the "il" (translated above as "he" but also meaning "it") could just as well refer to "body," a masculine word, as to the male lover: "it [the body] may have been ill, may be convalescent, it's hairless, nothing masculine about it [. . .]." The boundaries between feminine and masculine bodies are temporarily obscured in the textual lovemaking, not so much to deny sexual difference as to flout conventional (white, Western) traits denoting masculinity (toughness, hairiness, muscle, bulk, strength). As was the case in "The Seated Man in the Passage", or *The Ravishing of Lol V. Stein*, Duras disturbs inflexible definitions of gender through the ambivalences of textual identity.

Duras's family stories supply two very different readings of the love relationship that compete in shaping Duras's feminine portrait. In the realm of social interaction, the racist attitudes of the family represent the Chinese lover as an outsider and a racial inferior whose only merit is his money: "it's taken for granted I don't love him, that I'm with him for the money, that I can't love him, it's impossible [. . .]" [L, 5]. Duras insists upon the racial difference by repeatedly referring to herself as the *white* girl, and to her lover as the *Chinese* man. The family's racism, in particular the older brother's, even contaminates the girl's feelings toward her lover to the point that she's ashamed of him and does not speak to him in the family's presence. To avoid her mother's beatings, she denies the relationship in the family's racist vocabulary: "how could I do that with a Chinese, so ugly, such a weakling?" she cries [L, 59]. In the social reading, the family cuts the girl off from her desire—in its presence, the Chinese man is no longer her lover. The earlier purity of her feminine desire (that deconstructs the possessive moves of romantic love from within) is tainted by its resemblance with the family's racism: in both instances the girl avoids saying she cares for the man.

The psychic identifications between family and lovers transgress these social hierarchies and shape another, although related, story of impossible loves. Given the family prototype of the Oedipal triangle, the mechanism of identity substitutions is perhaps most evident in Duras's family configurations: the absence of the father opens up a position in the triangle that enables a series of taboo pairings. Incest is alluded to several times in *The Lover* and the girl's proscribed love affair becomes a substitute for censured family couples. In the tender lovemaking between Duras and her lover, for example, a parent/child relationship is enacted as she becomes her lover's child: "It was with his own child that he made love every evening" [L, 100]. What is intriguing about this rapport is that it compensates for Duras's exclusion from another incestuous duo: Duras's mother and older brother. Although Duras describes this brother as a brute, leading a mean and meaningless life of lies, theft, gambling, and bullying, she also traces the special rapport between him and their mother: in Duras's memory, he is the only one the mother calls "my child" and he can do no wrong in her eyes. In the title story of *Whole Days in the Trees and Other Stories*, Duras had already recounted the story of a mother's all-consuming love for her son.[65] What is interesting, in the context of the feminine identifications in *The Lover*, is the change in Duras's own reading of the principal characters (mother, son, and the son's mistress, Marcelle):

When I wrote the text of *Days in the Trees*, I thought, in fact I was convinced, that the subject was solely that of the love of a mother for her son—a passionate love, an oceanic current involving everything in its path. I think now that while this theme has remained a major one, another has claimed its own place in the play: that of the relationship between the two women . . . .[66]

Again, the hidden relationship is a bond between two women that is (inadvertently) mediated by a man. Although the affective resonances differ, we have seen that this structure is repeated in *The Lover*, as well as in Duras's remarks about Sarraute.

In *The Lover*, Duras reveals that her mother even asks that the older son be buried with her: "Both in the same grave. Just the two of them. It's as it should be. An image of intolerable splendor" [L, 81]. This despised older brother is symbolically killed off in *The Sea Wall*: the young girl Suzanne has only one (good) brother. In the context of *The Lover*, the early fiction appears as a dream fulfillment. First of all, the young girl's revolt against a morally bankrupt social system remains ideally pure, since she shuns the advances of the reprehensible Mr. Jo.[67] Next, Duras conveniently has the mother die near the end, thereby freeing son and daughter. Finally, the girl rides off into the sunset with her only brother (whom she idolizes) and his mistress.

While one brother fills the paternal role in *The Lover* (as the object of the mother's love),[68] the other is the daughter's beloved. Duras associates her Chinese lover's fears, his weakness before his father's will, with those same traits in her younger brother, whom the older brother relentlessly tyrannizes. In another incestuous twist, the Chinese lover becomes the replacement for Duras's younger brother whom she remembers having passionately loved, and who later dies of an illness during the War. Her brother's shadow, like her mother's before, symbolically passes through the room where the girl and her lover make love. In the guise of a hunter (double figure in *The Sea Wall* of Suzanne's beloved brother and the long awaited husband/lover who could rescue her from a desolate life), the younger brother intervenes in the lovemaking:

The shadow of a young hunter must have passed through the room [. . .] sometimes he was present in the pleasure and I'd tell the lover from Cholon, talk to him of the other's body and member, of his indescribable sweetness, of his courage in the forest and on the rivers whose estuaries hold the black panthers. Everything chimed with his desire and made him possess me. I had become his child [L, 100].

Imperceptibly in the last sentences, the narration switches focus, from the brother/hunter to the lover, or rather, it seems to include both of them in the same breath. Like two images fading into one, brother and lover are inextricably bound together in Duras's emotional/fictive landscape.

On the surface at least, the love for the younger brother appears as a core relationship that is compulsively "repeated" in the subsequent encounter with the Chinese man. But characteristically, Duras's "origins" never obey temporal hierarchy; they are never in their traditional "place." Autobiography for Duras does not trace a singular causality through a chronology: Duras's love for her brother is not fully recognized *until he dies* (many years after her affair). In fact, she remarks in her televised interview with Pivot that it is *in the writing* of *The Lover* that she realizes how much she loved (loves) him. It is only in death, as an absent object (of desire, of writing) that the brother *returns* as the primal figure of the painful, lost love: "The wild love I feel for him remains an unfathomable mystery to me. I don't know why I loved him so much as to want to die of his death. I'd been parted from him for ten years when it happened, and hardly ever thought about him" [L, 106]. Similarly, Duras's love story repeats this structure of delayed meaning: her love for the Chinese man, although intensely lived during the year and a half, is not fully admitted, to herself, much less to him or others, until she is en route to France: "suddenly she wasn't sure she hadn't loved him [her Chinese lover] with a love she hadn't seen because it had lost itself in the affair like water in sand and she rediscovered it only now [. . .]" [L, 114]. In the delayed reaction, the "she" of this passage is no longer the controlling agent of the story: just as the adult retroactively realizes how much she cared for her brother, the adolescent recognizes her feelings after the fact. *The Lover* is a voyage of textual discovery, not of a preestablished past, but of pasts as they become alive in the present of writing, and of presents as they are shaped by the representations of the past.

*

Although I have tended to stress the substitutional series that trace (gendered) identity as shifting, multiple, and fragmented, no doubt part of the allure of *The Lover* has as much to do with the radiant fiction of a romantic, prohibited love as with its disruptions of traditional notions (of genre, of gender . . .). In the Pivot interview, Duras herself speaks of the "dazzle of loving" ["*l'éblouissement d'aimer*"] and of the "happiness" involved in the writing of this text. For although the text asserts the interchangeability of partners in love, it also seems to attribute a primacy to Duras's love affair with the Chinese man. *The Lover*'s remarkably touching ending undoubtedly reinforces the work's romantic aspects. First, Duras realizes that she might have actually loved her lover. Then, years after the affair, the Chinese lover phones Duras and reiterates his undying love for her:

He said, I just wanted to hear your voice. She said, It's me, hello. He was nervous, afraid, as before. His voice suddenly trembled. And with the trembling, suddenly, she heard again the voice of China. He knew she'd begun writing books, he'd heard about it through her mother whom he'd met again in Saigon. [. . .] Then he didn't know what to say. And then he told her. Told her that it was as before, that he still loved her, he could never stop loving her, that he'd love her until death [L, 1 1 7].

There is a wonderful generosity in the lover's final declaration, a love that surpasses the limits of the contingent, the variable, the limited, the superficial. In her interview with Pivot, Duras says that this love eclipsed all others in her life. One wonders, then, how this image of the absolute works within Duras's conception of circulating desires and identities. Has Duras sacrificed the text's earlier (feminist) strategies concerning identity formation in order to reaffirm a tradition of romantic love? Perhaps "romantic love" should not be read here as a homogeneous, unified concept. From a certain "masculine" point of view, we saw that it represents values pertaining to (male) individuals who "possess" others in love: the man asserts his identity, his sense of self, and his relationship to others through the woman. She is the object of desire and returns to man the image of his masculinity and selfhood. Its feminine version, however, is entirely different, and this is the conception that Duras seems to invoke (regardless of the gender of those involved). This romantic love stresses unselfishness, generosity, and interdependencies that exceed the narrow, demanding "I" of the individual. It is not so much a sacrifice of the self (a frequent negative interpretation for the female victim who then becomes a slave or a martyr) as a joyful, outrageous expenditure (dispossession) of the self (selves), in love, drink, death, writing . . . . Duras thus manages to intertwine a certain seductive romanticism with her deconstructive assault on (masculinist) individualism.

Within the context of autobiography, Duras's personal alteration in the genre's format lies, paradoxically, in what makes it less personal. The anonymous lover, whose very lack of a proper name makes of him a function or position more than a specific individual, is the counterpart to the girl who strives to fill the "typical" place of woman in the sexual relationship. Duras's insistent use of the third-person pronoun ("she") within the first-person narrative lends an air of solemn ritual to the text, underscores the fictive (conventional) quality both of the love story and of the self,[69] and curiously extends the autobiographical voice beyond the confines of the private image. By this, I mean that autobiography becomes an exemplary springboard for tracing the movements of feminine identity in heterosexual love (with its physical, emotive, psychic, and sociolinguistic intertexts). The doubled subject, I/she, not only acknowledges Rimbaud's familiar dictum that "I" is another, it also ingeniously consecrates an allegiance among women. But Duras goes even farther: instead of imagining the self in terms of inherent (sexual) difference, Duras's autobiography celebrates her sexual initiation as the joy of becoming "like everybody else."[70] *The Lover* is the autobiographical testimonial that wishes to implicate us all in the circulation of desire.

Confusing the Genres: Autobiographical Parody and Utopia in Monique Wittig's *Across the Acheron*

4.

S trictly speaking, none of Monique Wittig's literary works fits a rigid definition of autobiography. There are no auto-biographical pacts, no formal guarantees of identity between author and narrative voice. More often than not, she writes in the present tense rather than in the traditional autobiographical past. And yet, because of the intensely personal, political investment she brings to literature, Wittig constantly transgresses the boundaries between genres. If autobiography is understood as a creative reshaping of itself, crossing personal and collective identities, referentiality, and intertextuality, in a continual re-evaluation of language's relationship to the subject(s) it engenders, then Wittig's fiction is indeed autobiographical.

Few writers have managed to couple a militant feminist agenda and the reworking of literary language and cultural myth as well as Wittig. Focusing almost exclusively on portrayals of women, her two novels from the seventies, *Les Guérillères* and *The Lesbian Body*, as well as *Across the Acheron* (*Virgile, Non* in French) in the eighties, poetically disassemble and reform the discourse and myths of androcentric culture. Cutting across standard categorizations of literary movements, Wittig's fiction presents a confluence of apparently contradictory trends, somewhere between de Beauvoir's conception of personally committed literature and Sarraute's explorations of language in the New Novel. Wittig's ties to literary tradition, both recent and past, constitute a post-modern feminist adventure in the imaginative reworking of our Western cultural heritage. In order to set the stage for an auto-biographical reading of her most recent novel to date, *Across the Acheron*, I will first be considering some of Wittig's theoretical positions on literature and feminism, her ties to de Beauvoir and Sarraute, as well as the autobiographical tenor of her earlier works.

As a lesbian writer adamantly opposed to any notion of an inherently feminine writing, Wittig has most often been placed either in opposition to Hélène Cixous, or in a tradition of lesbian writers.[1] Her ties to de Beauvoir and Sarraute are, however, equally significant, and position her work within a double history of feminism and avant-garde literature of the last half of the twentieth century. Like Duras and Cixous, she devotes her work to a rethinking of women's experience in writing, while her staunch opposition to a notion of "difference" that would be based on sexuality or biology aligns her more with de Beauvoir and Sarraute.

Wittig herself has taken care to articulate some of the junctures between her writings and those of de Beauvoir and Sarraute. Having worked with de Beauvoir in the seventies on the editorial board of the radical feminist journal *Questions féministes*, Wittig has repeatedly linked her own feminist positions to de Beauvoir's. Taking up again de Beauvoir's prophetic statement that "one is not born a woman," ("woman" is not a natural given but rather a cultural—and negative—creation as the other of man), Wittig goes one step farther by dispensing altogether with the concepts of "man" and "woman," because they represent an oppositional ideology in which women are continually dominated.[2] De Beauvoir had also proposed this in her own fashion in *The Second Sex*, when affirming that women should aspire to the full status of human beings, rather than to that of "Woman." But Wittig sees the humanist trap for women: humankind is always represented by the masculine, as mankind. Wittig eliminates the designations "man" and "woman" from her novels in order to conceive of female identity beyond or against the standard opposition, while also deconstructing the idea of an eternal feminine principle. For the most part, she concentrates on female communities (*Les Guérillères*' female warrior-guerillas), or couples in a lesbian community (as in *The Lesbian Body*), although her earlier novel, *The Opoponax*, portrays a community of children, both male and female. In the later works, male beings tend to be present in the form of a shadowy class or group that threatens the autonomy, development, and well-being of a female group. Because the family is a heterosexual institution that has historically confined women's potential and restricted the ways they could conceive of themselves, Wittig turns instead to utopian communities of women, a class of equals who do not rely on mother/child relations or male/female relations for their sense of self.[3] Lesbian is the one positive collective name that she uses in her novels. It provides her with a powerful critical perspective from which to point out historical and social inequities against women, as well as the possibility of imagining new female identities in language.

De Beauvoir's own treatment of lesbians in *The Second Sex* had already acknowledged lesbianism, contrary to the times, as a valid alternative life-style, rather than as a "perversion" or "a curse of fate."[4] By implication, her treatment suggests that lesbianism entails a political refusal to submit to heterosexual ideology, although in her case studies of lesbian writers she does not explore the relationship between their literary strategies and the specific ways they conceive of lived experience.[5] Nevertheless, her boldness in speaking of such a taboo issue in 1949 no doubt seemed as shocking as Wittig's lesbian literature does to some readers today.

In her 1977 interview with Alice Jardine, de Beauvoir, again shunning the feminine essence as a dangerous notion for women, said that a woman's point of view should be "singular and universal at the same time."[6] Wittig expands this idea by envisioning a strategy that brings the two in focus simultaneously. In order to refute the universality of the masculine point of view, Wittig fictively "universalizes the particular," that is to say, she turns her lesbian perspective into a worldview. The shock value of such a maneuver is obviously very powerful. When our assumptions about objectivity have for so long been a function of a universal male model, to dream of a woman-centered universe where men do not figure importantly is clearly anathema. But Wittig's strategy is not merely a simple reversal of the humanist model of an objective male universal. Her "universalized" point of view has more to do with the formulation of her own (and more generally, women's) concerns in the general body of literature and culture than with an offhanded rejection or exclusion of a male tradition.

On the contrary, the force of her work stems from the way she reimagines, fragments, and alters the tradition and its discourse from a lesbian point of view. In "The Point of View: Universal or Particular?" she writes:

A text by a minority writer is efficient only it if succeeds in making the minority point of view universal, only if it is an important literary text. *Remembrance of Things Past* is a monument of French literature *even though* homosexuality is *the* theme of the book.[7]

Both a personal perspective that extends beyond the individual subject and a set of literary strategies are necessary conditions for literary creation on the part of the minority writer. What may seem curious about Wittig's statement is that she sets the two at odds through her emphasis on the phrase *"even though."* Reference to personal experience is both a source of literary inspiration and a threat to the work's autonomy. Like the Proustian transformations of men into female characters, fiction for Wittig would appear as the necessary veiling—and expansion—of autobiographical concerns. Even more than the heterosexual woman writer, the lesbian writer always runs the risk of having her work reduced to a series of autobiographical particularities that quickly become stereotypes and obscure the literary transformations the work may entail.

Since writing represents at once a personal stake for Wittig, as she is "stirred heart and soul by [her] subject," a formulation of a feminist struggle on behalf of all women, and a literary operation, the reader might be tempted to associate Wittig's literary transformations of the (female) subject in language with a new form of committed literature.[8] Wittig avoids the move, however, and forcefully takes her distance from de Beauvoir on this issue. She reiterates the distinctions between a committed literature unequivocally "representing" the real, and a "pure" literature whose referents remain within textual borders. Wittig chooses the latter, because she defines committed literature as an objectionable dissolution of literary qualities on behalf of sociopolitical messages and themes, whereas literature's "primary aim" should be "to change the textual reality within which it is inscribed."[9] But she has also (rightly) maintained that discourse and reality are intertwined, mutually shaping each other. ("Discourse *is* reality," says

Wittig in "The Straight Mind.")[10] The stiff opposition she creates between committed literature and a literature that stands on its own belies the tensions in her works between representation and textual reflexivity. Gayatri Spivak has pointed out that critical readings of Wittig's fiction focus on her *"substantive* revision of, rather than [an] apparent *formal* allegiance to, the European avant-garde."[11] Although Wittig herself tends to position her works within the purview of the New Novel's formal inventions (what Spivak calls the "mainstream avant-garde"), *because* Wittig's innovations are intimately tied to her political, feminist rework-ing of language and culture, the formal transformations are readily subsumed under the political banner, an ultimate "signi-fied."[12] The question for Wittig and her readers that constantly recurs is: how does a text remain politically explosive without being reduced to a series of thematic axioms? Wittig's fiction, probably more than her essays admit, reproduces the tensions between the personal and the collective, and between literary polysemy and lesbian/feminist advocacy. Her novels' efficacy lies perhaps in the ability to invoke the suggestive power of language through nonrealistic discursive modes which offer themselves up to a multiplicity of readings.

If Wittig's essays of the late seventies and eighties tend to emphasize the literary aspects of fiction over the political or the personal, it is in part because her feminist readers of the seventies (in particular, after the publication of *Les Guérillères* in the U.S.), were quick to incorporate her books into a feminist polemic, almost as a form of propaganda. Wittig's insistence on the poly-valence of literature is paradoxically illustrated by the fact that *Les Guérillères* has sometimes been (mis)read as a celebration of the feminine principle or essence, contrary to the author's design.[13] Given that Wittig does distinguish between men's and women's relationships to language, her works necessarily run the risk of being read in this way. Literary indeterminacy is a double-edged sword.

*

Sarraute and Wittig have actively supported each other's literary endeavors throughout the years, bearing witness to a deep mu-tual respect and a long-standing friendship. In many ways, it may appear an unlikely alliance. Over thirty years Wittig's senior, Sarraute, as we have seen, has always veered away from female protagonists and narrators, and most often situates her narratives within the bourgeois family context. Her novels explore psychological interaction in its most ethereal, disembodied forms. Wittig, on the other hand, is attentive to the textual inscription of the female body in all its detail, to lesbian sexuality, to the recreation of (mythic) histories and futuristic societies of women, as well as to women's material struggles for freedom within patriarchal, heterosexual society. While Sarraute's novels portray the act of naming (people, sensations . . .) as the obliteration of the tropism which she strives to unearth, Wittig's novels abound in female names, as well as the names of famous men that have been feminized, as she searches for new ways of conceiving of the female subject through our cultural tradition. Wittig's prose, while experimenting with linguistic forms, is more clearly representational than Sarraute's, and includes stable characters.

But ultimately, both Sarraute and Wittig are interested in a gender-free writing and in the literary possibilities for reshaping the way we perceive human interaction and identity in language. Neither of them makes any definitive distinction in her novels between prose and poetry. Both are heedful of literature's intertextual resonances as they play with old forms (clichés, myths, traditional novels) in order to produce new configurations that affect our reading of the contemporary world. Taking steps similar to those in Roland Barthes's early structuralist critiques of sign systems,[14] Sarraute and Wittig literarily unravel the linguistic and cultural codes that rely on normative thinking to suppress individuals and groups. For both, literature enacts the discursive power struggles involved in human interaction.

On more than one occasion, Wittig has defended Sarraute's use of a "neutral" writing that uses the masculine as its base:

Gender is the linguistic index of the political opposition between the sexes. [. . .] There is only one [gender]: the feminine, the "masculine" not being a gender. For the masculine is not the masculine but the general. [. . .] It is this which makes Nathalie Sarraute say that she cannot use the feminine gender when she wants to generalize (and not particularize) what she is writing about.[15]

In an article on Sarraute's fiction, Wittig admires the New Novelist's ability to portray the tropism as "words before words, before 'fathers' before 'mothers,' before the 'you,' [. . .] before 'structurations' before 'capitalism.'"[16] The tropism is like the flip side of Wittig's lesbian utopias, where the characters live after the traditional family has been eschewed, after capitalism, after language has been reappropriated (or is in the process of being reappropriated) by women . . . . Between the two (and within each of their works as they evoke a present) lie the difficult struggles among (within) subjects in language.

Sarraute has also, upon occasion, showered Wittig's writing with praise. During the discussion of her own *Childhood* in her 1983 interview, Sarraute first evinced some reservations concerning the autobiographies of Sartre and Michel Leiris, before describing Wittig's *Opoponax* in the following way:

[. . .] I believe that it is possible [. . .] to write books on childhood that are true. I am thinking of the admirable *Opoponax* by Monique Wittig in which, while not indicating that it is about her own memories, she has succeeded in conserving all the soft tones of childhood. An extremely rare success.[17]

The Opoponax, Wittig's first novel, is no doubt her work that most clearly uses New Novel–style experimentation. Since it precedes Wittig's turn to feminist utopias, one might suspect that Sarraute's extremely favorable evaluation would not extend to her works after *The Opoponax*. But such is not the case.[18] For both Sarraute and Wittig, good literature (or theater) is neither a slave to, nor entirely independent of, its thematic choices. Wittig describes it as a Trojan horse or war machine that "pulverize[s] the old forms and formal conventions."[19] Where Wittig and Sarraute perhaps differ most is in the way that Sarraute's novels work against their own verisimilitude and apparent themes, whereas Wittig's feminist/lesbian advocacy works in tandem with stylistic innovations and textual construction.

Awarded the Médicis Prize in 1964, the same year that Sarraute received the International Publishers Prize for *The Golden Fruits, The Opoponax* ingeniously combines the personal touch of autobiography and a generalized treatment of childhood perception. Instead of the central "I" the reader might have expected to convey a little girl's growing consciousness of her world, its sensations, objects, rules, and lessons, an indefinite "on" (one) is the form through which young Catherine Legrand's sensory experiences are channeled. "One" is a neutral form designating anybody and nobody in particular. In colloquial French, it is the pronoun that can stand in for many other personal pronouns, "you," "we," "they". . . .[20] By using the indefinite pronoun, Wittig renders Catherine Legrand's meandering, heterogeneous, personal narrative emblematic of childhood in general. Mary McCarthy has in fact called it "everybody's childhood," and Duras, in a highly complimentary article devoted to *The Opoponax*, calls it a work of art, that belongs to all of us, that we've all written.[21] Already in *The Opoponax*, Wittig manages to "universalize the particular," creating a new form of autobiography in which the voice of one becomes that of anybody, thereby rendering the little girl's perspective paradigmatic of childhood perception.

Catherine Legrand is less an "individual" in a traditional (adult) sense, than a register of perception for whom all experience has equal value. New Novelist Claude Simon has pointed out that there are no hierarchies of significance: the death of a schoolmate or a teacher is at the same level as a fishing expedition with a friend.[22] This narrative leveling enacts the girl's experience at the moment of occurrence rather than as an adult remembering "important" moments selectively gleaned from the past. In this instance, fiction is more capable of portraying the autobiographical topoi of childhood than traditional autobiography. It is not so much the "facts" of experience that Wittig stresses as the allusive rhythms of its formulation, the twists and jumps in subjective attention.

It is not until Catherine Legrand develops a crush on another classmate, Valerie Borge, toward the end of the novel, that Catherine first uses the first person to express a personal point of view. The subject dramatically comes into being through the desire for and exchange with another. Subjectivity in Wittig's works is always formulated in *intersubjective* terms. The personal subject is not defined along the lines of the individual's uniqueness, but rather as a linguistic, cultural being whose apprehension of herself as "I" is filtered through the language of a (masculine) cultural tradition. Catherine Legrand's expression of love comes alive through quotation. Taking up the love texts she has memorized, Baudelaire's nineteenth-century "L'Invitation au voyage," as well as the love poems of the sixteenth-century poet Maurice Scève, Catherine Legrand finds her voice via citation. The masculine originals take on new meanings through the repetition, as they articulate the love between two young girls.[23] Catherine Legrand's mimetic performance sets the masculine poems adrift, takes them out of their context, and renders visible their lesbian inscription.[24] Identity formation, as our insertion in a discourse that is not our own, resembles the functioning of literature as it "change[s] the textual reality within which it is inscribed."[25]

Wittig's second novel, *Les Guérillères*, repeats *The Opoponax*'s passage from an indefinite narrating voice (this time resembling an omniscient narrator) to a personalized form at the end.[26] On the last page of the novel, the narrator actively becomes a part of the text when she includes herself in the "we" of the female community that has successfully fought a war against the males that oppressed them in language and in action. Published in French in 1969, at a time of revolutionary fervor in the French student left and the women's movement, *Les Guérillères* is Wittig's personal vision of the period's possibilities.[27]

Les Guérillères portrays a collective protagonist who, although temporally and spatially not locatable (an island where primitive and modern aspects of social life coalesce), is nevertheless an evolving group whose beliefs and conceptions of itself unfold in a history. Interspersed among the short texts recounting the young women's myriad daily activities are periodic self-evaluations of their trajectories in discourse. Acknowledging that the dominant discourse (of men) has excluded them ("the language you speak is made up of words that are killing you. They say, the language you speak is made up of signs that rightly speaking designate what men have appropriated"),[28] they write their own "feminaries" to extol their accomplishments and their bodies' sexuality. But the emphasis on their bodies' genital specificity is a temporary measure and the "feminaries" are eventually burned because obsolete:

The women say that they perceive their bodies in their entirety. They say that they do not favour any of its parts on the grounds that it was formerly a forbidden object. They say that they do not want to become prisoners of their own ideology. They say that they did not garner and develop the symbols that were necessary to them at an earlier period to demonstrate their strength. For example they do not compare the vulvas to the sun moon stars. They do not say that the vulvas are like black suns in the shining night.[29]

Les Guérillères is both the tale of a female collective's attempt to restructure its material and discursive identity, and a literary enactment of new directions for women in language. Identity is no doubt a problematic term here, since postmodern theories of the subject contest the integrity or wholeness of the body, as well as individual (or collective) self-identity and autonomy. But as seen in the foregoing passage, Wittig's characters manifest a critical self-awareness that refuses complacency. By refusing to privilege their sexual anatomical traits, they avoid duplicating the masculine move of fetishizing the body. And it is not so much a stable female identity that Wittig emphasizes as the possibility of imagining, inventing, and revising new self-definitions that phallocentrism has impeded. The process is similar to a passage in the novel when the character, Elsa Brauer, appeals to the community to remember the time when they were not slaves: "Make an effort to remember. Or, failing that, invent."[30] Identity as process is a creative fiction that engenders and is engendered by discourse.

If it is not feasible to control the unconscious structurings of the self, its repressions, women can at least channel their conscious energies into reevaluating their material positions (and this includes discursive positions) in the dominant social structures. Wittig states in "One Is Not Born a Woman":

For once one has acknowledged oppression, one needs to know and experience the fact that one can constitute oneself as a subject (as opposed to an object of oppression), that one can become *someone* in spite of oppression, that one has one's own identity. There is no possible fight for someone deprived of an identity, no internal motivation for fighting, since although I can fight only with others, first I fight for myself.[31]

In the militant context, the belief in "one's own identity" is not a final moment of self-fulfillment, but a point of departure from

which to engage in struggle. Wittig's literary attack on androcentric discourse consists of a disruption of male-centered definitions of women, an affirmation of new horizons for identity formation within an alienated language, and an ongoing self-
awareness of the dangers in claiming to fix identity once and for
all. But for Wittig, to eliminate the notion of a subject altogether
would too easily mean repeating women's already marginalized
relation to discourse and power. As Nancy Miller has noted:

> [. . .] the postmodern decision that the Author is dead, and subjective
> agency along with him, does not necessarily work for women and pre-
> maturely forecloses the question of identity for them. Because women
> have not had the same historical relation of identity to origin, institution,
> production, that men have had, women have not, I think, (collectively)
> felt burdened by too much Self, Ego, Cogito, etc. [. . .] the female
> subject['s] relation to integrity and textuality, desire and authority, is
> structurally different.[32]

Because women have historically been defined as "the sex," in
opposition to rational, thinking man, their relationship to their
bodies has tended to be filtered through masculine conceptions
and through masculine desire. From literature to the television
advertisement, woman recognizes herself as the desired sexual
object of man. We have already seen that Duras works within this
framework of heterosexual romantic discourse while subverting
its traditional masculine subject/feminine object dichotomy. In
her memoirs, de Beauvoir devotes relatively little space to descriptions of her body and her sexuality. A certain ("feminine")
modesty or even prudishness regarding her own sexuality reigns
throughout. In The Second Sex, however, she does study female
anatomy and sexuality, and insists on the interweaving of cultural
and biological representations of the female body. One sometimes senses, nevertheless, her revulsion for her own sex's characteristics as shaped by a dominant (male) discourse.[33] Sarraute
simply avoids the question of the sexual body altogether. Wittig,
on the other hand, violently wrests the female body from the
heterosexual politics that have made it a sign of man's desire, and
focuses instead on its material manifestations outside gender
opposition. Wittig prolongs de Beauvoir's project of understand-

ing the female body "in situation," that is, as a political, culturally constructed entity, but without de Beauvoir's tacit acceptance of a masculine-oriented reading.[34]

Wittig's third work, *The Lesbian Body*, addresses the question of female identity through the lesbian body. It is a first-person narrative addressing a "you," the loved one, and while it partakes of fiction, it also falls within the autobiographical realm as the subject defines herself in and through the discourse addressed to another woman. Lynn Higgins has called it a "nouvelle nouvelle autobiographie," in which "conflict, disarticulation and reconstruction produce a new identity of self and language."[35] Wittig emphasizes the materiality of both language and the body as she explores the female body's surfaces and articulations, as well as its internal organs.[36] "Sexuality" takes on new meaning as the body is valued in all its aspects. Intertwining the languages of the anatomist and the poet, the novel challenges the portrayal of the female body in traditional romantic literature as well as pornography. In both of the latter, the woman's body is divided into desirable and undesirable fragments, just as the narrative is ordered according to a hierarchical structure of significance. But in *The Lesbian Body* (as in *The Opoponax*), the narrative overturns any hierarchy among its parts, as well as among the characters' body parts. Instead, an incantatory enumeration of all the lover's anatomical traits is celebrated in a violent dispersion and reconstruction of the lovers' bodies in language. Interspersed in the poetic narrative are lists of the fragmented body parts.

You drift off suddenly, you sway from side to side, you are uplifted. Your hands cling to m/y hair, now you rise up, you drag m/e carried by m/y hair. You start to spin on yourself, *I* copy your

> THE DORSALS THE ILIACS THE
> TERES THE QUADRATI THE TRI-
> ANGULAR THE PYRAMIDS THE
> ABDOMINALS THE GLUTEALS THE
> BICEPS THE TRICEPS THE TENDONS [. . .]

movement, *I* effect the same slow rotation m/y hands seeking points of support. It is not then possible to arrest the movement it is so slow. An irresistible force emanates from you and sweeps m/e away.[37]

Instead of naming the body according to a restrictive, fetishized logic of desire, the lists of female body parts are articulated through anatomical convention, that is, they are organized according to function: muscles, bones, secretions, glands, and so on. No part will be cast away, for all are desirable. In the narrative segments, these parts are incorporated in the lovers' active, reciprocal explorations of each other.

The female subject joining with her companion lover is a self-conscious "I" who recognizes the difficulty of finding a voice that is not already defined by a masculine discourse. The narrator is a split "I" ("j/e" in French) who recognizes the alienated position from which she writes. In the "Author's Note," Wittig explains that "J/e is the symbol of the lived, rending experience which is m/y writing, of this cutting in two which throughout literature is the exercise of a language which does not constitute me as subject. J/e poses the ideological and historical question of feminine subjects."[38] The union between the lesbian lovers is thus not one of "whole" individuals in a language that fully represents them. Their bodies only meet as they are violently torn apart and reassembled in a narrative that itself is fragmented and riddled with gaps.[39] In its final words, the "Author's Note" confirms the auto-biographical dimension of the fiction by deliberately confusing the authorial voice and the reference to the split "I" of the narrator: "If *I* [*J/e*] examine m/y specific situation as subject in the language, *I* [*J/e*] am physically incapable of writing 'I,' [JE], I [*J/e*] have no desire to do so."[40]

*

From *The Opoponax* to *The Lesbian Body*, Wittig's autobiographical tack consists in bending, breaking, challenging, and reshaping the language of heterosexual culture in order to affirm her lesbian voice. Her works straddle conventional genre divisions in the effort to challenge old discursive orders and to posit new ones. Via the experimental novel, utopian fiction, the prose poem, even the dictionary,[41] Wittig explores the literary and historical possibilities of the personal voice in relationship to female communities. In *Across the Acheron*, however, the tacit alliance in her previous works between the personal voice and the collective female community is questioned as the lesbian reconsiders her position vis-à-vis heterosexual women.

In inscribing her own name in *Across the Acheron*, her personal, playful version of Dante's voyage transposed to modern San Francisco, Wittig nimbly juggles literary genres and the interaction between referential and self-referential writing. It plays upon the possibility of combining the personal, the literary, and the political, of mixing parody, utopia, and autobiography in a capricious but also serious endeavor. Wittig makes "Wittig" a character who owns up to the name by tackling ethical, social, and political problems that the author has addressed elsewhere, both in and out of print, in and out of fiction. As in classical autobiography, identity is (at least hypothetically) posited between author and the narrator-character via the proper name and the assumption of a first-person voice. To be sure, *Across the Acheron* is also a fantastic fiction that exceeds the constraints of mimetic realism and like her other works (in particular *Les Guérillères*, *The Lesbian Body*, and *Le Voyage sans fin*), it self-consciously points to its intertextual origins within the Western literary canon.[42] Through the mythified personal history, Wittig invites the reader to ponder women's collective problems. For "Wittig's" fabulous journeys through hell, heaven, and purgatory include serious reflections of a lesbian feminist contemplating in dismay the fear and distrust with which she is viewed by heterosexual women, as well as the general oppression of women.

Within the context of women's autobiography, I am interested in the way *Across the Acheron* reworks autobiography as both a political, feminist act—referentially bound to historic situation— and a formal fireworks of literary invention beyond historical contingencies. The power of her writing lies in the special way she makes literature responsive to women's issues through formal innovation (and renovation). *Across the Acheron*'s reworking of Dante's *Divine Comedy* offers the occasion for new considerations of the self. On a formal level, it is clear that the alterations Wittig makes to the literary pre-text (Dante) constitute significant marks of her "own" story as a radical lesbian: the author's choice of San Francisco as the site for her story is not innocent, for Wittig has been living in the U.S. for over ten years—fleeing the controversies and acrimony in France surrounding the connections between politics, feminism, and lesbianism. In addition, San Francisco is specifically renowned as a city with substantial gay and lesbian communities, where alternative life-styles are possible. But ultimately, what is perhaps most classically autobiographical about this text is Wittig's sustained dialectic between proud self-affirmation and humorous self-criticism, a modern allegory of lesbian/feminist consciousness.

*

Quite to the contrary of a Sarraute who displays a certain nervousness about initiating a work whose innumerable precedents leave little room for artistic innovation, Wittig almost gleefully displays the texts she rewrites. On the cover of *Virgile, non*, the original French text of *Across the Acheron*, the protagonists, "Wittig" and her guide Manastabal, are compared to Dante and his guide Virgil, and the book as a whole is likened to Dante's comedy, as both end happily in paradise.[43] Rather than rejecting literary antecedents of a male-centered tradition, or pretending that they do not exist, Wittig uses our Western literary heritage to forge her modern mythic quest. Modern autobiographies since the eighteenth century have tended to describe their particular mode of existing through the metaphor of the stage and performance. Wittig's work aligns itself with the earlier models of spiritual autobiography that have used what Janet Gunn calls "the trope of religious pilgrimage" as the appropriate form for a personal quest.[44] But Wittig's choice of *The Divine Comedy* combines both the dramatic—or comic—staging *and* the personal quest model. This mixture creates a timeliness (the evolving drama of self interrogation) within a utopian framework that posits an end to women's oppression.[45]

Wittig's references to *The Divine Comedy* clearly derealize the work by situating it within the intertextual realm of fantastic literature—*Across the Acheron* is immediately marked as a work of the imagination. We are outside "real" time, the chronology of history. The present of "Wittig's" search for paradise is not defined by specific dates. And its location, modern-day San Francisco, while supported by realistic references to specific places—Valencia Street, Golden Gate Park, the Golden Gate Bridge . . . is nevertheless a utopian place: "a nowhere that is either hell, limbo or paradise," as stated on the French edition's cover.[46] The coupling of a medieval model and contemporary touches including dress (from blue jeans to high heels), colloquialisms, slang, computers . . . produces many wonderful comic effects that distance the readers, keeping them from taking the story "literally." This novel, like its predecessor, has clearly defined protagonists, "Wittig" and Manastabal, rather than the shadowy voices of the New Novel. We are again within the tradition of "full, unitary subjects," of which contemporary readers might well feel suspicious, but because these characters are already situated within a nonrealistic fiction, replete with fantastic speaking animals (the ulliphant and the bourlababu), we accept "Wittig" and Manastabal as the utopian figures of an exemplary search for (women's) freedom. At the same time, however, the very polysemy of utopian fiction invites readers to ponder its links to a historical moment. And although Wittig's use of her own name in the first person repeats Dante's own gesture, the reader cannot help but read Wittig-the-author's name in that of the character. One suspects that the form of the personal quest is not totally devoid of experiential referents. Clearly, Wittig is playing upon the boundaries between parody, utopia, and autobiographical realism.

The explicit intertextual resonances of *Across the Acheron* (that is, those which the text itself points out) produce a series of displacements and transformations that call upon the reader to contrast *The Divine Comedy* and its modern counterpart.[47] Wittig's work stages its own representation of *The Divine Comedy*. Most obviously, this new journey is effectuated by two female characters whose rapport is quite different from their male counterparts (as indicated in the French title, Manastabal is *not* Virgil). And as "Wittig" points out on the first page, their trip is both classical and profane. This signpost (coupled with the humorous remark: "fortunately we don't have to wear tunics") establishes both proximity and distance from its predecessor.[48] The work is classical in that it is a variation on Dante's famous travels through hell, purgatory, and heaven. Certain stylistic traits reinforce the work's ritual repetition of the classical mode. In addressing Manastabal, for example, "Wittig" always uses the epithet "my guide," thereby lending a classical ceremoniousness to the text. It is also profane, however, because God-the-Father has nothing to do with "Wittig's" quest, and because hell is on earth in the form of women's suffering and oppression. Dante's heavenly female mentor, Beatrice, finds her equivalent in "she who is my Providence" [AA, 9], "Wittig's" unnamed celestial love who gives her a flacon of ether to help "Wittig" in difficult moments when she risks fainting at the horror of hell's visions. Thus the basic character configuration is maintained, although the content of each is radically different, as are the rapports among them. The loving female supporter in heaven obviously produces a very different textual effect when the protagonist is also female: the medieval (and contemporary) norm of heterosexual romance is reshaped to meet the needs of the lesbian perspective.

The damned souls of *Across the Acheron*'s contemporary hell are not the famous dead heroes of Dante's inferno, but rather an anonymous, agonizing group whose lot is not at all poetic, even in infernal terms. These souls are never named as "women." The fantasy aligns itself with Wittig's efforts to detach women from an essentialist view of "Woman." But because the French word for soul (*âme*) is feminine, the souls' gender is subsequently feminine. Concrete "men" are not present either, but occasional references to the "enemy," a masculine word in French, reinscribes the masculine as a dangerous "other."[49] The avoidance of "men" and "women" can be read both as a literary device (to wrest the text from mimetic realism) and as a political ploy. *Across the Acheron* is an allegory of strife, not a factual document. And by depriving the damned voices who address "Wittig" of names, the text stresses the collective quality of their plight.[50]

The contemporary narrative also differs structurally from the medieval one in important ways: Manastabal has no intention of having "Wittig" visit the circles of hell in any order [AA, 18]. The linear progression of the medieval poem is forsaken in favor of a meandering prose narrative that leaves the reader unsure of where the next location will be.[51] The text is composed as a serial repetition: before the finale, there are six visits to paradise, between which "Wittig" interposes sequences in limbo and hell. The lack of a progressive narrative order breaks up any possible monotony and suggests a notion of experience that does not adhere to a chronological structure. Like the character "Wittig," we never know what awaits us. In addition, the content of the three spheres is specifically oriented by "Wittig's" lesbian vision of the world and has precious little to do with Dante's particular saints and sinners. Hell, for example, is not a place of just punishments for past sins, but rather an imposed, unjustifiable suffering on earth. The novel's outrageous deviations from the literary classic, its transpositions, displacements, exaggerations, and incongruities, produce a narrative that is both familiar and strange: "Wittig's" stops at limbo, in the guise of bars where one can settle down with a shot of tequila, admire the (female) clientele, and relax, alternate with the explorations of hell's myriad forms of female torture and occasional incursions into a paradise where the air is soft like peach fuzz and where "Wittig" contemplates with pleasure "a string of dikes"—the English word "dikes" is used— "naked on their motorcycles, their skin gleaming black or golden [. . .]" [AA, 18].[52] Needless to say, this is a highly personalized vision, in tragicomic terms, of Dante's original three spheres. Wittig takes Dante's term "comedy" seriously.

The dialogues of *Across the Acheron* are curiously contained within parentheses, almost as if they were asides or digressions from the main course of action, thereby creating a certain tension between words and action. This tension between dialogue and narrative points all the more forcefully to the break for "Wittig" between her idealistic quest and her inability to interact positively with the damned souls.

Before visiting hell, Manastabal admonishes "Wittig" to avoid glorifying the plight of the suffering souls she will encounter:

(There is nothing where we are going, Wittig, at least nothing that you don't know already. [. . .] Sighs, cries of pain, anguish, terror and uncertainty are uttered there, and you'd need vast ingenuity to describe them as heroic. The condemned souls you are about to meet are alive despite their fervent wish to be dead. They are anonymous and I challenge you to find any quality about them that clothes them in glory [. . .].) [AA, 8].

Manastabal's warning is twofold. On the one hand, she stresses the collective group over the individual: these sufferings are fully typical, not just the particularized sufferings of a few, and the souls are not condemned because of their actions. On the other hand, she seems to refer to the way "Wittig's" narrative of what she sees will be handled: she must choose a concrete, unadorned language for the portrayal of the anonymous collective rather than a heroic, epic form that would legitimate the suffering by glamorizing it. Here, Dante's model is a temptation to be avoided.

The choice of the collective over the individual also distinguishes "Dante" and "Wittig" as characters. Whereas "Dante's" goal is to secure salvation for himself, "Wittig," armed with her rifle and ready for combat, has a mission that exceeds the purely personal. One's own salvation, equivalent to freedom from oppression, is contingent upon helping others do the same. Freedom, says Manastabal, is "a privilege so remarkable" that the only way to justify it is to "extricat[e others] from Hell," "at whatever cost" [AA, 33]. Like an "exterminating angel," a Robinhood, a Don Quixote, or more prosaically, a sort of tragicomic "Rambolina," "Wittig" sets out to reclaim the whole world for herself and the condemned. The task is, however, not as easy as the idealistic "Wittig" would have wished.

"Wittig's" rapport with the condemned souls is anything but harmonious. The numerous episodes charting the predicaments and pain of the souls forcefully stage a lack of understanding between the lesbian warrior and those whom she wishes to succor. The condemned souls' frequent attachment to their oppressed situations, their apparent unwillingness to throw off the enemy's yoke, frustrate and anger "Wittig." And the latter, in turn, is suspected of hubris and treachery by the condemned souls: "(You deserter, you renegade, have you come into this circle to insult me and laugh at me?)" [AA, 11]. Barely veiled by the imaginary anecdotes lies a vivid portrayal of the mutual distrust and misunderstanding between heterosexual females and the lesbian. In a hilarious episode occurring in a laundromat, "Wittig," "trying out [her] grand style in order to get their attention" [AA, 14], engages the souls in dialogue, presenting herself as their savior:

I raised my arms to Heaven (which I took as witness), calling out: (Sappho is my witness that I wish you no harm. On the contrary, I've come here to defend you and redress your wrongs, for I suspect that they [the masculine pronoun is used in French] multiply among you, like evil deeds . . . ()] [AA, 14].

But the occupants of the laundromat (a characteristic meeting place for those serving the enemy) offer no acknowledgment to her militant call, so "Wittig" tries another tack. She strips off her clothes "between two rows of washing-machines," "not like Venus emerging from the waves," but rather in "perfect human conformity with persons of [her] own sex," in order to show that she is made just like them [AA, 14]. The result is utter pandemonium, cries of rape, rioting, with one of these terrified and terrifying Bacchantes throwing herself into a churning dryer. The souls can see "Wittig's" body only through the grid of their prejudices and fears, that is, as radically different, displaying in turn "long, black shiny hairs," scales, and finally, something at the middle of her body, "long like a finger," whereby one soul cries "cut it off, cut it off" [AA, 16]. Like clothing, the body becomes a monstrous mask of itself, neither wholly female nor male, barely even human. The representation of the body is already encoded in such a way that the body cannot present itself. The power of words to shape a nonhuman or masculine image of "Wittig's" body is demonstrated by the fact that she too comes to see her own body in the way the others have described it.[53] In the nick of time, Manastabal rescues this luckless savior who is about to be mauled.[54]

The fear of the lesbian blight or the "lavender threat," as "Wittig" willingly calls it, turns the knight-errant into a monster. "Wittig" receives buckets of water on her head when gallantly serenading the souls imprisoned in their "master's" apartments [AA, 65]. And her efforts to help are deemed laughable by those who fear being "corrupted" by the "lesbian plague." Whether it is from the ones being tracked down at night (prostitutes or unsuspecting strollers), or from the ones who have failed in their battle and are dejectedly returning to hell, or again from those who have no lives of their own and exist only through their "annexes" (i.e., children), "Wittig" winces at each attack and is often tempted to return the hostility with her own.[55] The idealized female collectivity of *Les Guérillères* is threatened with extinction in *Across the Acheron*, as the different voices of women no longer recognize themselves as a homogeneous group. Wittig's outsider status makes her a perceptive critic, but it deprives her of support in the struggle for an uncompromised freedom.

In order to intensify the images of women's oppression, Wittig chooses the most glaring, horrendous forms it can take, but she also evokes its more subtle versions. By avoiding common names given to potential constraints on women in the present and the past (prostitution, pornography, clitoridectomy, marriage, child-rearing, foot-binding, impractical dress . . .), the text both dereal-izes itself (this is a fable of inequities) and sheds a more powerful light on what sometimes becomes so entrenched in our societies as to appear "natural" or at least tolerable. The lesbian, fantastic perspective refuses to let us take anything for granted, that is, to reduce heterosocial relations to a one-dimensional banality that would obfuscate the imbalances of power relations between men and women. The text produces an effect of estrangement, in order to make us see what "Wittig" sees.

As a character, "Wittig" manifests a certain number of fixed traits that make her both endearing and comical. She is a mixture of poetic idealism, combative energy, presumption, sarcasm, in-eptitude, an occasional (unsuccessful) seducer of condemned souls (for which she is continually reprimanded by Manastabal), but, most important, "Wittig" is an interlocutor whose mission is not only to secure freedom for herself and others, but to *tell* her adventures and interventions. "Wittig's" travels are recounted as a learning process for the character: an interrogation about her-self, about what she witnesses, and the linguistic formulation of the two. Narrated dramatically in the present, the work figures both as a representation of existing evils and as a questioning of the narrating subject's relationship to the situations. Clearly re-jecting the monstrous characterizations of "Wittig" by the lost souls and the enemy, the text portrays her awareness of herself as a series of idealized roles that she tries out. But the reader can never take her completely seriously in these roles, because they are so frequently disrupted by comic twists, in the form of puns, verbal anachronisms, or farcical situations. The text only ap-proaches a serious modality when "Wittig," overcome with grief at the sight of so much suffering, empathizes with the pain of others. It is something akin to compassion (but "that's a word which has lost all its meaning," says Manastabal) that enables "Wittig's" passage into paradise [AA, 19]. The word "compassion" comes from the Latin *com* (together) and *pati* (to suffer). "Wittig's" entry into an earthly heaven is contingent upon her ability to suffer *with* those who are different from her.

If the two protagonists, "Wittig" and Manastabal, are unreal figures in allegory, thereby quite distinct from the "author," their exchanges do, nevertheless, enact the dramatic split in the autobiographical subject. Wittig-the-author implicitly invests herself in the dynamic *between* the two (as well as in the virulent exchanges between "Wittig" and the condemned souls). Manastabal is both the knowing instructor (the "mana" of her name connotes a supernatural power and a principle of action), *and* a sparring partner for the protagonist, for she counterbalances "Wittig's" brash interpretations and actions. At one point "Wittig" thinks wistfully to herself that she "would have been satisfied with the gentle Virgil in this adventure" [AA, 30]. Manastabal deflates "Wittig's" chivalric balloon and persistently questions "Wittig's" self-righteous, judgmental remarks (both in terms of content and style) concerning the condemned souls. As mediator, Manastabal recommends that "Wittig" learn to nuance her thoughts, for hell is much too complex to be understood through simplistic reasoning.

The power and nature of language is a constant theme to which "Wittig" and Manastabal return in their discussions and it is an essential element of "Wittig's" apprenticeship with her guide. The text shows repeatedly its awareness of its own generative process. During their first brief visit to paradise, for example, Manastabal calls upon "Wittig" to "find words to describe this place, lest everything you see suddenly disappears" [AA, 20]. The existence of the lesbian ideal is contingent upon the ability to create it with words. "Wittig," in her early visit to paradise, can only think of the word "beauty" to describe it, and recognizes the pitiful inadequacy of the word. Later, as she gains confidence and waxes poetic in a prayer to paradise, Manastabal warns her not to get carried away with her words: "you don't take to the air by using figures of speech" [AA, 57]. Manastabal resembles Sarraute's censuring narrator: pretty words, stylistic tours de force, are to be rejected in order to avoid killing the object of description, just as are vague abstractions (such as "beauty"). In such passages, one reads Wittig's own concern for the materiality of language, its power, as well as the danger of facile metaphors and abstractions. Paradoxically perhaps, the rejection of "pretty language," as was the case for both Sarraute and de Beauvoir, can also be read as the distaste for a feminine language that reverts back to stereotypical, ladylike aesthetics, emphasizing a dazzling, flowery form over a tangible or logical content.

But "Wittig's" linguistic care is not just a restraint on language: *Across the Acheron* is a constant game in which clichés, maxims, and colloquialisms are transformed into new meanings in a celebration of language's potential. Such common expressions in French as *"un ange passe,"* figuratively meaning that there is a lull in conversation, and literally "an angel is passing over" [AA, 56], or *"rire aux anges,"* figuratively, "to smile in one's sleep, with a beatific look," literally, "to laugh to the angels," become the occasion for playful punning, of incorporating old expressions into the new celestial context.[56] The *pleasures* of linguistic creation are thoroughly a part of the narrator's experience. "Wittig" infuses new life into old or worn-out forms, much in the way that the work as a whole renovates and transforms Dante's classic.

From *The Opoponax* to *Across the Acheron*, all Wittig's works rethink the female subject in language through exchanges between female characters. In *Across the Acheron*, the dialogic principle is essential to the construction of an autobiographical subject, but not in the sense of a unitary being that would dominate through a global view of the action or the discourse. For although we follow the narrative of one character, the latter is in constant dialogue with others in such a way as to question her as an authoritative voice. Like Sarraute's doubled narrator, Wittig's duo of "Wittig" and Manastabal depicts the subject in process, a dialectic of visions and revisions that are as attentive to linguistic formulation as they are to a particular content of experience. And although a hierarchy is posited between "Wittig" and Manastabal, with the latter assuming the "superior" although secondary role (following its model), their rapport is primarily one of collaboration and companionship. On at least one occasion, the text actually undoes the hierarchy. At the "riches fair," where one can take away whatever one wants, Manastabal criticizes "Wittig's" desire to pick out a horse for herself, declaring: "What will you do with a horse in hell, Wittig? Remember that we aren't in a western. Your confusion of genres sometimes really seems barbaric" [AA, 63]. Wittig's text, however, relies *precisely* on a mixture of genres, styles, and tones, as well as on the fanciful blend of realism and the fantastic to convey a personal vision of heaven and hell. These are the trademarks of "Wittig's"—and Wittig's—literary investigation, the power of which lies in the breaking down of a homogeneous, unitary, rational discourse through playful parody. *Across the Acheron* does not do away with a sense of personal identity (even avant-garde deconstructions of the latter never stop identity from continually being reformulated from its own ashes), but the heterogeneity of the novel does keep the notion in movement, in play. "Wittig" and the text retain their polyvalence in the combining of the personal political allegory and literary intertextuality.

To what extent, then, is it possible to read *Across the Acheron* as an autobiographical piece, momentarily crossing Wittig with "Wittig," or at least Wittig's preoccupations with those of *Across the Acheron*? For readers familiar with Wittig's theoretical essays, *Across the Acheron*'s allegorical elements concerning women's oppression are already familiar. The fact that those condemned to hell on earth continue to be attached, in one form or another, to the masculine enemy, repeats Wittig's critique of heterosexuality as the primary structure that oppresses women as a class. The lesbian character "Wittig" considers herself outside the oppressed group because she is not involved in the heterosexual relationships, but it is nevertheless the principle of heterosexuality that keeps her from establishing a common ground of understanding with the condemned. In "The Straight Mind," Wittig had forcefully criticized the heterosexual, normalizing discourses of structuralism and psychoanalysis that confirm and maintain heterosexuality as a universal institution regulating "all human relationships but also [societies'] very production of concepts."[57] In "One Is Not Born a Woman," she again argued against heterosexuality as an oppressive, all-pervasive social system, adding that lesbians escape its naturalizing typology of "man" and "woman" (based on biological difference rather than on sociocultural forms of domination).[58] These ideas clearly inform the narrative of *Across the Acheron* in the way it avoids naming various forms of oppression and those concerned (victims and aggressors) with the old nomenclatures. Lesbian is the only name that remains and it is defined, positively or negatively, according to the speakers' perspectives (heterosexual or lesbian).

And yet the dialogues and debates in the novel recast her theories in such a way that they become less self-assured or self-evident. *Across the Acheron*, rather than merely *applying* Wittig's theories, reproduces in a very personal, literary form the debates and questions surrounding those theories. In addition to being an intertextual reworking of Dante's comedy, *Across the Acheron* can also be understood as an autobiographical reading of Wittig's break in 1980 with the radical feminist collective, *Questions féministes*, for which she had been writing since its inception.

The dissensions that led to the demise of *Questions féministes* involved the publication of Wittig's "The Straight Mind."[59] Wittig's indictment of heterosexuality as *the* form of oppression for both lesbians and female heterosexuals in "The Straight Mind" is countered, in the same 1980 issue of *Questions féministes*, with Emmanuèle de Lesseps's article, *"Hétérosexualité et féminisme"* [Heterosexuality and Feminism], which defends heterosexuality with all its contradictions as a part of most women's experience, and contests political lesbianism as a real choice for women, particularly if it means labeling heterosexual women as guilty "collaborators" with the (male class of) oppressors.[60]

Subsequent to the publication of these two articles, the rift between radical feminists and radical lesbians intensified: in meetings, tracts, and articles, name-calling and accusations of betrayal shot freely back and forth and the initial group was compelled to break up. In each instance, one group (whether radical lesbian or radical feminist) felt excluded by the others' working hypotheses. At the heart of the debates lay a fundamental division between, on the one hand, a radical lesbianism stressing political strategies involving class struggle (that do not ground themselves in sexuality or personal sexual preferences—this is

Wittig's radical lesbian line), and on the other, a radical feminism that entwines the personal and the political, combining women's personal experiences—including (hetero)sexual ones—with a feminist agenda. Although Wittig never directs attacks toward heterosexual women in "The Straight Mind," Lesseps's article (followed by other commentaries from radical feminists) tends to respond in personal terms, to defend heterosexual feminists against what they feel are implicit attacks against them (rather than against heterosexuality as a dominant, oppressive system).

Across the Acheron articulates the misunderstandings and strife between the two groups of *Questions féministes* through the episodic encounters between "Wittig" and the oppressed (heterosexual females). Of the latter, some struggle against all odds to free themselves (the feminists), while others are complacent in their subordinate roles. Because the tale is told from the lesbian's point of view, all the heterosexual females she meets are more or less incomprehensible to her. But it is the feminists in particular who puzzle her most, for they already recognize their oppression while remaining in heterosocial and heterosexual relations. "Wittig's" outsider status becomes a tenacious naïveté, best illustrated in two contrasting scenes. On the one hand, she takes a fancy to the romantic vision of the bandits in limbo who, while freed, must resort to crime in order to eat. To which Manastabal replies:

You speak of gestures, clothes, bearing. You celebrate the shady beauty of the bandits and pride yourself on being of their company [. . .] Ah, Wittig, all this is a token war. What can we gain from it [the struggle of a few hungry criminals] when it's the whole world we have to repossess?" [AA, 46].[61]

On the other hand, "Wittig" is disdainful of the two-headed souls she later meets. Manastabal explains the two heads in the following way:

(It's the strain, Wittig, that causes the doubling of the heads in these damned souls. In fact, all their intelligence makes them tend equally to quit Hell and not to quit it. From the front, they have a total awareness of the functioning of Hell, they are capable of mastering its techniques and sciences, they have acquired a taste for it and have become masters in their domains. From the back, they have a total understanding of the mechanism of domination that has reduced the majority of souls to the state of damnation. And they stand midway, not really knowing which side to take, both heads growing larger [. . .]) [AA, 72].

"Wittig" attributes these souls' hesitations, between choosing a hell they control and choosing freedom, to a certain dullness or stupidity on their part. The dilemma recalls Lesseps's reference to the contradictions of the heterosexual woman's situation, and "Wittig" seems to match the portrait of the uncompromising, reproachful lesbian that the radical feminists took objection to. But through the dialogue between "Wittig," a humorous, fanciful character, and Manastabal, an image of the critical sage, the acrimony is diffused, as Manastabal declares:

[. . .] your principle ["Wittig's"] is: either . . . or. You don't acknowledge any nuances. You see nothing complex in what constitutes the basis of hell. [. . .] I'm convinced, and by experience, that the highest human intelligence is found among the damned souls. The reason is this: once they are aware of what is happening, they set themselves the challenge of exercising their intelligence through all the laws that govern their world and immediately develop it in many more directions than is required in the dominant camp. Moreover, they have to act with a double intent and this duplicity sometimes leads them, as you have seen, to develop two heads. And it's a fact, I don't deny it, that I feel a near passion for intelligence at grips with itself and not letting go [AA, 74–75].

Manastabal's tribute to these souls who have not extricated themselves from the weighty contradictions of their heterosocial lives effectively counters the position of the lesbian purist.

In the referential allegory I have been sketching between *Across the Acheron* and the *Questions féministes* breakup, one must inevitably ask who is speaking at each turn of *Across the Acheron*'s dialogue.[62] In the above quotation, is the voice of Manastabal a repetition of that of the radical feminists who proclaim the necessity of facing the difficult, real contradictions of the heterosexual feminist? Is it the author's offering of reconciliation, by recognizing the complexity of the heterosexual feminist's situation? What does one make of a "Wittig" who is at once a puppet voice of chivalry, the author's namesake, and an incisive, critical voice that makes tacit oppression audible to our sometimes-deaf ears? Since Wittig has consistently kept separate the political dimensions of lesbianism and the lesbian's sexual preferences, how is one to read "Wittig's" occasional attempts at seduction? Is this self-criticism or an image of the lesbian by heterosexuals? More generally, are the comical actions of "Wittig" a form of self-mockery on Wittig's part, or an attempt to see herself as her critics might see her? Both perhaps, since in order to see "oneself," a certain doubling must already take place within the subject. As a plural text, *Across the Acheron* weaves through a dialectic of positions without providing an intentional authorial voice that would anchor the text in one set of meanings or "signified." But at the same time, the novel does not sacrifice Wittig's political stake: heterosexuality as the controlling system of discourse and action is continually put on trial. Wittig's personal investment in the text appears twofold: on the one hand, she creates a lesbian perspective, the voice of a minority view, along with its utopian separatist dreams of a noncontradictory society and a language that would articulate those dreams; on the other, the text produces a series of questions about the relationships between the personal and the political that acknowledge the complexity of the idealistic lesbian's relationship to other women. Ultimately, it is the problematization of free, unambiguous choice (heterosociality versus lesbianism) that the fiction acknowledges, an issue that her theoretical essays had at times elided. For the contradictions of heterosociality also involve the lesbian committed to a feminist struggle, even if those contradictions do not appear to be her own. In personal terms, *Across the Acheron* is indeed a courageous undertaking for the lesbian separatist.

*

In her analysis of what she considers to be superficial differences between French and Anglo-American feminisms, Gayatri Spivak calls upon both groups to consider a simultaneous "other focus," asking "not merely who am I? but who is the other woman? How am I naming her? How does she name me?"[63] Although Spivak is speaking specifically of the "colonized woman" of the Third World as this other, I think that in many ways, Wittig's condemned souls constitute a collective "other" that, from the point of view of the lesbian activist, is a colonized group, suffering under the yoke of heterosexual institutions that promote male dominance. *Across the Acheron*, through its dialogues between

"Wittig" and Manastabal, between "Wittig" and the condemned, poses all Spivak's questions. In the ambivalent relationships between authorial and narrative voices, between playful parody and serious polemic, Wittig dramatically creates the autobiographical space of self-quest-ioning.

Mediations of Identity through the Atlantic Triangle: Maryse Condé's *Heremakhonon*

"To be a woman and Antillean is a destiny difficult to decipher."

["*Etre femme et antillaise, c'est un destin difficile à déchiffrer.*"]

Maryse Condé, interview in *Notre Librairie*

For most white women writers, the question of race is a nonissue or the problem of others. For many black women writers, it just as frequently imposes itself as a major issue. We have already seen that while de Beauvoir nearly always takes class boundaries into account, race is not a personal issue in her memoirs. To be white was the norm of the French society in which she was raised.[1] For Sarraute, such accidentals as the subject's gender and color fall away in the discovery/enactment of the tropism. In Duras's case, race *is* an issue that complicates the conception of self, since her family's poverty clashes with its "superior" position as white in Indochina. Being white is thus not a "neutral" phenomenon in *The Lover*, but rather reveals itself as an automatic social privilege. In Wittig's utopian creations, because the (white) lesbian is sensitive to her own exclusion from heterosexual women's groups, she seeks to avoid exclusions in her own collective ideal by stressing its racial diversity—the "dikes" of heaven are "black and golden," and "Wittig's" situation is likened to that of a "maroon," that is, a runaway slave of the Antilles. In all of these instances, from de Beauvoir to Wittig, race is a relatively unproblematic phenomenon.

If we recognize that the concept of "race" or "racial difference," as a potential socioeconomic, cultural, and political marker, directly or indirectly affects us all, then it is imperative that we reiterate Spivak's questions for the white, Western feminist: "not merely who am I? but who is the other woman? How am I naming her? How does she name me?"[2] To this list, I would add another: how does "the other woman" name herself? As novelist, playwright, critic, radio producer, and scholar, black Guadeloupean author Maryse Condé offers a highly provocative, insightful perspective on a postcolonial black woman's questions about the self. For Condé, issues of gendered identity are inescapably embroiled in questions of race, language, and geopolitical origins. In her engrossing 1976 autobiographical novel, *Heremakhonon*, she stages a female identity quest that focuses on the intersections of traditional and modern values, and on the mediations of race, gender, politics, and history in the construction of the self.[3] Condé tackles the contradictions and challenges of an intellectual black woman striving for self-definition amid the structuring/ alienating images of the contemporary world. Her writing offers us an "other focus," to reuse Spivak's term, presenting new perspectives on autobiographical writing and issues of feminine identity.

Like Wittig, Condé has not chosen a strict form of autobiography in which to frame the interrogations of the self. Traditional autobiography's attention to factual accuracy concerning the individual's life data seems less of interest to her than the articulation of an open-ended, complex set of problems: readers must draw their own conclusions, provide their own interpretations. Although Condé has manifested a certain recalcitrance toward formal autobiography, especially toward its immodest, confessional tones, she is, nevertheless, creatively alert to the way elements of her personal history intersect with those of other women, particularly black Antilleans. Through the use of a first-person heroine who is distinct from herself (even if the resemblances are striking), Condé transforms the autobiographical issues of her novel into an exemplary performance of the personal: "one can find in her [the heroine of *Heremakhonon*] a series of conflicts, of contradictions that many Antillean women are certainly familiar with, even if they don't always feel like admitting them to themselves," says Condé in an interview.[4] For Condé, this adhesion and resistance to the character's dilemmas is representative of Antillean black women, but it also embodies the author's own involvement with her heroine, and incidentally our own. What is peculiar about Condé's autobiographical situation is that the love/hate relationship the heroine maintains with herself is symbolic of the author's ambivalence toward her narrator/ character—and indirectly toward herself.

*

Even more than the foreign settings of Sarraute's and Duras's childhood and adolescence, Condé's background traces a striking variety of multicultural experiences that articulate the twists, turns, and conflicts in identity formation. Born into the black bourgeoisie of Pointe-à-Pitre, Guadeloupe, in 1937 (she's two years Wittig's junior), Condé spent her childhood and adolescence in Guadeloupe, where the three-tiered society (black, white, mulatto) and the island's marginal position in relation to France made her aware of racial and cultural hierarchies at an early age. Her university years were spent in Paris and London, and after finishing her studies, she lived and taught for several years in West Africa (in Guinea and Ghana). More recently, she has been a professor of black African literature at the University of Paris IV (the Sorbonne), and has taught occasionally in the U.S. This biographical crisscrossing of the Atlantic is continually implicated in her literary and critical works as she approaches the thorny questions of origin and identity. In her first two novels, *Heremakhonon* and *Une Saison à Rihata* [A Season in Rihata], Condé is particularly attentive to the way the black Antillean woman sees herself through the discourses of Europe, Africa, and the U.S, as foreigner or outsider to others' cultures.[5] Each of these novels places a French-educated Antillean heroine in postcolonial Africa, in a (relatively unsuccessful) search for a "place" of her own, a sense of roots, belonging, and worth. These contemporary quests, set amid the complex, often bleak, political struggles of new black governments and their black oppositions, are tough-spirited, unsentimental novels that mock their heroines' delusions, while simultaneously sympathizing with their predicaments. Like the "Wittig" of *Across the Acheron*, Condé's heroines are fallible characters whose opinions can neither be faithfully accepted nor completely rejected. We are also reminded of de Beauvoir's ambivalent relationship to her narrative persona—vacillating between identification (approval) and disparagement, as well as the movement of Sarraute's tropisms (which invite both distance and identification on the part of the reader). We will be studying a similar ambivalence in *Heremakhonon*.

Condé's next set of novels, *Segu* and *Ségou, La Terre en miettes* [Segu, The Crumbled Earth], compose a two-volume, grandiose African saga of the decline of the Bambara kingdom of Segu (in today's Mali) at the end of the eighteenth century. The *Segu* novels portray the period when the holy wars of Islam were starting to overtake West Africa and when the white slave traders, with the help of local African rulers, were establishing their iniquitous commerce.[6] It is a spectacular historical novel written in the third person that dramatizes, through a seamless weave of fiction and fact, an ill-known story of African civilizations (Bambara, Toucouleur, Peul, Bozo . . .), before the arrival of Europeans, and during their first interventions in Africa. With a combination of fictive and historical characters, Condé concentrates on the fate of a prestigious fictional family close to the Bambara ruler, with the private and public histories intersecting in religious, political, and social conflicts of the period. Neither an idealization nor a condemnation of the African past—Condé does not attempt to provide an overriding explanation of Segu's decline—the novel sets in motion, from many perspectives, the actions and beliefs of the Bambara civilization as its foundations are gradually eroded. The characters, whether taking part in major political or religious struggles of the times, or quietly playing out their personal dramas in a local community, are richly drawn figures that resist one-dimensional evaluations. In this epic, Condé has placed male characters in the leading roles (as heroes and victims of history), with the muted tales of her female characters (as mothers, daughters, wives) filling secondary roles. In a 1986 interview, Condé explains this gender difference in terms of verisimilitude: for her, contrary to the Antillean literary (and social) tradition, in which woman occupies a central position, African cultural tradition places men in the limelight of social and familial events.[7]

In many ways, the Segu saga seems quite distant from any autobiographical concern—it is not a personal narrative, and deals with a past society whose customs and beliefs are, for the most part, alien to the author. In an interview, however, Condé admits a strong personal affinity for this region of Mali over other parts of Africa and calls her novel "a homage to a land that revealed to me a dimension of my past that I didn't know."[8] It is intriguing that *Segu* implicitly continues, on a literary track, the identity search outlined in *Heremakhonon*. The fictive heroine's desire to establish her African heritage in *Heremakhonon* is implicitly pursued by the author of *Segu*. In her 1986 interview, there is a certain slippage between the "I" of the author and the "I" of her earlier female characters, as Condé explains her rapport with Africa:

In the preceding novels, [*Heremakhonon, Une Saison à Rihata*] I had talked a lot about Africa, always as a land that I had a hard time loving, that I ended up loving, but that always remained rather foreign to me [. . .] Mali and the region of Segu gave me a profound happiness, a sort of dazzling vision [. . .].[9]

The distinctions that Condé is sometimes quick to uphold between author and narrator tend to fall away in her remarks about Africa. Condé even dedicates the first volume of *Segu* "to her Bambara ancestress," as if to confirm her personal investment in a work about Africa. It is noteworthy that, although women are not the dominant figures of the two Segu novels, Condé chooses to dedicate her work to a female ancestor rather than to a male one. In the 1986 interview, Condé stresses that she is not referring to a specific Malian relative of hers, that it is more a matter of an exemplary ancestry.

Condé's recent novel published in 1987 returns more explicitly to autobiographical models as it couples the intimate tones of the first-person narrative (already found in *Heremakhonon*) with historical fiction and the supernatural. *Moi, Tituba, sorcière noire de Salem* [I, Tituba, Black Witch of Salem] is the fictive autobiography—from beyond the grave—of the black Barbadian female slave who was imprisoned for witchcraft at the Salem trials in the late 1600s. Like *Segu*, *Moi, Tituba* uses little-known information to bring to life a black history that has been elided in Western knowledge. But this time, we are dealing with the narrative of a black *Caribbean woman* who tells her own story. The assumption of the fictive autobiographical voice constitutes the refusal to let a black woman's life be forgotten when, as the heroine laments, she feels she has been disappearing from history, with "no attentive or inspired biography recreating my life and its torments," whereas other (white) victims of the Salem trials were vindicated.[10] Not only does the black woman suffer from injustice, but she is also obliged to undergo the added insult of being consigned to oblivion in the annals of history. Condé uses the fictive autobiography to restore the specific black female figure's history to public awareness (occasionally using actual documents from the trials). But she also seems concerned with showing the representative quality of Tituba's situation as a black Caribbean woman. By writing from beyond the grave and creating encounters between Tituba and figures like Hester Prynne (Hawthorne's white heroine transformed into a feminist separatist), or black rebels in the mountains of Barbados, or the friendly, maternal spirits of the dead, Condé asks exemplary questions about the (modern) black woman's relationship to feminism, political revolution, and Caribbean tradition. Belief in the supernatural, as embodied in a dialogue with spirits, in spells, in curative herbs . . . is integral to the character of Tituba, but it also represents more generally an Antillean heritage. In her critical writing, Condé has observed that even in modern urban Antillean society, the trace of a belief in *"quimbois"* or magic (the lesser Antilles' equivalent to Haitian voodoo) rarely ever disappears entirely.[11] The fictive autobiography of a distant past becomes a modern forum for exploring (creating) the female slave's forgotten history, her misfortunes, suffering, and will to survive, as well as for general, contemporary questions involving gender, race, religion . . . .

Stylistically, Condé works within a literary tradition that has retained its faith in literature's ability to represent complex, polyvalent sociopolitical realities. Her name has not really been associated with the French literary avant-garde or the French feminist movements of the seventies (although her portrayal of Tituba as a traditional healer and consoler—rather than an evil witch—parallels French feminists' analyses of the "sorceress").[12] Her textual points of reference are instead the black authors of the Caribbean and Africa: Aimé Césaire, Frantz Fanon, Léopold Senghor, Mayotte Capécia, Simone Schwartz-Bart . . . , coupled with European classics (Pascal, Marivaux, Marx . . .), Afro-American authors (Booker T. Washington, Langston Hughes . . .), and a feminist like de Beauvoir. Condé's novels are not designed to challenge the formal elements of character, plot, chronology, syntax . . . the way those of the New Novelists do, although she certainly does upon occasion offer her own particular twists and innovations to each of these. Nor is she interested in exploring the possibilities of a specifically feminine language. There is, however, what one might call a "postmodern flavor" in the way her texts playfully attest to their intertextual borrowings and create mosaics of linguistic, cultural fragments that cut across geographic and chronological boundaries. It is as if the content of her particular concerns involving racial, sexual, linguistic identity—as a black, female, heterosexual French Caribbean writer—were a particularly propitious terrain for the heterogeneous moves of the postmodern. Condé is extremely alert to the creation of networks that graft together classical French literary language and culture with contemporary slang, popular Creole proverbs, Antillean and African myths, literatures, and vocabulary, Afro-American dictums . . . . As the "outsider within" Western (French) language and culture, as well as having lived as a foreigner within African societies, Condé molds an eclectic style that engages both the frictions and the harmonies of multicultural junctures.

Given the complexities that such polyvalent value systems engender, it is not so surprising that personal and collective identities remain crucial issues for Condé, even if they are often considered outmoded by the (white) postmodernist. Instead of putting on trial the notion of personal identity, her heroines (particularly in *Heremakhonon*), long for a secure sense of self. In some ways, Condé's writing seems to fit quite well into Teresa de Lauretis's characterization of women writers based on race: "Verisimilitude, realism, positive images are the demands that women of color make of their own writing as critical and political practice; white women demand instead simulation, textual performances, double displacements."[13] But if Condé's personal writing demands include a certain amount of verisimilitude and realism, one must also note that her particular version of the literary real is defined by its heterogeneity, contradictions, myriad assimilations (re-sistances, displacements), and, most important, its critical self-consciousness. One of the most salient features of her writing is its persistent recourse to irony, sarcasm, and humor. Condé is suspicious of both negative and positive images—but especially positive images—as identity models when they simplify the shift-ing, multiple intersections of race, gender, language, and culture. If anything, Condé is more comfortable with critical (negative) constructions of the self, because for her, positive images so readi-ly fall prey to simplification. In this context, realism is designed to evoke the multifaceted, equivocal stories of life, when there is no single model to follow, no transcendental truth to obey.

For Condé, identity is a fragile construction that runs two opposed risks rooted in "racial" difference. First, as a series of borrowings from other cultures (and races), the collective identity (of a Guadeloupe) is easily lost through assimilation (into the cultural values of a France). The inferiority of blacks is ratified when they are encouraged (forced) to adopt the values of the colonizer. It is not by accident that the first assignment in Condé's school manual on the Antillean novel is: "Explain the importance for a society or a people of knowing its past."[14] For the Guadelou-pean, this means acquiring a sense of Antillean identity, even though (or rather because) the island is a department of France.[15] One remembers, in contrast, colonial times when West African or French Antillean children had to puzzle through the first line of their history books, reading: "Our ancestors the Gauls . . . ." The child's feelings of perplexity and cultural alienation could hardly have been greater. At the other end of the spectrum, Condé distrusts what she feels are simplified, idealized identities, as found in the "black is beautiful" movement, and has at times displayed a good deal of wariness toward the Afro-Caribbean Négritude movement.[16] Condé sees in Négritude's affirmation of racial pride and a black cultural aesthetic the danger of compla-cency, of glossing over, for example, the aspects of black history that do not support a positive image—such as the institution of slavery that already existed in Africa before the Europeans' ar-rival. She is particularly leery of a romanticized, uncritical view of blacks as "natural" (an image frequently suggested in the African

Négritude poetry of Léopold Senghor). And she reacts vehemently against any essentialist position that recognizes the
"Negro" ("nègre") as a real category rather than a false mythol-
ogy invented by the Europeans (or the West in general). In her
critical and literary writings, Condé walks the tightrope amid the
extremes of overly facile negative and positive images of race. In
the political arena, her fictive works frequently displace (but do
not eliminate) the issue of race, by portraying postcolonial conflicts of black against black. The tensions in her writing, with all its
ironies, articulate the extremes as they inevitably intervene in her
heroines' attempts at self-definition.

In her
critical and literary writings, Condé walks the tightrope amid the
Like many women writers of color, Condé is a feminist who has
often been critical of the ways white Western feminism has either
ignored the particular problems of women of color, or has tried to
impose its own values and solutions on them. Condé steers clear,
for example, of a militancy that would set in simple opposition
the oppressed black man and the oppressed black woman, although many of her works do perform a tacit, feminist questioning of male/female relations from a black Caribbean woman's
point of view.[17] In *Moi, Tituba*, although the maternal spirits that
visit Tituba continually warn against becoming involved with a
man, that it will bring her ill fortune (which it does), the narra-
tor/heroine is unwilling to renounce male companionship and
the pleasures of heterosexual lovemaking. She does come to realize that as a black woman, she is made to suffer more than her
black male companion, John Indien: "The color of John Indien's
skin hadn't caused him half the rebuffs that mine had caused
me."[18] Although Tituba does not wish to blame the black man for
this differential treatment, she is forced to recognize that Hester
Prynne's feminist analysis of gender inequality applies to her
situation, too. Condé does not "resolve" the issue once and for all,
but rather stages several positions within the framework of the
historical tale.

In the opening to *La Parole des femmes* [The Discourse of
Women], her book on women novelists of the French Antilles,
Condé takes care to distinguish her approach to the black
woman's image from those of the West and Africa:

Everything that concerns the black woman is an object of controversy. The West is horrified by her subjection to man, has taken pity on her "sexual mutilations," and has wanted to be the initiator of her liberation. On the opposite side, a school of Africans has never stopped celebrating the considerable place that she occupies in traditional societies, the status that she used to enjoy and [. . .] has come to a total idealization of her image and her functions. We will refrain from defending either thesis [. . .].[19]

Condé introduces her analysis of the problems raised by women novelists of the Antilles against the backdrop of the classic opposition (victim/idol) concerning the black woman's social position. Displacing these Western and African attitudes about black women (both of which she shows to be somewhat self-righteous), Condé turns her attention to the representations Antillean women create of themselves and to the peculiar difficulties they face.

Condé's work as a feminist critic resembles the American feminist project of creating and reforming literary canons: her analysis is in part designed to enlarge the audience for women writers. Although certainly unwilling to consign their novels to the realm of anonymous textuality (the classic move of the deconstructor), Condé does not simply return to the traditional emphasis on the individual writer's specificity. Rather, she insists on the group issues, those they all raise, and on the range of their solutions. (A good example pertains to their use of French and Creole in their works—the sign of a problematic relationship to their own and their readers' linguistic identities.) For Condé, it still matters who is writing, because identity is not an issue that is ever "settled." Although the Antillean novelists she considers have different backgrounds, Condé is most interested in the collective feminine image they offer, the set of issues that they hold in common, over and above each island's particularities (and whether or not they are independent). What emerges in Condé's investigation is the depiction of a world of tribulations, questions, and malaises that can be recognized as specific to Antillean women without dissociating them from other women of the world:

This discourse [of Antillean women writers] is neither optimistic nor triumphal. It is charged with anguishes, frustrations and refusals. But that isn't particular to the Antilles. Throughout the world, women's discourse is rarely triumphant. The feminine condition is lived everywhere as a condition of the exploited and dependent. However, given the particular context of the Antilles, anguishes, frustrations, refusals are enunciated differently. It is this difference that it was important to apprehend.[20]

This mark of a different enunciation—the linguistic signature of a problematic identity—is precisely what we will be exploring in *Heremakhonon*. Two issues are to be considered: first, with a sort of double vision, I want to study how the black Antillean heroine's situation is articulated as distinctive—different from those of African, North American, and European women—while also suggesting that her conflicts and contradictions are representative phenomena not limited to the black Antillean woman. Second, I am interested in the place *Heremakhonon* occupies in Condé's writing, and the concurrent ties and tensions between author and narrator. Condé's publications after *Heremakhonon*, especially *Moi, Tituba*, seem to play off the identity issues raised in this first novel. If *Heremakhonon* is not autobiography in the strict sense, it is nevertheless a powerful enactment of the way language articulates the multiple, contradictory fictions of the self.

HEREMAKHONON'S CRACKED MIRRORS

Heremakhonon is a polyphonic work whose dissonances and concordant tonalities are filtered through the tricultural grid formed by the Antilles, France, and West Africa. For the French or Antillean, its Malinke title, literally meaning "wait for happiness" and figuratively "welcome house," retains the foreign, opaque allure that Africa presents for the heroine. Presented explicitly as a quest for cultural and sexual identity, *Heremakhonon* is a first-person narration that probes the painful, funny, and self-conscious queries of an educated black woman, whose wit and erudition are as provocative as they are engaging.[21] Veronica Mercier, the narrator and heroine, investigates the possibility of a self rooted in a cultural heritage, but still free to move in societies without being labeled or stereotyped. Condé's novel is distinct from those of many Antillean writers in that we are not looking at society through the eyes of a rural or underprivileged individual.[22] Veronica Mercier is a philosophy teacher from the black bourgeoisie of Guadeloupe. Her language is sophisticated, ironic, irreverent, and decidedly attuned to the dilemmas of a modern black woman. *Heremakhonon* is similar, however, to the works of many other *women* writers of the Antilles, in that its heroine does not bear children (she is sterile): feminine identity questions are not posed in terms of motherhood.[23]

Veronica Mercier is an alluring, outrageous voice that is both tough-minded and extremely vulnerable, and that elicits both our sympathy and disapproval. Condé's novel often reminds the reader of Frantz Fanon's *Black Skins, White Masks*, for like the latter, *Heremakhonon* confronts the various forms of intellectual alienation in the black bourgeoisie. It also recalls Toni Morrison's and Paule Marshall's penetrating critiques of bourgeois society.[24] In *Heremakhonon*, the focus on the self, through cultural mediations in the heroine's speech, takes the form of myriad displacements in a primarily alienated process. The novel's variegated linguistic features, from its shifts and layering of tone and imagery to the use of clichés, quotations, slang, and historical reference, set the notion of identity adrift. Ultimately, the whole conception of the identity quest is put on trial by the need to affirm a political stance, however qualified or interrelational it might be.

On a physical level, Veronica Mercier carries out her identity quest as a journey from Guadeloupe to France and then to West Africa, and through a series of sexual relationships: first, with a young Guadeloupean mulatto, then with a white French architect, and finally, with a black African politician of noble origins. In each of these encounters she is forced to face the political implications of her sexual choice, and in each she finds herself judged guilty by society's racial and/or ethical codes. The reader can only piece together this sequential chain, however, through flashbacks to the narrator's earlier life in Guadeloupe and France. The reflections on the past and on the difficulty of breaking out of racial and sexual stereotypes interrupt and punctuate the flow of the story in the present, which entails Veronica's stay in West Africa (where she has come to teach), from arrival to her return to France. The plot is double: on the one hand, Veronica's attempts to understand who she is, in a continual return to the past; on the other, political strife in West Africa between a postcolonial socialist government and its socialist opposition. Two men embody this political struggle in which the heroine finds herself embroiled despite her wishes: the Minister of Defense and Interior, Ibrahima Sory, who becomes Veronica's lover, and the leader of the opposition, Saliou, who becomes her friend. Refusing to take sides during most of the novel and trying to shut out the political present of Africa, Veronica gradually realizes that her love affair with a government official has placed her on the side of political oppression. When Saliou is arrested and mysteriously dies in his cell, Veronica is forced to recognize that she has let herself be lulled "in the arms of an assassin" [H, 176]. She ultimately chooses to leave for France because of her untenable situation.

On a historical level, *Heremakhonon*'s extraordinarily rich textures launch the reader into another intertextual journey. On nearly every page, Veronica's personal preoccupations weave together the pasts of Africa, Europe, and the Caribbean. Already on the first page, the African police officer who questions Veronica about the purpose of her visit becomes the link between Africa and Veronica's Caribbean past:

The thin, nervous type. Somewhat distinguished. Surely from that part of the coast that produced my father's ancestors. He too was somewhat on edge and somewhat handsome. He reminded me of that Mandingo marabout I had seen in my history book when I was seven. And not from the South either, but from Dahomey or Nigeria, men who had paid their fair share to what they called the New World. The New World? All that for a few Venetian glass beads, a few rolls of red cotton, a portable organ for Agadja and a carriage for Tegbessu. All that for so little! [H, 3].

Looking for resemblances between her Antillean heritage and contemporary Africa, Veronica retraces the slave trade links, when African kings like Agadja and Tegbessu were selling other Africans (perhaps Veronica's ancestors) to the Europeans. Amid the present of Veronica's encounters in Africa is inscribed, in abrupt fashion, Veronica's personal past—her education, her love affairs, her family—but also Antillean history and its ties to Africa. The reader plunges into a narrative that makes few distinctions between Veronica's spoken discourse and her silent thoughts, between present and past. During her first dinner with her new friend and boss, Saliou, Veronica's personal reflections about her Antillean past and Africa invade her conversation with him:

The niggers [from the Antilles] had to build their own Pantheon of famous men, didn't they? The Mandingo marabout [Veronica's father] was proud of his ancestors and he was right. This tastes good, what is it?
    "Chicken with groundnuts."
    Even so, it's nice to be welcomed by this stranger. My boss. Three centuries and a half wiped out.
    The whites are coming! The whites are coming!
    It seems they [the Africans] took them [the whites] for ghosts [H, 5].

Through multiple allusions (which the European or American reader can sometimes only piece together through context), Veronica's running narrative conjures up the images that have shaped her awareness of herself in history and tradition. As the plot progresses, the relative proportions of text dealing with the past and with the present are reversed—the African present gradually imposes itself on Veronica's consciousness. But the interlocking of the two never disappears. Stylistically, the oscillations between oral exchange and intimate thoughts, and between multiple pasts (personal and collective) and a chaotic present, are somewhat reminiscent of Sarraute's tropisms. Since it is not always possible to attribute the origin of a given discourse (Is Veronica talking to herself or to others? Is she serious or ironic? Even she is sometimes uncertain . . .), the reader's hold over the text is always precarious. The reader reenacts the loss of direction or uncertainty of meaning that troubles the heroine. The latter becomes a filter or mediator of the multiple, often contradictory, discourses that traverse her existence. And as we mentioned earlier, by the end of the novel, even the identity quest itself is seriously questioned.

ORIGINS AND MODELS—COPIES AND QUOTATIONS

What Veronica hates most in life is slavish imitation. The copy never seems to equal in value the original or model. Similar to Sarraute's narrators in *Childhood*, Condé's heroine manifests dis-

comfort at the idea that her personal pursuit belongs to a fashion-
able (or conventional) trend. *Heremakhonon* opens with a series of
intertextual acknowledgments and denials:

Honestly! You'd think I'm going because it is the in thing to do. Africa is
very much the thing to do lately. Europeans and a good many others are
writing volumes on the subject. Arts and crafts centers are opening all
over the Left Bank. Blondes are dyeing their lips with henna [. . .] Well,
I'm not! [H, 3].

Veronica quickly (and somewhat defensively) distinguishes a fad-
dish interest in Africa from her own journey there. Arriving from
Paris, she describes herself as "a tourist, but one of a new breed,
searching out herself, not landscapes" [H, 3]. In search of her own
reflection, Veronica disdains the "dubious thrill of exoticism" [H,
9] that a European might feel in Africa and concentrates on the
ways Africa can explain her own past in Guadeloupe to her.
Veronica turns to Africa as the key to the Antillean past.

Veronica's self-absorption, which brings all dialogue with others into a dialogue with and about herself, is a desire for an
unassailable self-love, with an established identity replete with
origins. But identity is that curious fiction that requires absolute
difference (I am like nobody else), while situating its subject in a
preexisting signifying chain of culture (my sense of self is dependent upon my "place" in relation to others). In Veronica's case,
individual identity is intimately connected to the problematic
collective identity of the Antilles. In the assimilated culture of her
parents who look toward France for the stamp of value, any
African origin is irretrievably lost and it is for the better since for
them, what bears the mark of that origin is an inferior, "natural"
condition that must be transcended. Veronica's major objection to
her bourgeois upbringing lies in its duplicitous position on Antillean identity, with "its talk of glorifying the Race and its terrified
conviction of its inferiority" [H, 52]. In the name of freedom and
dignity, Veronica's father says that blacks should not dance [H, 8]
and that his daughters should not go barefoot at the beach [H, 4].
"His freedom was an iron weight encircling his feet and ours" [H,
8]. "Négritude" and attempts at assimilation form an uneasy
union in Veronica's early life. France not only signifies high cultural achievement, it also implicitly represents white superiority

in Guadeloupean society where a strict racial hierarchy is maintained—white, mulatto, black, in descending order. Veronica's family—characteristic of its class—maintains its "superiority" by proving to itself and to the world that it is better than the poor, uneducated blacks (particularly those in rural areas), who maintain close ties to Antillean customs and religion, and who speak Creole. Veronica's trip to Africa is an exploration of another heritage that her parents have ignored.

As a child, Veronica envisions her parents as so refined and culturally elevated that she falls ill when she learns that they too engage in sexual intercourse. She feels that her father should have at least invented a more dignified manner to do it. The following is the adult's imagined newspaper announcement about the invention:

Our distinguished compatriot, Mr. Mercier, whose work and untiring devotion to the cause of the Race are known to everyone, has invented a noble, delicate and simple method of conceiving children, thereby replacing the vulgarity of mother nature. Henceforth we shall leave the sweat of fornication to the niggers of the lower town. To them and the whites [H, 84].

Veronica then adds her editorial comment: "No, on this point, like on all the rest, he was content to imitate. Imitate" [H, 84]. The humorous parody does not conceal Veronica's bitterness toward her father. Her mother even seems to mimic European fragility in her body. Whereas Condé has remarked that Antillean women are noted for their survival instincts, their ability to endure hardship,[25] Veronica remembers her mother as a faded, weak, Victorian-style figure who suffers from allergies and hay fever. When Veronica remarks on the difference between Saliou's wife, Oumou Hawa ("the black gazelle extolled by the poet"),[26] working hard although eight months pregnant, and her own mother, who was allergic to the sugarcane in flower, she comments wryly:

Can you imagine it! [. . .] It's as if the sight of coal made a miner's daughter sick. After all, where would we be if Christopher Columbus hadn't crossed the Atlantic with his ship's hold full of sugarcane plants taken from the Moslems in Cyprus. We ought to make it our emblem, our standard. If man is a (thinking) reed, the West Indian is a stalk of sugarcane [H, 13].

This passage is characteristic of Veronica's inherited ambivalence toward the Antilles: on the one hand, she longs for parents who would be "at home" in Guadeloupe. But on the other, when she alters Pascal's dictum to suit the Guadeloupean framework, what becomes clear is that the "emblem" of West Indians—sugarcane—is precisely what associates them with the blacks' enslavement. In addition, Veronica's historical remarks stress that this sign of the West Indies is an *importation*. What is "natural" or characteristic in the islands is a function of an economic enterprise. In an interview, Condé observes that both vegetation and people in the Antilles have been "imported," so that "the Antilles are totally artificial creations of the capitalist system."[27]

When it happens that Veronica's first intimate love relationship in Guadeloupe is with a mulatto, it causes an uproar in a community that accuses Veronica of prostituting herself in order to rise socially, something she vehemently denies. Her family exiles her to France to continue her studies, but it is also to insure distance between her and her mulatto lover. In France, Veronica seems (paradoxically) to feel more or less integrated into the culture and strikes up a warm, casual relationship with a white architect, Jean-Michel. Interestingly enough, white discriminatory attitudes and practices are not what trouble Veronica in Paris. Rather, it is the look of other blacks at the biracial couple—whether neutral, as the local black street-sweeper's, or excruciatingly accusatory, as the Antillean black militants'—that leave Veronica haunted by the idea that she has forsaken her race. As in the Antilles, she is called a "Marilisse," a slave/whore exchanging status or security for sex. In Africa, then, she hopes to reconcile herself with her collective origins and her race. Turning to West Africa's past, which she discovers through her readings, Veronica remarks: "Perhaps these ancestors were mine and I'm not a bastard" [H, 49]. The sense of a legitimate lineage (naming her neither as whore nor as bastard) is integral to her pursuit.

*

Now, *Heremakhonon*'s scenario could seem like a Francophone version of Alex Haley's *Roots*, were it not for the novel's incisive self-consciousness that points out the illusions of the "return to origins" and "natural identity," even as it dramatizes the heartfelt nostalgia. Through irony, parody, and intertextual reference, *Heremakhonon* is always displaying its own textual debts and literary echoes. Despite her distaste for her parents' imitations of the white French, Veronica is forced to recognize that her own identity search is an imitative form whose gravity and uniqueness are persistently deflated. When asked by a stranger if she is an American, she exclaims to herself in exasperation: "These damned black Americans have captured the limelight because of Mahalia, Aretha and James Brown. All we can offer is the cooing of Gilles Sala who is obviously no match" [H, 103]. When she pours out to her lover, Ibrahima Sory, the jumble of past memories, of her "escape" from her family's contradictions, he comments, somewhat mockingly: "In other words, you have an identity problem?" and then adds: "There was a young black American girl here who had the same sort of problem, I believe. She ended up having her hair plaited like our women and having herself renamed Salamata" [H, 52]. Veronica's identity quest is transformed into a cliché because of American blacks who have preceded her, and the "solution" to her problems is comically reduced to a few superficial alterations (a change in hairstyle, in name . . .). At every turn, the heroine's claim to originality/worth is denied.

Heremakhonon's self-conscious style is also evinced in Veronica's attempt to understand herself through quotations and allusions to the literatures, religions, and myths of the Caribbean, Africa, the U.S., and France. Although they are too numerous and resonant to deal with adequately here, we can at least note a couple of the references and their uses. In the context of her forays into Caribbean and American black history and culture, for example, Veronica quotes from Aimé Césaire's *Return to My Native Land* and alludes to Booker T. Washington [H, 12]. If Césaire and "good old Booker T." [H, 12] insist upon the black's rise out of slavery, Veronica, for her part, wants to know what came *before* slavery. In another passage, Veronica returns to Césaire, agilely combining a brief commentary on Césaire's *Tragedy of King Christophe* with a discussion of popular French and Creole sayings:

It's been drummed into me since childhood—work is healthy ["*le travail, c'est la santé*"]. Idleness is the root of the devil ["*L'oisiveté est la mère de tous les vices."*][28] *Quant nèg pas ka travaill, i ka fé quimbois.* When the nigger doesn't work, he casts spells. We were forgetting, however, the unfortunate lot who worked for nothing for two centuries [. . .]. I don't agree with Christophe when he proclaims by the grace of Césaire:

"I ask too much of men? But not enough of black men, Madame."

I've read Césaire like everybody else. I mean like everybody from our world. In my opinion, it's high time they left the niggers in peace, let them dance, get drunk and make love [H, 81–82].

Veronica rebels against the work ethic clichés of both French and Creole, as well as their literary version in Césaire. The emphasis on continually proving one's worth—and incidentally the worth of the (black) race—is rejected. This is no doubt why Ibrahima Sory's noble origins are so attractive: he has nothing to prove. At the same time, however, it should be noted that Veronica's remarks are made at the very moment she has accepted work with a doctor friend of Saliou. Her commentary thus contradicts her actions and points up the tug-of-war that pulls Veronica in opposite directions.

The socioliterary references fulfill a double function. Veronica allusively avows her debt to major texts of black literature—Condé's work offers many common concerns with Césaire's—while the heroine (and implicitly the author) positions herself in oblique fashion to this (modern) tradition. The autobiographical fiction creates its voice or position by bouncing off other texts.

While Veronica's language openly garners the resources of a rich cultural background, she is extremely wary of clichés and stereotypes, both as facile representations that preclude thinking and as linguistic taboos that limit expression. Her ironic perspective erodes their noxious potential. When describing a young African student, she comments: "He has a lovely smile, rounded teeth, very white. Careful! Beware of clichés: the nigger with the flashing white teeth. All the same, his teeth are very white" [H, 8]. The trace of the possible racial cliché/slur in her words causes a hesitation which she forces herself to overcome. She does not ignore the racial stereotype that has become attached to the words, but neither does she let it deny her access to them. Another way Veronica maintains and mocks her own use of clichés or ready-made expressions is by pointing them out through hyphenation, something Frantz Fanon often does in his work. When the heroine refers to the "chaos-that-set-in-after-the-whites-left" [H, 164], she uses the expression to connote (in a critical way) the bigoted tendency of Europeans or Americans to explain away quickly an African insurrection against an African government. But at the same time, Veronica's own unwillingness to become involved in the struggle makes her complicitous with the viewpoint. Her use of the coined phrase acknowledges and challenges the foreign view of Africa, a perspective that has been her own.

The narrative's biting humor is ever present in Veronica's monologues, but because of the elliptical style, the point of view is often revealingly unclear. The following passage is about Veronica's mulatto lover's family, the de Rosevals in Guadeloupe. The imagery comically plays on the ups and downs of racial hierarchy and on the commercialization of history:

De Roseval. The name sparkled on the bottles: of rum, liqueur, and punch, below the traditional Arawak, scarfaced and bedecked in feathers. The family lived a few miles from town [. . .]. And the tourists doing Island Tour No. 5 [. . .] were driven past the Roseval mansion [. . .]. Those who, like [my father], knew their colonial history by heart, would laugh. The mansion was a fake, a mere copy of the Marins de St Sorlins mansion which had stood a few miles higher up only to be brought down in a slave uprising. The light-skinned Rosevals claimed descendance from the Marins de St Sorlins. One of them had even attempted to prove it. All the whites rose up against him. Pretentious bastard [H, 6].

The elliptical final remark here is characteristic of the ambivalent perspectives in *Heremakhonon*. To whose point of view are we to attribute the remark, "Pretentious bastard"? Is it ironic? We can interpret the elliptical sentence as Veronica's indirect quotation of the rich colonial whites mentioned in the preceding sentence, for whom distinctions between black and mulatto are insignificant. It also comes from Veronica as a black who has been scorned by the mulatto class. She is only a *"négresse rouge"* [H, 13], a red Negress, slightly lighter in skin color because her grandmother was the daughter ("illegitimate of course") of a black woman and a white plantation owner. Veronica thus takes pleasure in seeing the mulatto class's bogus pretensions to superiority denied. The remark encompasses two of the three positions in the color triangle and reproduces the ambivalent inferiority/superiority complex.[29]

Veronica, in fact, refuses and adopts her parents' inferiority/ superiority complex vis-à-vis the racial question. From among Veronica's chaotic recollections of a veiled racial inferiority in Guadeloupe emerges the painful confession of a repressed memory: "We [Veronica's family] were not intruders at Saint-Claude [a "mulatto stronghold"]. *We simply did not exist*" [H, 129, my emphasis]. Veronica's sense of black pride and of her own worth are crushed by the mulattos. She is no Mayotte Capécia, she says [H, 30], who would seek to lighten the race; but on the other hand, she remembers her envy and shame as a child in wanting to be a mulatto girl [H, 130].

Because of the corrosive satire concerning the mulattos, Veronica's love affair at age sixteen with the de Roseval boy can be read in more than one way: even the narrator wonders if her love didn't bear in it a desire to appropriate the other's power or to carry out a scandalous revenge on a hateful racial hierarchy. Condé refuses to sketch a clear-cut psychological portrait of the heroine, preferring instead to posit conflicting motives and interpretations, over which the speaker/heroine does not/cannot offer an authoritative version. Her intentions in the sexual relationship are described according to two interpretations. On the one hand, she professes to have cared for Jean-Marie de Roseval beyond/ despite any question of race; on the other, she concedes that it is his status as a mulatto—his freedom—that attracted her to him. Rather than choose between these two readings, the text acquiesces to both.

Africa is to be the place of truth for the heroine, where racial difference vanishes, thereby delivering Veronica from the racial complexes inherited from her parents. Africa is also to serve as a point of origin because its people have a long history. Veronica is most drawn to the Africans of noble descent, because they are and have always been free: "I came to see a land inhabited by Blacks not Negroes" [H, 56]. But why then does she refer to her lover, Ibrahima Sory, as "my nigger with ancestors"? [H, 37]. The expression is almost an oxymoron, suggesting in an ironic twist a link between the Antillean black slave and the black African with a pedigree, a member of African royalty. To be successful in her quest, Veronica must somehow connect these opposites. What she tries to overlook (but keeps mentioning) is that the one was involved in the enslavement of the other.

*

From Césaire to Senghor, from *Ebony* magazine to the slave-trading kings of Dahomey, from Antillean proverbs in Creole to maxims and sayings in English, from the Golden Gate Bridge to "the Venus de Milo minus the arms" [H, 9]—Veronica's intellectual juggling, most often critical or ironic, is a means to thread her way through the maze of cultural attributes without clearly espousing any one of them in a definitive way. It is the same movement as in her use of clichés. At the same time, however, she searches desperately for something to hold on to amid the cultural fragments that articulate her. One senses that she is in effect seeking an untainted, ideal language, one that would not be marked by racism, sexism, social hierarchies . . . . For Veronica, cultural and linguistic identity are formed in a double movement of construction and disruption, particularly through ambivalent quotation. If Veronica's verbal moves follow Jane Gallop's belief that, "identity must be continually assumed and immediately called into question,"[30] it is also necessary to recognize that the perception of such instability can produce a great deal of discomfort and anguish. A completely mobile (or borrowed) identity may feel like none at all, even when one grants that all identity is simulation, echoing, borrowing, transposing . . . . When power and personal worth are already grounded in a system maintaining the illusions of "inherent value" (origins, race, sex . . .)—as they are in our societies—the lure of authenticity (whether in a "new" or "old" identity) is particularly intense.

In an interview, Condé remarks that the Antilles lack the kind of "serious or sacred" oral literature that invents a creation myth: "It is useless to invent a myth of origin for the Antilles when one knows that in 1492 Christopher Columbus arrives in Guadeloupe, and that a few years later a slave ship unloads hundreds of Africans."[31] For Condé, this literary lacuna is borne out in the Antillean people's feeling that "the terms of their identity are dictated to them."[32] To a certain extent, *Heremakhonon* articulates the effects of this absence of an Antillean origin myth. Although Veronica's language successfully registers the contemporary psychoanalytic notion of identity in terms of "position within an intersubjective [and intercultural] network,"[33] it is also quite clear that race, gender, and homeland continue to mark out her various positions despite her wishes.

"Through him [Ibrahima Sory] I shall at last be proud of what I am" [H, 42].

Veronica's relationship with Ibrahima Sory is a one-sided affair that places her in a subordinate role as sexual object—a role that she adopts for its masochistic pleasure ("there's a secret unhealthy voluptuousness in being treated like an object" [H, 89]), and as a trade-off for the identity she thinks he can bestow on her. As in Duras's *Lover*, the woman portrays herself as a prostitute, although the exchanges differ. Whereas in *The Lover* money is an integral part of the sexual transaction, Veronica is more concerned with appropriating another kind of social currency: Sory's royal origins and thus a "legitimated" identity. Rather than highlighting the idea that women, money, signs . . . are all in circulation—and thus belong to nobody—Veronica insists on the idea of ownership. Sory will possess her body and she will in exchange possess his genealogy. But we will also see that Veronica's utter (outrageous) dependence on Ibrahima Sory to define herself—as a woman, as a black . . .—is a lure that the text—Veronica's own commentary—will gradually, but persistently, question. Veronica, at odds with herself, challenges her own scandals and contradictory poses.

Veronica's love affair with the African Minister of Defense reproduces on an individual scale her desire vis-à-vis Africa in general. In her eyes, the minister represents a power, knowledge, and authority that his regal ancestry confirms and authenticates. He is less an individual than a symbol of freedom for the heroine. Sory thus embodies the imaginary "autonomous subject" whose autonomy is paradoxically ordained by ties to a family tree. (He owes his political power in the government to his family's prestige.) In Veronica's schema, the desired other, Ibrahima Sory, clearly occupies the illusory place of wholeness. Jacqueline Rose's explanation of Lacan's "Other" is useful here:

Subjects in language persist in their belief that somewhere there is a point of certainty, of knowledge and of truth. When the subject addresses its demand outside itself to another, this other becomes the fantasied place of just such a knowledge or certainty. Lacan calls this the Other—the side of language to which the speaking subject necessarily refers. The other appears to hold the "truth" of the subject and the power to make good its loss. But this is the ultimate fantasy. Language is the place where meaning circulates.[34]

In *Heremakhonon*, Sory (on the individual level) and Africa (on the collective level) fill the position of the all-powerful male "Other," whereas both Veronica and the Antilles belong to an illegitimate, feminine, slave world, without a history, without "forefathers."[35] The strength of this fantasy is attenuated, however, because Veronica is not entirely duped by her own creations: "Loving a man is the myth you create around him. Or with him in mind. In my case perhaps it's a bit more serious because the idea I have is so vital and yet so vague [. . .], that of an Africa, of a black world that Europe did not reduce to a caricature of itself" [H, 77]. Veronica thus recognizes that her minister is a projection of her own desire to be a total subject, one that is impervious to the imitations of Europe. What shatters the specular relationship is the introduction of a third term that challenges Sory's position of absolute authority and truth. The opposition leader to the government, Veronica's friend Saliou, insists on his right to truth, power, and to the same ethical discourse as the minister. Both have served the revolutionary cause and are even brothers-in-law. The similarity of their claims (another specular opposition) confuses Veronica:

Perhaps if they drew two camps, one imperialist, the other socialist, one pro-Washington, the other pro-Moscow, despite my hatred of slogans, I could work it out. But these subtleties! Because in fact these men are fighting and killing each other in the name of Africa [H, 94].

The fable of an Africa identical to itself breaks down, that is, its political reality harbors a heterogeneity that is not, significantly enough, reducible to the East/West caricatural opposition which Veronica is tempted to use.[36] Finally, in a passage near the end, Veronica endorses Saliou's fight against Sory's government: "Perhaps what I'm witnessing in such a fragmentary and imperfect way, like [Stendhal's] Fabrice on his battlefield, is the fight of a people for their liberty and justice" [H, 160]. Concurrently, Veronica recognizes that Sory is not (could never be) the mythic "full" subject that the heroine projected.

If it takes Veronica a long time to rally to the side of the oppressed opposition, it is because she has longed for a position from which to determine absolute truth (yet knowing all the while that it is not attainable), and because she has not wished to acknowledge the cracks invading the smooth image she has created of her lover. More than an escape, her departure from Africa at the end of the novel combines a new interpersonal and political awareness. First of all, Veronica recognizes the value of the opposition's struggle against the government. Despite the complexities of political struggle, she realizes that there *is* a difference between government and opposition that she cannot ignore. In a similar vein, Veronica increasingly reasserts the general possibility that value can exist despite the cliché or stereotype: "Cliché? What does that mean? That you are hardened, inured to major ideas and the words that translate them. That you are ashamed of them" [H, 134]. Veronica refuses more than ever to let important issues be debunked merely because they have been uttered before.[37] This vindication of what underlies the cliché is crucial: Veronica's quest and Saliou's opposition are not deprived of value merely because they "repeat" the acts or words of others. Ibrahima Sory's mockery of the heroine's problems is thus retrospectively undermined. In addition, Veronica comes to acknowledge her filiation to her parents: "Perhaps I've been too hard on them. They mimicked because they hadn't been taught anything else. They were victims. Like me" [H, 135]. Finally, Veronica's departure is predicated upon her understanding that the African past is not the "key" to her Antillean identity, and also that she cannot be blindly dependent on men for meaning and worth. In a Proustian ending, Veronica projects Condé's telling of the failed—but necessary—identity quest: "One day I'll have to break the silence. I'll have to explain. What? This mistake, this tragic mistake I couldn't help making, being what I am. [. . .] I looked for myself in the wrong place" [H, 176].

Condé's interview with Ina Césaire a few years after the publication of *Heremakhonon* affords intriguing insights into Condé's particular resistances to, and affinities for, autobiography. In the first part of the interview, Condé takes her distance from formal autobiography in a categorical way: "Everything one writes has autobiographical roots. But Veronica's story is not mine and I have no desire to recount my life."[38] Even the first-person "I" turns out to be a lure, "simply an artifice of writing,"[39] says Condé, since she had originally written the work in the third person and only switched to the first person when the fiction did not have the appearance of the "firsthand testimony" ["récit-témoignage"] that she wished. The "I" reveals itself as a literary convention capable of producing certain textual effects, but does not represent a specific individual.

It would be inaccurate to say, however, that this artificial, constructed "I" is wholly devoid of referential attributes. Condé says she conceives of her character as an "anti-me," "fabricated from what I am not or perhaps what I believe myself not to be."[40] Condé states this in the context of the novel's political dimensions: "I had a precise, very sad story to tell about imprisoned African friends, in flight, in exile [. . .]."[41] The author's active support of the leftist opposition during her years in Africa sets her at odds with Veronica's initial refusal to take sides. But this "anti-me" also turns out to be an integral part of Condé's thinking. Veronica's dislike, for example, of dogmatic political positions, which often leads her to be critical even toward the groups she supports, is consonant with Condé's exorbitant political statements[42] that often seem designed to shock:

I[na] C[ésaire]:—Doesn't there appear through Veronica a sort of provocation in the absence of commitment? Isn't it true that you wanted to shock a certain militantism? Of the extreme left?
M[aryse] C[ondé]:—Of course, because a certain militantism that becomes sectarianism really bores me. Deep down, I have a lot of sympathy for anarchy . . . .[43]

The "anti-me" role that Veronica fills for Condé's thinking is not so much an external figure for the author as a language of negativity within the subject, part of the doubled subject's ongoing battle with herself as well as others. The form of the fictive autobiographical narrative bears this out quite well: as we already noted, Veronica's dialogue with others turns into a dialogue with and about herself. The voice of the "I" is portrayed as multiple shifts and even an incorporation of the other's (negative) voice. One senses Condé's personal inclination for a special kind of negativity: the "anti-me" embodies the fascinating, if troubling, contradictions of the self. Veronica's jibes at the Antilles, her parents, her lover, Africa, political parties . . . bear witness as much to struggles within the subject—a fundamental ambivalence about herself in relation to the world—as to her particular criticisms of that world.[44]

Once Condé projects Veronica as another in the interview, she spends much of her time defending the heroine from Césaire's criticisms. She even freely acknowledges some of the ways in which the "anti-me" articulates her biography. For example, Condé admits to having lived the contradictions of the superiority/inferiority complex concerning Race, that is, extreme pride, even arrogance, in being a "Negro," coupled with an "absolute imitation" of Western values: "It's an ambiguity that I have lived and that, very early, I felt like resolving by going to seek out people who were really Negroes, who had the right to say: 'Let's be proud to be Negroes' [. . .]."[45] She adds that the criticisms and irony directed toward Veronica by the other characters are "the reflection of questions that I myself was asking my character."[46] The autobiographical novel is thus an active interrogation and elaborate dramatization of contradictions displaced onto the fictional character—just as the arguments, criticisms, and compliments of other characters become part of Veronica's deliberations with herself.

If, at the end of *Heremakhonon*, Condé's own "precise, very sad story" of an African left-wing appears to overtake Veronica's identity quest, one must not, I think, infer that the character's new political stance "solves" the personal issues, or that it supplants them.[47] As I noted earlier, *Heremakhonon*'s ending not only marks the logic of Veronica's "mistake" (looking for herself through Africa, through a man), but also the necessity of its telling: despite the author's role as critical interlocutor (adopting/creating Sory's, Saliou's, and others' points of view), her position ultimately fades into the character's: the writing of the quest and its valorization are affirmed—by Veronica *and* Condé—and their political positions merge. For Condé, *Heremakhonon*'s written adventure signals the beginning of a novelistic career that pursues the issues of origins and Antillean feminine identity.[48] And although Condé asserts (doubly after the fact) that it is not necessary for the Antillean to turn to Africa for roots,[49] it is clear that Africa does provide her with literary sources, another kind of "origin": through the writing of the Segu saga, Condé mythically, literarily, creates her own African heritage. This is all the more the case when one takes into account that the Segu novels not only tell a story of Bambaras in Africa, but deal with the diaspora as well. In the context of feminine identity patterns in *Heremakhonon*, Condé's consecration of a matrilinear heritage ("to my Bambara ancestress") marks the shift from male-centered structures of identity and ancestry to female ones. Despite the fact that the African family saga focuses on male characters, the Antillean woman writer, in accordance with Antillean oral tradition, implicitly traces her own feminine genealogy, not just as character portrayed (the object of discourse), but actively, as *storyteller*. It is as if Condé were responding to a call similar to the one in *Les Guérillères* to remember the time before slavery: "Make an effort to remember. Or, failing that, invent."[50] The Segu novels are the engendering of Africa *and* the Caribbean woman writer through the storytelling.

Condé's journey in writing eventually brings her back to slavery and to the New World. With *Moi, Tituba, Sorcière noire de Salem*, she renews her ties with the brutal history of the slave, but instead of the shame that marked Veronica Mercier's childhood, with her feeling that the slave had no history, *Moi, Tituba* celebrates the female slave's story, her amazing courage and endurance, as well as a whole array of Antillean customs and beliefs. Although the slave recounts her story as a series of hardships and sorrows, Condé has traded some of her mordant sarcasm and irony for the lighter, more poetic tones of fantasy and personal reconciliation. Tituba's eventual return to the Antilles (from the U.S.), where she

dies and becomes an invisible spirit, seems to suggest metaphorically Condé's literary return to her native land (and one also
thinks of the intertextual echoes of Aimé Césaire's *Return to My
Native Land*). In a mixture of realism and the fantastic, Condé
again suggests the continuation of a female community, not
through "natural" means (that is, biologically giving birth), but as
a consciously chosen form of feminine guidance: repeating the
structures of Tituba's own childhood at the beginning of the
novel, the spirit of Tituba, in the last pages, "adopts" an orphan
daughter, whom she watches over, while she also consoles and
comforts slave women tempted by suicide. The tradition of Antillean animism (part of an African inheritance) metamorphoses
Tituba's identity/presence into the physical attributes of her island, while sustaining a continuum of feminine support and
caring.

   This model of a constructed feminine lineage is perpetuated in
the writing of *Moi, Tituba*: author and narrator are supportively
bound together through classic literary conventions: Condé
opens *Moi, Tituba* with the premise that Tituba has told her her
story during a year of intimate conversations. Although this preface metaphorically suggests that Condé has spent a year research-
ing and thinking through Tituba, it is also a self-conscious literary
performance that situates her first person narrative within two
long-standing traditions: first of all, the Antillean playfully gives
voice to her history through a fictive form common to eighteenth-
century Europe: like Marivaux's *Life of Marianne*, the "author/
editor" is the repository of a poor girl's sad, supposedly true,
story. Second, Condé's story has clear ties to the tradition of the
Afro-American slave narrative. Condé's text thus mediates an
Antillean woman's perspective through her version of Europe's,
and the U.S.'s literary traditions.

   With *Moi, Tituba*, Condé's writing responds more readily to the
affirmative image-making (of the Antillean woman) that Teresa
de Lauretis found in the critical and political writing strategies of
many women of color. The female writing subject articulates the
bonds between generations and cultures: autobiographical narrative becomes the exemplary voices of women as they confront
the contradictions in their lives and in discourse. What remains

distinct in Condé's work, however, is her self-conscious literary formulations of the notion of identity: it is an artificial construct, made up of heterogeneous borrowings, and it shifts according to one's relative position in the signifying chain of culture. In both *Heremakhonon* and *Moi, Tituba,* Condé weaves together the multiple discourses of Africa, Europe, and the U.S. in order to articulate the contradictions (internal and external) informing an Antillean woman's sense of self. "The paradox," says Condé, "is that in the end, although born from a truly artificial creation, the Antillean people nevertheless exists."[51] As a woman, Condé finds in the paradoxical identity of the Antilles the means for artistic self-creations.

Conclusion: Dialogues with the Other

I n accounting for the interactions between personal experience and writing, Barbara Smith offers the following remarks at the end of her article, "Toward a Black Feminist Criticism":

[I want] the most expansive of revolutions as well as many words to tell us how to make this revolution real. I finally want to express how much easier both my waking and my sleeping hours would be if there were one book in existence that would tell me something specific about my life. One book based in Black feminist and Black lesbian experience, fiction or nonfiction. Just one work to reflect the reality that I and the Black women whom I love are trying to create.[1]

Smith's call to a revolution that is enacted in language rises out of the desire for a book that is both a reflection of personal (and collective) experience and a creation of it. In many ways, this is also the feat to which the autobiographer continually aspires. In walking the tightrope "between" fact and fiction, experience and language, the autobiographer hesitates "between" performance, description, and interpretation, while balancing the demands of truthfulness and literary inventiveness.[2] As a genre that includes rules and a weighty tradition, autobiography is a model with which the writers must come to terms through their own strategies. Breaking generic rules becomes an integral part of the (artistic, personal) signature of the autobiographer, as well as a sign of the particular sociohistorical period of the writer. Writing in the last half of the twentieth century, de Beauvoir, Sarraute, Duras, Wittig, and Condé all know that autobiography is anything but an innocent genre, whether one is considering it as a function of a literary tradition, or as a social, historical, and political negotiation with the postcolonial, Western world.[3] What marks these modern texts (but does not separate them from the tradition in any absolute way) is that their self-consciousness becomes so fully a part of the experiential account. The experiences of gender, class, and race are ultimately bound to the self-conscious text in such a way that linguistic experiment and referential experience are inseparable.

Autobiography is in some sense an impossible strategy to bridle or control otherness. Otherness means here not only one's difference from others (intersubjectively), but also internal difference, as embodied in the past selves that a writing in the present strives to resurrect/imagine, or in a life recounted. We have noted at various points that although traditional autobiographical rules require the identity of author, narrator, and protagonist, the alienation of the subject is also a necessary condition for the self-recognition of autobiography. The split between subject narrating and object narrated constitutes the distance needed to see oneself (as another). What is striking about this structure for the writers I have been considering is that they all openly adopt *dialogic patterns* to sustain the figure of an interactive subject. Ultimately, the texts dramatically incorporate the other into the portrayal of the self. And in each instance the autobiographical dialogue reveals the use of a decisive *fictive element* in the exploration of textual identity. It is as if the true stories of the self, of life, could only be traced through a double/other in a dubious act of invention, fantasy, disguise, imitation . . . as fabrications of history and reality. This cheating—to use de Beauvoir's description of fiction—is both constitutive and disruptive of the autobiographical project. The element of fiction forcefully challenges the validity of the author's claims to have faithfully reported on the past, or to have honestly described her search for identity, even though it also enables her story to unfold. Thus the uneasy relationships between the reality of experience and literature, or between memory and the translation of memory into words, are continually mediated by the detours of fiction.

In de Beauvoir's case, the innocent, straightforward recounting of her youth in the *Memoirs* proves a double disguise. On the one hand, the *Memoirs* are a means to distance her from the painful reality of the Algerian War. On the other hand, de Beauvoir's guilt in the present of writing is itself the double of a guilt in the past recounted. *It is through her best friend Zaza's death that de Beauvoir is able to fashion her own literary persona.* Zaza's story as a dutiful daughter who rebels and fails is woven into Simone's, and it shapes de Beauvoir's self-image as a woman and as a writer. (It is important to remember that de Beauvoir's first writing attempts dealt with Zaza's death.) In the dialogue between Zaza's and Simone's stories, de Beauvoir eventually appropriates her friend's character and death, folding them into her autobiography. Zaza's historical death is textually repeated—Zaza dies again—when de Beauvoir borrows her personality, her past, and propels her own history forward with the romanticized death of her friend. The appropriation of Zaza's death is also, paradoxically, de Beauvoir's attempt to repay her "debt" to Zaza. In writing about her friend, de Beauvoir confesses that her own writings are nothing but the artificial creation of a young woman called Simone, who is in fact the image of Zaza. The ironic resemblances between the tensions in Zaza's life and those in de Beauvoir's own situation at the time she was writing the *Memoirs* ultimately challenge de Beauvoir's vehement rejection of the bourgeoisie, as well as her claim to truth and authenticity. The moving fiction of Zaza's feminine dilemma and her demise becomes the displaced, gendered origin of de Beauvoir's ambivalent critique of the bourgeoisie.

Sarraute's fiction of the self's otherness is clearly embodied in the dueling voices of *Childhood*'s dialogue. Since she is, among the five writers considered here, the one who has most tenaciously denied that literature is marked by gender, her dialogue between feminine and masculine voices, as they generate the autobiographical subject, is truly intriguing. Rather than a mere denial of gender, the introduction of the masculine voice becomes a complication of gendered identity: Sarraute posits an internal male interlocutor who is integral to the female autobiographical "I." The fiction of the doubled voice reproblematizes the relationships between gendered linguistic codes and sexual identity. This is why, for example, the parallels between Sarraute's opening hesitations to engage in autobiography—in a discussion between female and male narrators—and the sexually charged scene of the child's sofa-slashing are so fascinating. Each scene contains instances of the feminine and the masculine, but the juxtaposition of the two scenes defies any tidy categorizations of a unitary (gender/sexual) identity. The fiction of the censuring male voice produces in the female narrator the desire to tell, and thus provides both a constraint *and* the impetus to recount/interpret important moments of the girl's past. Similarly, under the law of the father, the little girl takes pleasure in transgressing his rule. And although her violent gesture (sticking the scissors in the sofa), coupled with her new mastery of German, seems to correspond to a *masculine* conception of individualized identity and power, the structure of the child's rebellious desire is clearly analogous to that of the *female* narrator. In addition, the gaping sofa traces the image of a provocative, excessive feminine sexuality that corresponds to the linguistic exuberance of the tropism.

Within the parental drama, Sarraute's masculine speaker suggests two conflicting interpretations, neither of which ever really prevails at the expense of the other. First, the inclusion of the masculine voice can be read as a total acceptance of the father as the most important person in Sarraute's life. Second, it symbolizes a repetition of the mother's act of covering up her feminine gender with a masculine pseudonym (hence, a negative identification with the mother). By borrowing, on a linguistic level, a masculine identity, a fictive self, Sarraute is able to create the critical space in which to tell the madness of desire ("I compose in madness and reread in reason"[4]). It is the madness of a feminine break with(in) the paternal order and its logic, and a mad desire to possess the maternal other through the repetition of her feminine erasure.

By writing an autobiographical text that points to itself as a rewriting/reading of the early novel, *The Sea Wall*, Duras most forcefully acknowledges the fictive aspects of autobiography. Thus *The Lover* unabashedly *reappropriates a fiction* that was itself already an indirect version of autobiography. Not only is autobiography for Duras a fictive form by definition, but her writing also continually implies that the apprehension of experience as such is bound up in an interpretative process that denies facts any exteriority to their fictive elaboration. Duras is drawn—and draws her readers—into the ways the subject is itself shaped in the forms of circulating fictions that no longer have any ultimate referent.

The dialogue with otherness is performed in *The Lover* in several ways. On an intertextual level, it is a dialogue with her other works, as the echoes of voices and events cross from one text to another. The autobiographical fiction cannot be closed upon itself and it has no privileged status over the other fictive works. Next, otherness is constituted as an internal difference in *The Lover*, with the autobiographical "I" harboring a foreign "she." This is not just the clean split between past and present "I"s, since we saw that both pronouns ("I" *and* "she") could apply to either temporal subject, past or present. Rather, the distance between "I" and "she" enacts the celebration of feminine sexuality and identity through the traditional fiction of the woman-as-object. At the same time—and here the dialogic pattern in *The Lover* tends to explode—the woman-as-object enters into the exemplary circulation of the prostitute and, like language, becomes exchangeable, without a "proper" place. The specificity of the heroine's identity is challenged through the way Duras exploits the grammatical ambiguities of French. The confusion, for example, between references to her lover's body and to her own emphasizes the exchange of identities, so that objects—and subjects—are in continual flux.

Duras stresses her active role in *The Lover* as stage director of her own performance. In the past, she is the initiator of the sexual encounter, thereby turning the passivity of her fictive past (in *The Sea Wall*) into an active lure. In the present, she engages in an autobiographical project that equates writing with seduction. In my reading of *The Lover*, I have tended to focus on the positive force of Duras's erotically charged writing and its ambivalent use of tradition, although there is a potentially objectionable side as well. What is so troubling about Duras's staging of the self's otherness is that it adopts traditionally alienating, repressive forms of feminine representation—woman-as-object, as other, as spectacle, as prostitute—to make a case for a new, revolutionary understanding of all subjects in language. In *The Lover*, it becomes difficult, for example, to set apart the effective critique of individualism and representation from the self-indulgent, exhibitionist performance of the woman autobiographer (and from that of the young girl she was).

It could be said that, by borrowing the theme of an old novel, Duras creates a case of double prostitution: on the one hand, the young girl prostitutes herself for money; on the other, the aging writer prostitutes her past for publication and glory. Duras's autobiographical strategies to undermine feminine repression/oppression always run the risk of reaffirming questionable feminine images and roles.[5] Duras willingly plays with this risk, forcing us to think through our assumptions about representations of women.

In the dialogue between "Wittig" and Manastabal in *Across the Acheron*, we return more clearly to the fictive externalization of the split subject. As autobiography, Wittig's *Across the Acheron* posits through dialogue the virtual "place" of the lesbian writing subject. The character of Manastabal is in many ways an extension of "Wittig," an alter ego that challenges "Wittig's" more strident harangues against the condemned (heterosexual women). The dialogue shakes up what otherwise might have become a complacent self-image of the lesbian purist. The picaresque exaggerations of the fantasy, coupled with the critical dialogue, shatter the uniform seriousness of the radical lesbian's position.

Whereas Sarraute introduces a masculine other within the female subject through dialogue, Wittig seems, at first glance, to be doing just the opposite in *Across the Acheron*. The doubled subject, created through the "Wittig"-Manastabal exchanges, imagines a society where difference (or self-definition) is supposedly *not* a function of gender, either internally or externally. There are, after all, no "men" and no "women" in this book. And yet the clash between "Wittig" and the condemned feminine souls is a critical allegory of heterosexuality as an institution, so that as an implicit theme, gender cannot be dismissed. In addition, the "war between the sexes" is still present, although reintroduced as a war between an oppressed (feminine) class and a (masculine) class of oppressors. The gender markings in French (masculine "enemy"; feminine "souls") are not neutral. Similarly, the relationships between the character's name and the author's, or between Dante's comedy and Wittig's, are not innocent. Wittig's attempts (in interviews) to keep literature intact—safe from its own referential potential—are belied by her works, which openly invite the social, political, and personal connections.

Although Wittig tends to avoid making correspondences between her political affinities and her novels, she clearly welcomes intertextual references to the (masculine) literary tradition. (Literature, in this context, is supposedly an unmarked writing.)[6] But here, too, gender clearly makes a difference: Wittig's playful mockery and self-conscious appropriation of Dante's *Divine Comedy* implicitly acknowledges that her own affirmation of a female utopian fiction can only take place against the disrupted but implicit order of the universal masculine.[7] Her brash take-off on the male masterpiece consistently recalls its origin, since the allusions to that earlier fiction are part and parcel of Wittig's text. *Virgile, non,* the French title, reminds us that while Virgil was Dante's guide, this new version will in some way be a negation ("*non*") of its antecedent. The intertextual borrowings from the masculine tradition are constitutive of the lesbian's autobiographical fiction. That is, many of the effects of the *feminine* borrowing are obtained by staging it against the backdrop of the *masculine* text.

In Condé's works, the dialogue with otherness is perhaps the most far-reaching and the richest in structure. In *Heremakhonon*, Veronica Mercier's private dialogues with herself—dialogues that juxtapose her past (in Guadeloupe; in France) and her present in Africa—powerfully reveal the alienated, ironic self caught in a series of borrowed cultures and borrowed identities. This "anti-me," with whom the author enters into a sometimes critical, sometimes sympathetic dialogue via her characters, articulates the problems of race and gender in the search for a (self) legitimating *origin*.

Two questions come back repeatedly in Condé's writings and in those of black women in general: how is my identity as a woman affected by my being black? How is my black identity affected by my being a woman? There are no easy answers and *Heremakhonon* first appears as a general denial, as a refusal to answer any questions regarding identity. I am not Veronica, says

Condé of her heroine. And in the book, Veronica, who goes to Africa in search of her roots, of her identity, leaves disillusioned by her experience. The lack of legitimating origins is in fact thematized as a break with a natural genealogy in Condé's works. As we already saw, the Guadeloupean writer tends to phrase her questions about a black woman's identity outside natural reproduction: Veronica (and Tituba) do not give birth to children and their own parents do not give them a legitimated identity. Veronica's funny newspaper announcement about a new art of human reproduction without sex is her sarcastic rejection of the artificial identities of her parents. They copy Europe, so that (black) identity is merely an alienated fiction (of whites). What is remarkable about Condé's point of view, however, is that it will ultimately transform the structure of borrowed identity and artificial filiation into a positive construction. Condé turns to *fiction* as the means to reformulate the quest for identity and origins. Tituba, for example, who has no natural children, becomes in Condé's tale the spirit-mother of a young Barbadian girl. As autobiographical fictions, Condé's *Heremakhonon*, the *Segu* saga, and *Moi, Tituba* all metaphorically give birth to the Antillean black writer who realizes that the "artificial creation" of the fictive self, although it appropriates other cultures, other people, nonetheless operates most effectively. Condé makes us aware that the artificial constructions of the self, in all its contradictory poses, are valid and real. As an Antillean woman writer, she lays claim to a fictive, multicultural genealogy that she produces and that produces her in turn.

*

All five writers have thus engaged in various forms of autobiographical writing by searching for an identity that can only be reached through the appropriation of a fiction, *an element foreign to their history, their background, their gender.* Through dialogic forms, they systematically borrow something beyond their personal experience, and this borrowing becomes the key support, the organizing element of their autobiographical writing. De Beauvoir borrows at the thematic level (a friend's identity); Sarraute borrows at the grammatical level (a male speaker); Duras borrows at the narrative level (a fiction appropriated as autobiography); Wittig borrows at the textual level (from Dante's classic); Condé borrows at the intercultural level (I need Africa to understand myself).[8]

Not only do these writers attest to the notion of autobiography as distortion, they also make us suspect that reality is somehow always already bound up in distortions and fabrications. De Beauvoir, Sarraute, Duras, Wittig, and Condé all walk the tightrope between fiction and experience to the point where one wonders whether they experience anything but fiction.

As women autobiographers, they consistently show that the gendered subject continues to be an issue in the fictions of identity, even in the cases where they aspire to an unmarked, neutral writing. Their negotiations with a masculine/feminine dichotomy refuse the authority of a masculine universal or an essential feminine. By keeping the terms in play, they open up autobiography to the multiple affirmations, negations, and displacements of the feminine subject.

Notes

INTRODUCTION

1   For a useful introduction to the particularities of modern textual
    criticism and its relevance for women writers and readers, see
    Nelly Furman, "Textual Feminism," in *Women and Language in
    Literature and Society*, edited by Sally McConnell-Ginet, Ruth
    Borker, and Nelly Furman (New York: Praeger, 1980), 45–54.

2   Jacques Derrida has described the problematic status of auto-
    biography in the following way: "wherever the paradoxical prob-
    lem of the border is posed, then the line that could separate an
    author's life from his work, for example, or which, within this life,
    could separate an essentialness or transcendentality from an em-
    pirical fact, or, yet again, within his work, an empirical fact from
    something that is not empirical—that very line itself becomes
    unclear. [. . .] When this identity is dislocated, then the problem of
    the *autos*, of the autobiographical, has to be totally redistributed."
    Derrida's argument insists that each element of the opposition
    life/text is already not identical to itself, thereby compounding the
    complexities. See *The Ear of the Other: Otobiography, Transference,
    Translation*, texts and discussions with Jacques Derrida, translated
    by Peggy Kamuf, edited by Christie V. McDonald (New York:
    Schocken Books, 1985), 44–45.

3   Paul de Man, "Autobiography as Defacement," MLN 94 (1974):
    920.

4   Sidonie Smith, *A Poetics of Women's Autobiography: Marginality and
    the Fictions of Self-Representation* (Bloomington: Indiana Univ. Press,
    1987), 26.

5   Jane Gallop has also pointed out our culture's gender-marked
    expectations of men's and women's writing: "Women write let-
    ters—personal, intimate, in relation; men write books—universal,
    public, in general circulation." We might rewrite this as: Histor-
    ically, women have written diaries, letters, journals . . . ; men have

written autobiographies. In both stereotypes, the "male activity" and its product are valued over the female ones. See Jane Gallop, "Writing a Letter with Vermeer," in *The Poetics of Gender*, edited by Nancy K. Miller (New York: Columbia Univ. Press, 1986), 139.

6 Nancy K. Miller, "Women's Autobiography in France: For a Dialectics of Identification," in *Women and Language in Literature and Society*, edited by Sally McConnell-Ginet, Ruth Borker, and Nelly Furman (New York: Praeger, 1980), 262.

7 Mary Russo introduces her convincing essay on carnival and theory with this resonant phrase. See Mary Russo, "Female Grotesques: Carnival and Theory," *Feminist Studies/Critical Studies*, edited by Teresa de Lauretis (Bloomington: Indiana Univ. Press, 1986), 213.

8 See Sigmund Freud, "On Narcissism: An Introduction," edited by James Strachey, *The Standard Edition of the Complete Psychological Works*, vol. 14 (London: Hogarth Press, 1953), 67–102. For an ingenious, subtle, deconstructive study of Freud's "narcissistic woman" (one that turns her into a self-sufficient, double subject), see Sarah Kofman's *The Enigma of Woman: Woman in Freud's Writings*, translated by Catherine Porter (Ithaca, N.Y.: Cornell Univ. Press, 1985).

9 Julia Kristeva, "Le sujet en procès," in *Polylogue* (Paris: Seuil, 1977), 55–106.

10 Roland Barthes, "The Death of the Author," in *Image-Music-Text*, translated by Stephen Heath (New York, Hill & Wang, 1977), 143–48.

11 Michael Sprinker, "Fictions of the Self: The End of Autobiography," in *Autobiography: Essays Theoretical and Critical*, edited by James Olney (Princeton: Princeton Univ. Press, 1980), 342.

12 See Steven Shapiro, "The Dark Continent of Literature: Autobiography," *Comparative Literature Studies* 5 (1968): 421–54.

13 "[S]e distingue de l'autobiographie par l'*absence* d'un récit suivi" (my translation). Michel Beaujour, *Miroirs d'encre: Rhétorique de l'autoportrait* (Paris: Editions du Seuil, 1980), 8. *Childhood*'s narrative self-consciousness also makes it resemble Beaujour's definition of the self-portrait.

CHAPTER 1

1 I will be considering the following autobiographical works by Simone de Beauvoir: *Memoirs of a Dutiful Daughter*, translated by James Kirkup (London: World Publishing, 1959); *The Prime of Life*,

translated by Peter Green (London: André Deutsch and Weidenfeld and Nicholson, 1959); *Force of Circumstance*, translated by Richard Howard (New York: G. P. Putnam's Sons, 1965); *All Said and Done*, translated by Patrick O'Brian (New York: G. P. Putnam's Sons, 1974). All further references to these works will be included in the text in brackets.

2   "[*La Cérémonie des adieux*] détonne par l'ambiguïté de son statut, l'ambivalence de ses motivations, l'insignifiance de son écriture. [. . .] les critiques expriment presque tous le malaise et l'incertitude sur le sens et la valeur d'un ouvrage à la fois ordinaire et imprévu." See Geneviève Idt, "*La Cérémonie des adieux* de Simone de Beauvoir: rite funéraire et défi littéraire," *Revue des Sciences Humaines* 4:192 (1983):15–16.

3   Konrad Bieber, *Simone de Beauvoir* (Boston: Twayne Publishers, 1979), 17.

4   Judith Okely, *Simone de Beauvoir* (New York: Random House, Virago/Pantheon series, 1986), vii.

5   Alice A. Jardine, *Gynesis: Configurations of Woman and Modernity* (Ithaca: Cornell Univ. Press, 1985), 183. Jardine's description of the "feminine operation" appears in her discussion of Jacques Derrida's metaphorical equation of the feminine and writing.

6   *Memoirs of a Dutiful Daughter* spans the years from de Beauvoir's early childhood to the completion of her studies and her meeting with Sartre (1908–29). *The Prime of Life* (1929–44) tells of her early teaching assignments, her first attempts at writing, her life with Sartre, and the impact of World War II on her life. *Force of Circumstance* (1944–62) narrates the period when she and Sartre became controversial literary and political celebrities; it contains accounts of her affairs with Nelson Algren and Claude Lanzmann, as well as long passages dealing with events during the Algerian War. *All Said and Done* (1962–72) includes accounts of various friends' deaths, dreams, her numerous trips with Sartre (to Cuba, Brazil, the Soviet Union . . .) as well as de Beauvoir's political and feminist activities. In the latter three volumes, de Beauvoir devotes much space to establishing connections between her fiction, theoretical essays, and daily thoughts and actions.

7   For the account of her mother's death, see *A Very Easy Death*, translated by Patrick O'Brian (New York: Penguin Books, 1983).

8   Simone de Beauvoir, *The Second Sex*, translated by H. M. Parshley (New York: Random House, 1974), 786.

9   "[L]'histoire de sa personnalité." See Philippe Lejeune, *Le Pacte autobiographique* (Paris: Seuil, 1975), 14.

10 Judith Butler, "Sex and Gender in Simone de Beauvoir's *Second Sex*," *Yale French Studies* 72 (1986): 40.

11 Butler, "Sex and Gender," 45.

12 Deirdre Bair, "'My Life . . . This Curious Object': Simone de Beauvoir on Autobiography," in *The Female Autograph*, edited by Domna Stanton and Jeannine Parisier Plottel (New York: New York Literary Forum, vols. 12–13, 1984), 242.

13 Bair, "'My Life . . . ,'" 242.

14 See de Beauvoir's article, "Littérature et métaphysique," *Les Temps Modernes* 1 (April 1946): 1155.

15 "[I]l n'y a pas de vérité antérieure à celle que le langage exprime." Francis Jeanson, *Simone de Beauvoir ou l'entreprise de vivre* (Paris: Seuil, 1966), 270.

16 De Beauvoir, *Tout Compte fait* (Paris: Gallimard, 1972), 633. Rather than using the published translation, I have provided my own translation for this passage of the last volume, because the published one strays too far from the French.

17 Paul de Man, "Autobiography as De-facement," MLN 94:5 (1979): 922.

18 "Rares sont les autobiographies qui choisissent de s'en tenir à un pur récit, et s'abstiennent de tout discours autobiographique. Par exemple Simone de Beauvoir, dans les *Mémoires d'une jeune fille rangée*, loin d'afficher la subjectivité liée au récit autobiographique, a l'air de raconter les choses 'telles qu'elles furent': il n'y a aucun pacte autobiographique au début du livre, et les interventions *avouées* du narrateur se comptent sur les doigts de la main. Au lecteur de décider si cette feinte objectivité est inspirée par la discrétion, ou par la ruse. Mais dans les volumes suivants, S. de Beauvoir revient à une attitude plus naturelle: chaque volume est précédé d'un pacte en bonne et due forme, qui développe le traditionnel discours autobiographique." Philippe Lejeune, *L'Autobiographie en France* (Paris: Armand Colin, 1971), 79–80.

19 De Man, "Autobiography as De-facement," 921.

20 According to Rodolphe Gasché, autobiography inevitably presents itself as "a discourse of authority, as a discourse where the *other* is transformed into a barbarian [. . .]." See the foreword to the special issue "Autobiography and the Problem of the Subject," MLN 93:4 (1978): 573.

21 As Candace Lang has remarked, "the theoretical problems inher-

ent in the traditional autobiographical project appear most clearly when they are explicitly denied." See "Autobiography in the Aftermath of Romanticism," *Diacritics* 12:4 (1982): 9.

22 In her discussion of de Beauvoir's novel, *She Came to Stay*, Martha Noel Evans convincingly shows that this ambivalent attitude of narrator toward character also operates in de Beauvoir's fiction: "The technique of *style indirecte libre* allows the author to identify with the characters of her novel but in an ironic, disrupted way that points up their self-delusions. [. . .] It activates, then, a doubly charged connection between author and character, a relationship that hovers unspecifiably between identification and condemnation." Martha Noel Evans, "Murdering *L'Invitée*: Gender and Fictional Narrative," *Yale French Studies* 72 (1986): 76. Although de Beauvoir, according to Evans, characterizes fiction as the "arena of feeling and connection, the same domain as that allotted to women in our society," and nonfiction as "the sphere of reason, lucidity, the province of men" (69), de Beauvoir's autobiographical writing breaks up the tidy division. I am arguing that the narrator of the *Memoirs* adopts both positions (empathic and disparaging), giving rise to a double vision.

23 Elaine Marks, "The Dream of Love: A Study of Three Autobiographies," in *Twentieth Century French Fiction: Essays for Germaine Brée*, edited by George Stambolian (New Brunswick: Rutgers Univ. Press, 1975), 79.

24 This is also the period when de Beauvoir's book on China, *The Long March*, was ill received by the critics. See 345.

25 Autobiography as the revelation (and eradication) of guilt belongs to a long tradition of which Jean-Jacques Rousseau's *Confessions* are no doubt the most famous example.

26 See Claude Roy, "Beauvoir, par Simone," *La Nef* 22 (1958): 77.

27 Robert D. Cottrell, *Simone de Beauvoir* (New York: Frederick Ungar, 1975), 8.

28 Paul de Man, "The Rhetoric of Temporality," *Blindness and Insight: Essays in the Rhetoric of Contemporary Criticism*, 2nd edition revised (Minneapolis: Univ. of Minnesota Press, Theory and History of Literature Series, vol.7, 1983), 213.

29 De Man, "Rhetoric of Temporality," 212.

30 For an insightful discussion of the way the young Simone identifies with, and separates herself from, female figures in her early childhood, see Catherine Portuges's article: "Attachment and Separation in *The Memoirs of a Dutiful Daughter*," *Yale French Studies* 72 (1986): 107–18.

31 It is very interesting to note that in her book on Brigitte Bardot, de Beauvoir has Bardot's female detractors in France say practically the same thing about the star: "On New Year's Eve, Brigitte Bardot appeared on French television. [. . .] Lounging on a sofa, she plucked a guitar. *'That's not hard,'* said the women. *'I could do just as well.'* She's not even pretty. She has the face of a housemaid" (5; my emphasis). De Beauvoir's analysis of the Bardot image could be a description of her own defense. She explains that the beautiful BB threatens women because she flouts conventional moral codes without assuming the role of the "bad woman" (18–19). Structurally, the dilemmas of this female movie star and the female autobiographer are quite similar. See Simone de Beauvoir, *Brigitte Bardot and the Lolita Syndrome* (New York: Arno Press, 1972). The book was originally published in French in 1959, thus within a year of the publication of de Beauvoir's *Memoirs*.

32 Cottrell, *Simone de Beauvoir*, 8.

33 Cottrell, *Simone de Beauvoir*, 7.

34 De Man, "Rhetoric of Temporality," 214.

35 De Man, "Rhetoric of Temporality," 215.

36 Jeanson, *de Beauvoir*, 269.

37 Lejeune, *Le Pacte autobiographique*, 236. Lejeune seems to assume that it would in fact be possible to remain "master" of the writing and the production of meaning, which is debatable at the very least.

38 Jean-Paul Sartre, *Nausea*, translated by Lloyd Alexander (New York: New Directions, 1964), 3.

39 Mary Evans astutely notes in her book, *Simone de Beauvoir: A Feminist Mandarin* (New York: Tavistock, 1985), 4, that during Simone's adolescence, the de Beauvoir family was at the margins of the bourgeoisie, thus Simone was already in a position to take her distance from it: "[. . .] the relative poverty of the de Beauvoir family made it impossible for them to play any real part in bourgeois social life. There was no money for entertaining, or attractive clothes, or the acts of apparent spontaneous generosity that support bourgeois entertaining's claim to originality and liveliness. Deprived of the material means to fulfil bourgeois expectations the de Beauvoirs had to fall back [. . .] on exaggerated adherence to the forms of bourgeois life. [. . .] the de Beauvoirs elevated standards about 'breeding' and 'good taste' to semi-religious importance [. . .]."

CHAPTER 2

1   If de Beauvoir's portrait of her friend Sarraute does not seem
    particularly friendly, it is because *Force of Circumstance* was written
    when the two were already on distant terms.

2   Sarraute's biographical data would in fact make an interesting
    novel or film (whether traditional or not). In skeletal fashion, the
    following are a few facts about Sarraute's background. Born in
    1902 in Ivanova-Voznessensk, Russia, of Russian Jewish parents,
    she spent most of her childhood traveling between France and
    Russia to live with either of her parents (who divorced when she
    was two), before eventually settling in Paris with her father and
    stepmother. After receiving her baccalaureate degree, she studied
    history in England, sociology in Berlin, obtained a B.A. in English
    at the Sorbonne, and then a law degree. While studying law, she
    met Raymond Sarraute (also a future lawyer) whom she married in
    1925. During the late twenties and thirties, she practiced law (with-
    out much enthusiasm), bore three daughters, and began to write
    Tropisms in the thirties. Her political affinities during this period
    leaned toward the Communist Party, but after witnessing the vio-
    lent repressions in the Soviet Union during a trip in 1936, she
    turned away from any formal affiliation. During the Occupation,
    Samuel Beckett, who was a member of the Resistance, took refuge
    with his wife in Sarraute's home. Because of her Jewish origins,
    Sarraute found herself obliged to change domiciles several times.
    She was denounced by a local shopkeeper, and at one point posed
    as the governess of her own children in order to avoid being caught
    by the Gestapo. For a more complete account of episodes from
    Sarraute's life, as well as for her sometimes comically violent re-
    sistances to talking about herself, see Sarraute's interview with
    Marc Saporta, "Portrait d'une inconnue," in the issue of *L'Arc*
    devoted to her: 95 (1984): 2–23.

3   Nathalie Sarraute, *Enfance* (Paris: Gallimard, 1983). I will be using
    the English translation: *Childhood*, translated by Barbara Wright
    (New York: George Braziller, 1984).

4   See "From Dostoievski to Kafka" and "The Age of Suspicion" in
    Tropisms, and *The Age of Suspicion*, translated by Maria Jolas (Lon-
    don: Calder, 1964).

5   Nathalie Sarraute, *Portrait of a Man Unknown*, preface by Jean-Paul
    Sartre, translated by Maria Jolas (New York: George Braziller,
    1958), ix.

6   Jean-Paul Sartre, "The Look," *Being and Nothingness*, translated by
    Hazel E. Barnes (New York: Citadel Press, 1964), 228–78.

7 Sartre quoted by de Beauvoir in FC, 14.

8 "Les clichés, les lieux communs, il n'y a que ça dans la vie courante, pourquoi taper dessus? Il n'y a même pas à s'en méfier: s'il fait beau, il fait beau. Ce qui est intéressant, c'est de savoir pourquoi je vais dire ça à mon voisin, sur quel ton, etc." "Nathalie Sarraute: Sartre s'est trompé à mon sujet," interview by Jean-Louis Ezine, *Nouvelles Littéraires* 2552 (September 30–October 6, 1976): 5.

9 "New Movements in French Literature: Nathalie Sarraute Explains Tropisms," *The Listener* (March 9, 1961): 428. Sarraute borrows the term tropism from the biological sciences where it refers to an instinctive response to external stimuli, as when a plant turns toward light or heat.

10 "Nathalie Sarraute," interview with Pierre Boncenne, *Lire* (June 1983): 88.

11 The advent of the "New Novel" as a recognized, avant-garde literary phenomenon was very important to Sarraute because through it, she no longer felt as if she were working in a void; others shared similar concerns about the necessary transformations to be carried out in the novel if it were to remain viable. Because of the critical attention paid to the New Novel as a group phenomenon, the label also greatly helped to increase Sarraute's reading public.

12 Sarraute's book continually prefigures and acknowledges the kinds of attacks that de Beauvoir wages: she describes her male writer as socially maladjusted and obsessed. The narrator of *The Age of Suspicion* provides the "outside" view, de Beauvoir's, only to prepare better the revelation of another, more sympathetic one.

13 De Beauvoir's criticisms in *Force of Circumstance* appear within the context of a general disappointment about literature, as it proves inadequate to the task of measuring up to contemporary events, in particular the Algerian War. Literature is insignificant in comparison, and although she includes her own writing in this indictment, her attacks are most vehement against the New Novelists. One wonders if this isn't a case of displaced guilt on her part.

14 See "Dix Romanciers face au roman," a survey by Bernard Pingaud, *La Pensée française* (December 12, 1956), 56.

15 Roland Barthes, *Sade/Fourier/Loyola*, translated by Richard Miller (New York: Hill & Wang, 1976), 10.

16 Bettina L. Knapp, "Interview avec Nathalie Sarraute," *Kentucky Romance Quarterly* 14:3 (1967): 293.

17 Boncenne, *Lire*, 88. Women obtained the vote in France in 1944.

18 "[L]a condition féminine, c'est la dernière chose à laquelle je pense en écrivant." Boncenne, *Lire*, 92.

19 I realize that these characterizations of women's movements in France and in the U.S. greatly oversimplify their complexity and diversity. My intention here is merely to point out that Sarraute has never felt a *literary* affinity for any of them.

20 "Du réel qui n'est pas encore pris dans les formes convenues." See "Conversation avec Nathalie Sarraute," by Serge Fauchereau and Jean Ristat, in *Digraphe* 32 (April 1984): 16. This is a special issue devoted to Sarraute.

21 It also should be noted that Hélène Cixous, probably the most visible advocate of "écriture féminine" in France in the seventies, also associates fluidity and the woman's body through abundant metaphorical references to blood and milk. And she too anchors women's writing in a sexual pleasure ("jouissance") that is characterized as diffuse and multiple. "I think in terms of overflow, in terms of an energy which spills over, the flow of which cannot be controlled." See "Rethinking Differences," in *Homosexualities and French Literature*, edited by George Stambolian and Elaine Marks (Ithaca, N.Y.: Cornell Univ. Press, 1979), 71.

22 Luce Irigaray, "The 'Mechanics' of Fluids," in *This Sex Which Is Not One*, translated by Catherine Porter and Carolyn Burke (Ithaca, N.Y.: Cornell Univ. Press, 1985), 106; see also *The Speculum of the Other Woman*, translated by Gillian Gill (Ithaca, N.Y.: Cornell Univ. Press, 1985), her deconstructive critique of psychoanalysis, and "One Doesn't Stir without the Other," translated by Hélène Vivienne Wenzel, *Signs* 7:1 (1981): 56–67, a lyrical monologue of daughter to mother.

23 Irigaray, *This Sex*, 111.

24 Irigaray, *This Sex*, 77.

25 Irigaray, *This Sex*, 134.

26 Irigaray, *This Sex*, 68.

27 See Julia Kristeva, *Revolution in Poetic Language*, translated by Margaret Waller (New York: Columbia Univ. Press, 1984); *Desire in Language: A Semiotic Approach to Literature and Art*, translated by Leon S. Roudiez (New York: Columbia Univ. Press, 1980); "Héréthique de l'amour," *Tel Quel* 74 (1977): 30–49; "Maternité selon Giovanni Bellini," in *Polylogue* (Paris: Seuil, 1977).

28 Kristeva, *Revolution in Poetic Language*, 28–29.

29 Kristeva, *Revolution in Poetic Language*, 29.

30 Although there are by now innumerable accounts of French feminisms and French theories of the feminine, I have found the following to be particularly useful: *New French Feminisms: An An-*

thology, edited by Elaine Marks and Isabelle de Courtivron (New York: Schocken Books, 1981); Elaine Marks, "Women and Literature in France," *Signs* 3:4 (1978): 832–42; Ann Rosalind Jones, "Inscribing Femininity: French Theories of the Feminine," in *Making a Difference: Feminist Literary Criticism*, edited by Gayle Greene and Coppélia Kahn (London: Methuen, 1985): 80–112; Jane Gallop, *The Daughter's Seduction: Feminism and Psychoanalysis* (Ithaca, N.Y.: Cornell Univ. Press, 1982); Michele Richman, "Sex and Signs: The Language of French Feminist Criticism," *Language and Style* 13 (1980): 62–80; Josette Féral, "Antigone or the Irony of the Tribe," *Diacritics* 8 (September 1978): 2–14. For an appreciation of some of the differences between American and French critical theories of the feminine, see *The Future of Difference*, edited by Hester Eisenstein and Alice Jardine (New Brunswick, N.J.: Rutgers Univ. Press, 1985); Toril Moi, *Sexual/Textual Politics: Feminist Literary Theory* (New York: Methuen, 1985); *Yale French Studies*, "Feminist Readings: French Texts/American Contexts," 62 (1981). A historical account of the numerous women's movements in France can be found in Claire Duchen, *Feminism in France: From May '68 to Mitterand* (Boston: Routledge & Kegan Paul, 1986) and *French Connections: Voices from the Women's Movement in France*, edited and translated by Claire Duchen (Amherst, Mass.: Univ. of Massachusetts Press, 1987).

31 Sarraute's works show a progressive elimination of conventions that obscure the tropism. In her first three novels, *Portrait of a Man Unknown*, *Martereau*, and *The Planetarium*, she still retains a semblance of plot and named characters, whereas in later ones, *Between Life and Death*, *Do You Hear Them?*, *"fools say,"* and *The Use of Speech*, plots dissolve (action, in de Beauvoir's sense, disappears), and speakers, for the most part, are unnamed.

32 This is clearly not the case for other New Novelists. In the works of Robbe-Grillet, Duras, and Simon, for example, sexuality is a major structuring component.

33 Boncenne, *Lire*, 91.

34 Boncenne, *Lire*, 92.

35 Nancy Chodorow, *The Reproduction of Mothering: Psychoanalysis and the Sociology of Gender* (Berkeley: Univ. of California Press, 1978).

36 Judith Kegan Gardiner, "On Female Identity and Writing by Women," in *Writing and Sexual Difference*, edited by Elizabeth Abel (Chicago: Chicago Univ. Press, 1982), 184.

37 "[. . .]s'il y un absolu que mes personnages recherchent, c'est

toujours le besoin de *fusion* et de *contact* avec autrui"; see Knapp, "Interview avec Nathalie Sarraute," 293.

38 In her analysis of the difficulties in heterosexual relationships (caused by the fact that women are the primary or sole caretakers of infants), Chodorow does not try to turn the tables in any overt way, that is, she does not turn masculine identity into the negative pole and feminine identity into the positive one. Nevertheless, it is difficult not to see value differences in the asymmetry between women's and men's conceptions of self. As Judith Kegan Gardiner points out: "Dinnerstein, Chodorow and Rich describe gender differences in terms that imply women are nicer than men. Empathy, responsibility and interdependence seem preferable to defensive aggression, destructive rage against women and nature, and a compulsion for control." See "Mind Mother: Psychoanalysis and Feminism" in Greene and Kahn, *Making a Difference*, 134–35. Although Kristeva's "semiotic" is most often described as a fundamental negativity, it is positive in the sense that it energetically disrupts phallocentric discourse.

39 Sarraute herself is oblivious to this negativity until it is pointed out to her by readers. In her interview with Knapp (286), she says: "I was surprised when I was told that my vision of man is pessimistic [. . .]." "J'ai été étonnée quand on m'a dit que ma vision de l'homme est pessimiste [. . .]."

40 It is interesting to note that the novels Sarraute uses as examples of this commanding talent are all by men: Proust, Gide, Genet, Rilke, Céline, and Sartre. As was the case for de Beauvoir, it would appear that the dangers of narcissism or solipsism are greater for those who are not (male) "masters" of the art. But in a characteristic move, Sarraute complicates the gender question by listing only the works, not the authors. Both individual and gender identity are passed over in favor of the production.

41 Nathalie Sarraute, *The Use of Speech*, translated by Barbara Wright (New York: George Braziller, 1983), 19–20.

42 Sarraute, *The Use of Speech*, 35.

43 In a provocative, insightful commentary on *The Use of Speech*, Ellen Munley, using Chodorow's theories, reads the dynamic exchanges between narrator, narratees, and various characters as an example of "écriture féminine," a feminine writing in which the personal is not sacrificed in favor of the dissolving voices of anonymous discourse (as was the case in many of Sarraute's earlier novels). Thus, a feminine "I" can merge with others without losing "herself." The

argument persuasively maintains that fusion and identification do not preclude individual separateness, although it does require that Munley neutralize or soften the negative, strife-ridden tenor of several of the texts. Following these arguments, one would be tempted to call the work a form of feminine autobiographical writing in a broad sense, were it not for one problem concerning the gender attribution: while Munley insistently refers to the narrator as "she," implicitly associating author and narrator, the adjectives qualifying the narrator in the text are *all* in the *masculine* form. This oversight seriously hampers the claim for Sarraute's "feminine writing," if one means by that a discourse that posits a personal female voice. It is not until *Childhood* that the mark of the feminine "I" will fully make its appearance. See Ellen W. Munley, "I'm Dying but It's Only Your Story: Sarraute's Reader on Stage," *Contemporary Literature* 24:2 (1983): 233–58.

44 As Foucault has shown, nothing is more common in the West than the avowal or confession: "[. . .] one confesses in public and in private, to one's parents, one's educators, one's doctor, to those one loves [. . .]. Western man has become a confessing animal." See Michel Foucault, *The History of Sexuality, Vol. I: An Introduction*, translated by Robert Hurley (New York: Pantheon, 1978), 59.

45 Already in *Between Life and Death*, Sarraute had used this device to dramatize the act of the writer who rereads his work.

46 Mary Jacobus, "The Law of/and Gender: Genre Theory and the Prelude," *Diacritics* 14:4 (1984): 50.

47 Boncenne, *Lire*, 90.

48 The blank spaces between memories also contribute to the fragmentary quality of the subject.

49 In accordance with Lejeune's pact, and contrary to the beginning of de Beauvoir's *Memoirs*, Sarraute situates her autobiography in the narrating present, as well as in the context of the genre's tradition. Where she deviates from tradition is through the use of the present to go over experiences of the past.

50 Sarraute, *Enfance*, 8–9.

51 See Gretchen R. Besser, "Sarraute on Childhood—Her Own," *French Literature Series* 12 (1985): 154. Bettina L. Knapp offers an archetypal reading of Sarraute's androgyny in "Nathalie Sarraute's *Between Life and Death*: Androgyny and the Creative Process," in *Women in Twentieth Century Literature: A Jungian View* (University Park, Pa.: Pennsylvania State Univ. Press, 1987).

52 In his review article, "The Way of Disobedience," *Times Literary*

Supplement (June 10, 1983): 596, John Sturrock aptly describes Sarraute as a "novelist supremely gifted in the slicing open of our human upholstery."

53 Germaine Brée, "Nathalie Sarraute," interview in *Contemporary Literature* 14:2 (1973): 139.

54 See Sigmund Freud, "On Narcissism: An Introduction," edited by James Strachey, *The Standard Edition of the Complete Psychological Works*, vol.14 (London: Hogarth Press, 1953), 67–102.

55 Knapp, "Interview avec Nathalie Sarraute," 293–94.

56 The father's mark is traced in the passages of her fiction where one returns to solid characters and positions that shield from the discomfort of the tropism.

57 See Helen Watson-Williams, *The Novels of Nathalie Sarraute: Towards an Aesthetic* (Amsterdam: Editions Rodopi BV, 1981), 150–51.

58 Even Sarraute's strategic comparison of Dostoevski and Kafka in *The Age of Suspicion* plays out her autobiographical economy. Sarraute sees in both writers (her own emphasis on) the violent, relentless need for contact with others. Interestingly enough, whereas she avoids establishing links between her heritage and her writing, she makes nationality and race important factors in her literary analysis of Kafka and Dostoevski. She turns the latter's need for contact with others into a distinctive Russian trait, and Kafka's German Jewish origins into factors that allow him to prefigure the horror of the Holocaust. It would seem as if she had eloquently displaced the ties between her own heritage (Russian, Jewish) and her writing onto those she admires.

59 De Beauvoir, ss, 666.

60 What the child and the New Novelist might, nevertheless, have in common is the attention given to the effects produced in the reader.

61 In many respects, Sarraute's family situation is strikingly similar to that of Gothic novelist Mary Shelley, author of *Frankenstein*. Her mother, Mary Wollstonecraft, was a feminist writer from whom she was separated (the mother having died giving birth to Mary); her father, William Godwin (also an author, as was the second husband of Sarraute's mother) remarried someone who was, in Barbara Johnson's words, "a staunch housewifely mother of two who clearly preferred her own children to Godwin's." This latter description resembles Sarraute's portrait of her stepmother, Vera. In addition to these circumstantial similarities, a case might be made for a

certain resemblance in their works as these women deal with the gender tensions of their lives. Although Mary Shelley's *Frankenstein* focuses ostensibly on male characters (as do Sarraute's works), Johnson makes a compelling claim that the work stages the repression of female contradictions: "It is thus indeed perhaps the very hiddenness of the question of femininity in *Frankenstein* that somehow proclaims the painful message not of female monstrousness but of female contradictions." I have been arguing here that Sarraute's ambivalence toward her mother(s)—her contradictions about gender identification—resurface in her works as a repressed identification with the feminine. See Barbara Johnson, "My Monster/My Self," *Diacritics* 12:2 (Summer 1982): 9.

62 Boncenne, *Lire*, 92.

63 See her interview with Brée, 138.

64 Besser, "Sarraute on Childhood," 154.

65 Boncenne, *Lire*, 92.

66 In a curious coincidence, we may note that Sarraute's novelistic career begins about the same time that she is bearing her own children. Between 1927 and 1933 her three daughters are born. In 1932, Sarraute begins to write the first texts for *Tropisms*. The connection between maternity and writing, assuming the mother/writer's role, is thus fulfilled in the daughter.

67 This is particularly evident in a work like *Portrait of a Man Unknown*, in which Sarraute admits to having used Balzacian-style characters (the miser and his daughter in *Eugénie Grandet*), and then destroys the "types" by multiplying perspectives.

68 The feminine narrator of *Childhood* enacts this fusion with the child's point of view, whereas her masculine counterpart veers away from it.

69 Unlike other (male) New Novelists such as Robbe-Grillet, Sarraute refuses to believe that all texts point nowhere but to themselves. In the heyday of the New Novel during the sixties, when textual self-reflexivity was the password, Sarraute was often taken to task for maintaining that her object was not exclusively linguistic. For although she never claims to "represent" the tropistic experience—it is literally unrepresentable—she does strive to make her words provoke the reader's own tropistic reaction. The excess of this "experience," beyond the written word, sets in motion new rapports and new struggles within the reader. Sarraute is one of the most successful modern women writers to rehabilitate the notion of experience without reverting back to a naive belief in mimetic

representation. For the debates concerning representation in Sarraute's work, see *Nouveau Roman: hier, aujourdhui*, vol.2, edited by Jean Ricardou and Françoise von Rossum-Guyon (Paris: Union Générale d'Editions, 1972), 41–57.

70 This is not to devalue the importance or necessity of her father's influence: his enduring, stable concern for his daughter is primordial in the construction of Nathalie's sense of self. Her gleeful violation of the sofa in the opening scene is contingent upon an already extant security within the paternal law. Her transgressions, in actions and writing, rely upon an understanding and acknowledgment of the laws she breaks.

CHAPTER 3

1 Although Sarraute and Duras belong to the same literary generation, Duras, born in 1914, is twelve years Sarraute's junior.

2 See Marc Saporta, "Le Regard et l'école," *L'Arc* 98 (1985): 50. In this same issue of *L'Arc* devoted to Duras, Madeleine Borgomano manifests a certain discomfort with *The Lover*'s success: "I would like [. . .] to see in these confessions—in spite of their success—an ultimate form of destruction." ("J'aimerais [. . .] voir dans ces aveux—malgré leur succès—une forme ultime de destruction.") For her, *The Lover* (or autobiography in general) appears to impoverish the mysteries of fiction, for it "stops the incessant movement of the written, reducing [the works] to 'the truth'" ("arrête le mouvement incessant de l'écrit: en les réduisant à 'la vérité.' "). See Madeleine Borgomano, "Romans: La Fascination du vide," *L'Arc* 98 (1985): 47. Coming from such a perceptive critic as Borgomano, this reductive conception of autobiography is rather surprising.

Some of the negative reactions to *The Lover* recall readers' reactions to *Adieux*, de Beauvoir's account of Sartre's death, since neither work met literary critics' expectations.

3 Duras appeared on the televised program "Apostrophes" on September 28, 1984, in an interview with Bernard Pivot.

4 Marguerite Duras, *La Vie matérielle* (Paris: P.O.L., 1987), 7.

5 The only consistency Duras grants herself in the introduction to *La Vie matérielle*—and it is not negligible—concerns her thoughts on social injustice.

6 Marguerite Duras, *The Sea Wall*, translated by Herma Briffault (New York: Harper & Row, 1986).

7 Marguerite Duras, "Whole Days in the Trees," in *Whole Days in the*

Trees and Other Stories, translated by Anita Barrows (New York: Riverrun, 1984). This story first appeared in French in *Des Journées entières dans les arbres* (Paris: Gallimard, 1954); *Agatha* (Paris: Minuit, 1981). Duras's *L'Eden Cinéma* (Paris: Mercure de France, 1977) is a theatrical adaptation of *The Sea Wall*, so *The Lover* is not the only work to reconsider this early material.

8   See Marguerite Duras and Xavière Gauthier, *Woman to Woman*, translated by Katharine A. Jensen, European Women Writers Series (Lincoln, Nebraska: Univ. of Nebraska Press, 1987), 161.

9   Duras and Gauthier, *Woman to Woman*, 160.

10   The pieces written in an overt first-person female voice before *The Lover* are: the early short story entitled "The Boa," published in French (as "Le Boa") in *Les Temps Modernes* and then in the collection *Des Journées entières dans les arbres* (Paris: Gallimard, 1954), and translated in *Whole Days in the Trees and Other Stories*, translated by Anita Barrows (New York: Riverrun, 1984), and two more recent works: *L'Eté 80*, a collection of chronicles written for the newspaper *Libération* (Paris: Minuit, 1980), and the short narrative *L'Homme atlantique* (Paris: Minuit, 1982). In "The Seated Man in the Passage" (another short narrative), although the "I" who watches a couple's lovemaking is not marked so as to identify gender (there are no past participles or adjectives present that would determine gender in the French), Duras has nevertheless linked that narrative voice to her own. (See Marguerite Duras, "L'Homme assis dans le couloir," *Les Cahiers du Cinéma* 312/313 (June 1980): 32–33.) In all these works, the narrating female "I" fills the role of spectator to a drama.

   Since *The Lover*'s publication, an increasing interest in overtly combining autobiography and fiction has become more evident in Duras's writings. See *The War* (translation of *La Douleur* by Barbara Bray, New York: Pantheon, 1986), *La Pute de la côte normande* [The Whore of the Normandy Coast] (Paris: Minuit, 1986), *La Vie matérielle* (Paris: P.O.L., 1987), and *Emily L.* (Paris: Minuit, 1987). All these works are first-person female narratives (journal, essay, personal reflection, novel . . .) that in varying degrees focus on the question of the author's life in connection with her writing and history.

11   Duras published in *Les Temps Modernes* the following stories: "Le Boa," 3:25 (October 1947): 613–22 and "Madame Dodin," 7:79 (May 1952): 1952–81. For a discussion of Duras's and Mitterand's shared memories of the Resistance, see the interview: "Le Bureau

de poste de la rue Dupin," *L'Autre Journal* 1 (February 26–March 4, 1986): 32–40.

12 Marguerite Duras, *The Lover*, translated by Barbara Bray (New York: Harper & Row, 1986), 68.

13 Germaine Brée, "An interview with Marguerite Duras," *Contemporary Literature* 13:4 (1972): 421.

14 Maurice Nadeau includes Duras under the rubric "Existentialisme et ses à-côtés" [Existentialism and Its Asides] in his book, *Le Roman depuis la guerre* (Paris: Gallimard, 1970), 129–30.

15 Marilyn R. Schuster, however, makes a convincing case for a Durasian feminist irony vis-à-vis Hemingway's novels, so that the "influence," as acknowledged in the work itself (Hemingway is referred to in *The Sailor from Gibraltar*), is (already) playfully twisted. See "Reading and Writing as a Woman: The Retold Tales of Marguerite Duras," *French Review* 58:1 (October 1984): 48–57.

16 This is really only true for the first part of *The Stranger*. As Sarraute convincingly points out in *The Age of Suspicion*, Meursault's inner feelings and psychological make-up are amply revealed in the second half of the book.

17 Alain Vircondelet, *Marguerite Duras* (Paris: Seghers, 1972), 159–60.

18 The qualifications are rather reminiscent of how Sarraute conceived of (undistinguished) traditional writing: full of events and strong, compelling characters that tend to function like puppets because they are so pat.

19 Roland Barthes, *Writing Degree Zero*, translated by Annette Lavers and Colin Smith (New York: Hill & Wang, 1981), 77. Madeleine Borgomano, in her article "Une Ecriture féminine? A propos de Marguerite Duras," *Littérature* 53 (February 1984): 63, calls Duras's later, spare style an "écriture blanche" (a "white writing").

20 In "Une Ecriture féminine?" (63), Borgomano says that "the absence of expressed emotions suggests indefinite possibilities of diverse emotions" in Duras's texts. ["l'absence d'émotions exprimées suggère des possibilités indéfinies d'émotions diverses."— my translation). This is precisely the opposite effect Camus obtained in the first part of *The Stranger*, where the simplest words seem to connote an absence of emotion.

21 Duras in Marks and de Courtivron, *New French Feminisms*, 111.

22 Madeleine Chapsal, *Quinze Ecrivains* (Paris: Juillard, 1963), 63.

23 See *Nouveau Roman: hier, aujourd'hui*, vol.I (Paris: Union Générale d'Editions, 10/18, 1972).

24 Duras and Gauthier, *Woman to Woman*, 37. Of the five writers I am considering, Duras is no doubt the one who most eagerly points out the interaction between her personal life and her writing style.

25 See *Force of Circumstance*, 620–21.

26 The term "l'école du regard" was originally coined by François Mauriac.

27 Marc Saporta has noted many of the points in common between Duras and the New Novelists' attention to the gaze in his short article, "Le Regard et l'école," *L'Arc* 98 (1985): 49–50.

28 In *The Ravishing of Lol V. Stein*, Lol is continually watched by Jacques Hold who desires this madwoman and wishes to tell her story. But Lol also watches, or "stages" the watching, of Jacques Hold making love to Lol's friend, Tatiana Karl. (For Lol, the duo fantasmatically repeats the lovemaking of Lol's long-lost fiancé with another woman, Anne-Marie Stretter). Desire and the gaze enter into a circuit of substitutability as Lol tries to capture through repetition the original love scene from which she was excluded. In the later work, *L'Homme atlantique*, the speaker/viewer ("I") is a woman/camera eye, while the addressee/spectacle ("you") is a man. Again, Duras interferes with accepted gender codes, making us self-conscious of our position (as female or male readers) in relation to the text. The female subject addressing the male object is an infrequent situation that jolts. When the text says "you," the female reader is at once implicated and excluded, since this "you" is male. Gender's relation to representation and the gaze is mobilized, so that gendered "subjects" and "objects" appear as relative positions in the symbolic chain rather than as fixed or essential. We are constantly called upon to reconstruct our gendered position, instead of taking it for granted. In her book on Lacan, Jane Gallop creates a similar effect by alternately using masculine and feminine pronouns and adjectives to designate individuals (psychiatrists, patients, readers . . .). As Gallop explains, this usage de-universalizes the masculine, makes it a gender instead of an all-encompassing neuter. See Jane Gallop, *Reading Lacan* (Ithaca, N.Y.: Cornell Univ. Press, 1985), 21.

29 Marcelle Marini, "L'Autre Corps," in *Ecrire dit-elle: Imaginaires de Marguerite Duras*, edited by Danielle Bajomée and Ralph Heyndels (Brussels: Editions de l'Université de Bruxelles, 1985), 25–27. Marini is one of the rare critics who does mention similarities between Sarraute and Duras. Her insightful article associates Sarraute's *Use of Speech* and Duras's remarks about the stupidity of theory.

30 Michel Foucault and Hélène Cixous, "A propos de Marguerite Duras," *Cahiers Renaud-Barrault* 89 (1975): 9.

31 In Duras's novel, *Destroy, She Said*, translated by Barbara Bray (New York: Grove Press, 1970), 64, the young, outspoken Alissa's declaration of "I love and desire you" to another woman, Elisabeth Alioune, is a fierce invitation to break away from a suffocating, bourgeois life, but Elisabeth can only respond "You're insane" to the overture.

32 Marguerite Duras and Michelle Porte, "The Places of Marguerite Duras," translated by Edith Cohen, *Enclitic* 7:1 (1984): 59.

33 Duras and Gauthier, *Woman to Woman*, 45.

34 Foucault and Cixous, "Marguerite Duras," 22.

35 Foucault and Cixous, "Marguerite Duras," 8–9.

36 Foucault and Cixous, "Marguerite Duras," 55.

37 See Mary Lydon's illuminating article, "Translating Duras: 'The Seated Man in the Passage,'" *Contemporary Literature* 24 (1983): 259–75.

38 "Vous considérez-vous comme une femme écrivain?—Jamais." See Chapsal, *Quinze Ecrivains*, 62. In this early interview (published in 1963), Duras also dissociates herself from her characters.

39 Duras and Gauthier, *Woman to Woman*, 18.

40 Since her disillusionment with the outcome of the events of May 1968, Duras has favored more and more a *passive* resistance as an effective political form of revolt for workers, women, Jews, and all others who are oppressed.

41 Duras in Marks and de Courtivron, *New French Feminisms*, 111.

42 Makward says the reader (and characters) are "penetrated by" or "infused with" Duras's writing. See "Structures du silence/du délire: Marguerite Duras/Hélène Cixous," *Poétique* 35 (1978): 315.

The strange effect of the Durasian text recalls a passage in a poem by René Char entitled "Centon," in which the poet resists the reader's attempt at mastery or possession because the poet/poem is not a solid being to ensnare or control: "You are looking for my weak point, my fault? Its discovery would permit you to have me at your mercy? But assailant, don't you see that I am a sieve and that your small brain dries up amongst my expired rays?" ["Vous cherchez mon point faible, ma faille? Sa découverte vous permettrait de m'avoir à merci? Mais, assaillant, ne voyez-vous pas que je suis un crible et que votre peu de cervelle sèche parmi mes rayons expirés?"—my translation] See René Char, "Centon," in *Commune Présence* (Paris: Gallimard, 1964), 222.

43   Cixous in Marks and de Courtivron, *New French Feminisms*, 249.

44   Duras in Marks and de Courtivron, *New French Feminisms*, 174–75.

45   Duras criticizes Colette for responding to a masculine version of femininity in Marks and de Courtivron, *New French Feminisms*, 174.

46   Borgomano, in her article, "Une Ecriture féminine?" (59), says that Duras takes the empty signifier "woman" and, through the dynamics of writing, multiplies the signifieds, so that any idea of essence becomes impossible.

47   In a later interview conducted in 1977, Duras insists that it is *not* a question of "writing the body," following Cixous's injunction to women in "The Laugh of the Medusa." By 1977, the issue had come up so frequently that Duras says she doesn't even want to hear of it any more. See Marguerite Duras, *Le Camion, suivi de Entretien avec Michelle Porte* (Paris: Minuit, 1977), 10.

48   Makward, in her *Poétique* article (316), has also indirectly suggested this connection between Sarraute and Duras. Without mentioning Sarraute's name, she nevertheless says that Duras's "somatization of silence" and her "passion/affectivity" (that springs from banal words), are quite similar to the "affectivity of tropisms."

49   Sarraute, AS, 135. Sarraute makes this statement when refuting existentialist notions of "committed literature."

50   Monique Gosselin, "Voyage au bout de la féminité: Figures féminines dans quelques romans de Marguerite Duras," in *Figures féminines et roman*, edited by Jean Bessière (Paris: Presses Universitaires de France, 1982), 149. Gosselin says that Duras's anesthetized women not only reveal the pain of living through daily events, but that they also enact the more fundamental "pain of being a woman" ("la douleur d'être femme").

51   In Duras and Gauthier, *Woman to Woman*, 117, Duras insists that her character Lol V. Stein is not representative of "Woman" in general. But at the same time, she admits that many readers write to her saying: "Lol V. Stein is me."

52   In her insightful psychoanalytic study of Duras's fiction, Sharon Willis identifies two definitions of woman in the figure of the Mother as castrated or phallic: "Parading, alternately, the figure of the woman as lack—Lol V. Stein, the beggar—and the woman as phallic mother, the narcissistic, full, self-referential body—Anne-Marie Stretter, Tatiana Karl, the beggar's mother—the texts re-inscribe and disfigure a certain imposing libidinal economy." See Sharon Willis, *Marguerite Duras: Writing on the Body* (Chicago: Univ. of Illinois Press, 1987), 120.

53 For some readers of *The Lover*, the affirmative, feminine power of the young girl in *The Lover* is tainted by the girl's potential complicity with her family's racism toward her Chinese lover. Although this is a reading that I am not stressing, I do think that the text leaves room for it, particularly when one remembers that Duras is always heedful of the "impurity" of ethical positions.

54 In Duras and Gauthier, *Woman to Woman*, 25, Duras says "if a woman is prostituted, *she* has to want it. It shouldn't have to be dictated by men [. . .]." Characters like Anne-Marie Stretter (*The Vice Consul*), Lol V. Stein, or the anonymous woman in *The Malady of Death* directly or indirectly play the part of prostitute. Martha Noel Evans, in her lucid study of *The Ravishing of Lol V. Stein*, says that in this novel, "as Duras uncovers and explores the indecency of female writing, she discloses that indecency as a cover for something else: the hidden whoring of all language." Although she never mentions it, *The Lover*'s insistence on the figure of the author as prostitute gives additional weight to Evans's reading. See "Marguerite Duras: The Whore," in *Masks of Tradition: Women and the Politics of Writing in Twentieth Century France* (Ithaca, N.Y.: Cornell Univ. Press, 1987), 124.

55 *The Sea Wall* is the English translation of *Un Barrage contre le Pacifique* (Paris: Gallimard, 1950).

56 As Jean Pierrot has pointed out in his recent book, *Marguerite Duras* (Paris: José Corti, 1986), 52, *The Sea Wall* was written during Duras's Communist period and reveals Duras's contempt for the sociopolitical bankruptcy of France via its colony.

57 Unlike the professional prostitute who is called upon to play (fake) the role of lover, to make the man believe he is someone exceptional who can arouse her, the girl, instead, stresses that neither partner is exceptional and that her arousal depends initially on the existence of her desire.

58 Luce Irigaray, *This Sex Which Is Not One*, translated by Catherine Porter and Carolyn Burke (Ithaca, N.Y.: Cornell Univ. Press, 1985), 76.

59 And, of course, when publication is involved, writing, like prostitution, also includes a monetary exchange. This is particularly evident for *The Lover*, since the book was commissioned.

60 In "Une Ecriture féminine?" (63), Borgomano notes a "troubling resemblance" between the woman Duras invents and her writing.

61 Claude Lévi-Strauss, *The Elementary Structures of Kinship*, translated by James Harle Bell, John Richard von Sturmer, and Rodney

Needham (Boston: Beacon Press, 1969), 36–37. From a woman's point of view, Lévi-Strauss's uncritical discussion of women as essential commodities for men is harrowing.

62 Irigaray, *This Sex,* 170–91.

63 In *The Sea Wall,* the young heroine Suzanne tends to represent a commodity link between men (or between a man and the family—which comes to the same thing). For example, when her suitor, Mr. Jo, gives her a phonograph, the gift passes immediately into the hands of Suzanne's brother, Joseph.

64 Because her lover is rich, Chinese (rather than Vietnamese), and has just spent two years in France, he too is an "outsider" to Saigon society. And like Betty Fernandez's, his life is caught up in a public/private split. Duras reduces it to its simplest expression: "his heroism is me, his cravenness is his father's money" [L, 49]. In other words, his courage is manifested in a love that braves the social and paternal interdiction; his cowardice consists of his inability to accept being disinherited for his love. As in Duras's own case, love is caught up in financial concerns.

65 See Carol J. Murphy, *Alienation and Absence in the Novels of Marguerite Duras* (Lexington, Ky.: French Forum, 1982), 53. This story, which Murphy aptly describes as a sort of sequel to *Un Barrage contre le Pacifique* (*The Sea Wall*), later continues to circulate when Duras turns it into a play that is first performed in 1964. (Duras then films the play—performed by the Renaud-Barrault company—in 1976.)

66 Duras, cited in Murphy, *Alienation and Absence,* 54.

67 The girl's innocence in the novel also protects Duras's mother from the truth. In the television interview with Pivot, Duras says she never told her mother (or older brother) about her affair, never admitted to it, because her mother would not have been able to stand the idea of her daughter's "dishonor." Even her novel keeps the secret.

68 We may remember that the daughter has also filled the father's role (as financial supporter of the family), causing a structural analogy between her and the brother she hates. Interestingly enough, Duras also notes a strong physical resemblance between the two [L, 53] and the fact that she is the only one in the family whom her older brother fears. Finally, Duras associates the older brother with the horror of the War and refers to him as an assassin, but in effect, it is she who novelistically kills him off by excluding him from *The Sea Wall.*

69   Barthes, in *Writing Degree Zero*, 34–35, notes that the use of the third person narrative in the novel unveils the genre's own artifice. In the case of autobiography, the use of the third person to refer to the narrating subject makes the reader aware that the autobiographical "I" is in fact like a disguised third-person, a convention that presents itself as a coherence, while masking the heterogeneity of the subject. Barthes's own autobiographical text, *Roland Barthes by Roland Barthes*, translated by Richard Howard (New York: Hill & Wang, 1977), playfully weaves in and out of first- and third-person voices, thereby dislodging enunciation from any fixed point.

70   Duras emphasizes this in the Pivot interview.

CHAPTER 4

1   The differences between Cixous and Wittig are in fact drastic, in writing strategies and ground concepts. Contrary to Cixous, Wittig willingly calls herself a feminist, proclaims the legitimacy of her political lesbianism, and rejects psychoanalytical and structuralist discourses which, for her, reduce human beings' histories to a set of totalizing invariables. "Ecriture féminine" constitutes for Wittig the return to a debilitating, stereotypical conception of "Woman." In addition, Wittig's writing style tends to be more accessible to a wider public because she deviates less from standard syntax and storytelling. In shorthand, one might say that Wittig is concerned with fighting the oppression of women in language and action, whereas Cixous seeks to unlock woman's repression in the body and/of discourse. For comparisons of their work, see Hélène Vivienne Wenzel, "The Text as Body/Politics: An Appreciation of Monique Wittig's Writings in Context," *Feminist Studies* 7:2 (Summer 1981): 264–87; Diane Griffin Crowder, "Amazons and Mothers? Monique Wittig, Hélène Cixous and Theories of Writing," *Contemporary Literature* 24:2 (1983): 117–44; Dina Sherzer, "Postmodern Feminist Fiction," in *Representation in Contemporary French Fiction* (Lincoln: Univ. of Nebraska Press, 1986). It should be noted that Wenzel's and Crowder's articles take Wittig's "side" in the debate. An example of Wittig's inclusion in the lesbian tradition can be found in Elaine Marks's "Lesbian Intertextuality," in *Homosexualities and French Literature*, edited by George Stambolian and Elaine Marks (Ithaca, N.Y.: Cornell Univ. Press, 1979), 353–77.

2   Similar to Michel Foucault's proposition at the end of *The Order of*

Things that "Man" is a phenomenon destined to disappear, Wittig dreams the end of "Woman," a (future) time when to be female would not mean to be defined by essences or in opposition to "Man." See Michel Foucault, *The Order of Things: An Archaeology of the Human Sciences*, translated by Alan Sheridan-Smith (New York: Random House, 1970).

3   The sole direct references to family (another heterosexual grouping) appear in her first novel, *The Opoponax*, but even there, the focus is so much on a child's experience and perspective that the portrayals of relationships between child and parents become matter-of-fact, unquestioned, as they would be by a child.

4   De Beauvoir, ss, 473.

5   Although de Beauvoir's chapter on lesbians in *The Second Sex* is from the point of view of a heterosexual woman who identifies with male values, she does, nevertheless, counter many of the negative biases of her time. Elaine Marks describes de Beauvoir's favorable attitude toward lesbians in the following way: "Simone de Beauvoir transgresses the boundaries of accepted discourse at several points: she writes against that common sense discourse whose reliance on nature and what is natural nullifies any serious analysis of ideology and makes political constructions impossible; she writes against the reigning determinist discourse of psychoanalysis with its case histories and its established categories of masculine and feminine; she opposes, by not mentioning it, any religious discourse in which procreation becomes the definition of woman's functions." Marks also recognizes, however, de Beauvoir's lack of analysis of the relationship between textual properties and (the lesbian's) lived experience. See Elaine Marks, "Transgressing the (In)cont(in)ent Boundaries: The Body in Decline," *Yale French Studies* 72 (1986): 190–91.

6   Alice A. Jardine, "Interview with Simone de Beauvoir," *Signs* 5:2 (1979): 231.

7   Monique Wittig, "The Point of View: Universal or Particular?" *Feminist Issues* 3:2 (1983): 66. One may well question the opinion that homosexuality is *the* theme of Proust's work, but it is certain that much has been made of it in the traditional analysis of character and in the connections between the author's biography and his creation. It is no doubt what Gayatri Spivak calls the "regulative psychobiography" that Wittig wishes to avoid.

8   Wittig, "Point of View," 65.

9   Wittig, "Point of View," 65.

10 Monique Wittig, "The Straight Mind," *Feminist Issues* 1:1 (Summer 1980): 106.

11 Gayatri Chakravorty Spivak, "French Feminism in an International Frame," *Yale French Studies* 62 (1981): 167.

12 Spivak, "French Feminism," 166. Spivak rightly distinguishes the "mainstream avant-garde" of Duras and Sarraute from the neo-feminist avant-garde represented by Kristeva and Cixous.

13 In her article, "A Cosmogony of O: Wittig's *Les Guérillères*," in *Twentieth Century French Fiction* (New Brunswick, N.J.: Rutgers Univ. Press, 1975), Erica Ostrowsky describes *Les Guérillères* as a work which creates a "unified vision of the Female Principle" (241). And Christiane Makward cites *Les Guérillères* as a fictive precursor to the theoretical developments concerning feminine writing. See Christiane Makward, "To Be or Not to Be . . . a Feminist Speaker," in *The Future of Difference*, edited by Hester Eisenstein and Alice Jardine (New Brunswick, N.J.: Rutgers Univ. Press, 1985), 95.

14 See, for example, Roland Barthes, *Mythologies*, translated by Annette Lavers (New York: Hill & Wang, 1972).

15 Wittig, "Point of View," 64.

16 "Le Lieu de l'action," in *Digraphe* 32 (March, 1984): 71: "les mots d'avant les mots, d'avant les 'pères' d'avant les 'mères', d'avant les 'vous,' [. . .] d'avant 'structurations' d'avant 'capitalisme.'" Although Sarraute would no doubt agree with Wittig's description, I have tried to show in the preceding chapter that the ties to family structures may not be so innocent in the creation of the tropism.

17 "Je crois qu'il est possible [. . .] d'écrire des livres vrais sur l'enfance. Je pense à l'admirable *Opoponax* de Monique Wittig où, en n'indiquant pas qu'il s'agit de ses propres souvenirs, elle a réussi à conserver tout le duvet de l'enfance. Une réussite rarissime." Interview with Boncenne, *Lire*, 90.

18 Sitting next to Sarraute at the last performance in Paris of Wittig's 1985 play, *Le Voyage sans fin* (Journey without End), I learned that it was the third time that Sarraute had come to watch and admire a play whose feminist reworking of *Don Quixote* was amply clear.

19 Monique Wittig, "The Trojan Horse," *Feminist Issues* 4:2 (Fall 1984): 45.

20 In the English translation, the idiomatic French "on" is translated as "you," causing Wittig's novel to resemble Michel Butor's New Novel *Change of Heart*, translated by Jean Stewart (New York: Simon & Schuster, 1958). In this work (entitled *La Modification* in French), Butor uses the second person "vous" (you) in the text.

The resemblance is only superficial, however, since the pronouns "on" and "vous" fulfill very different functions in the novels.

21　See Mary McCarthy, "Everybody's Childhood," in *The Writing on the Wall and Other Literary Essays* (New York: Harcourt, Brace, 1970), 102–11; and Marguerite Duras, "A Brilliant Work: *L'Opoponax*, by Monique Wittig," in *Outside: Selected Writings*, translated by Arthur Goldhammer (Boston: Beacon Press, 1986), 228–31. Duras's article originally appeared in the newspaper *France-Observateur* in 1964, when *The Opoponax* was first published in French.

22　Claude Simon, "Pour Monique Wittig," *L'Express* (November 30–December 6, 1964): 69–71. *The Opoponax* shares with both modern autobiographies and the New Novel an attention to the daily, "uneventful" rhythms of existence. It does not attempt to "sound the depths" of personal psychology and abstract emotion, but rather to glide with an equal, intense interest along the surfaces of everything Catherine Legrand sees, touches . . . etc.

23　In her article, "French Feminism in an International Frame," Spivak astutely calls Wittig's *Lesbian Body* a prose poem that has ties to a Baudelairian "'evocative magic'" (166). All Wittig's works do in fact invoke "the power of indeterminate suggestion rather than determinate reference that could overwhelm and sabotage the signifying conventions" (Spivak, 166). Wittig herself has referred to Baudelaire as a lesbian poet because he underscores pleasure for pleasure's sake rather than sexuality's reproductive function. (See Monique Wittig, "Paradigm," in Stambolian and Marks, *Homosexualities in French Literature*, 117.) Spivak's formal association between Wittig and Baudelaire, and Wittig's substantive association between Baudelaire and lesbian sexuality, are not unrelated: in both, a signifier (language, sexuality) works against a utilitarian order (referential, reproductive).

24　Wittig's mimetic strategy undermines the dominant (masculine) culture's hold on its great works, and reveals that, because language belongs to no one, its repetitions are capable of creating new meanings—and new subjects—beyond traditional gender boundaries. Although writing in the context of a search for a feminine language, Luce Irigaray also advises women writers to use a playful mimetism as a strategy to undo the masculine logic that they deliberately imitate, in order to expose "what was supposed to remain invisible: the cover-up of a possible operation of the feminine in language." See Luce Irigaray, *This Sex Which Is Not One*, translated by Catherine Porter and Carolyn Burke (Ithaca, N.Y.:

Cornell Univ. Press), 76. For Wittig, the process does not reveal a feminine language or a feminine writing, but is rather a reappropriation or theft within the dominant culture. Nancy K. Miller, in her essay, "Changing the Subject: Authorship, Writing, and the Reader," in *Feminist Studies/Critical Studies*, edited by Teresa de Lauretis (Bloomington: Indiana Univ. Press, 1986), 111, associates Wittig, as well as Cixous and Irigaray, with the Barthesian tactics of "dispersion and fragmentation" within the dominant culture. But Wittig's works, in contrast to those of Cixous if not Irigaray's, display an unwillingness to relinquish the possibility of a female subject or personal identity, even if it entails a recognition that the subject is perforce alienated, not identical to herself.

25   Wittig, "Point of View," 64.

26   The two novels also bear a resemblance in their beginnings, but with an important difference. *The Opoponax* opens with the repeated, humorous cry of a little boy proudly exclaiming: "Who wants to see my weewee-er?," while *Les Guérillères*'s early pages contain the description of a woman urinating in the rain, as others gather round to watch. Both passages focus on sexuality and the body, but the pleasures of masculine exhibitionism are replaced by those of female voyeurism. See *The Opoponax*, translated by Helen Weaver (New York: Simon & Schuster, 1966), 5; and *Les Guérillères*, translated by David Le Vay (New York: Viking Press, 1971), 9.

27   Some of the ethos of the late sixties is integrated into the details of *Les Guérillères*: for example, the daily activities of the group suggest a simpler life-style that is reminiscent of the communal experiments of the sixties. In addition, drugs are a part of the women's festivities and the men who rally to the women's cause near the end are young and long-haired. Finally, on the last page, the women come together to sing the Internationale. *Les Guérillères* resembles a collective autobiography of the period at the same time that it explores future possibilities for women.

28   Wittig, *Les Guérillères*, 114.

29   Wittig, *Les Guérillères*, 57–58.

30   Wittig, *Les Guérillères*, 89.

31   Monique Wittig, "One Is Not Born a Woman," *Feminist Issues* 1:2 (Winter 1981): 51.

32   Miller, "Changing the Subject," 106.

33   In "Transgressing the (In)cont(in)ent Boundaries," Elaine Marks persuasively suggests that de Beauvoir's description of an incontinent Sartre in *Adieux: A Farewell to Sartre* is in fact a displacement of

her disgust and embarrassment vis-à-vis the female body. Aging and female bodies are envisioned as uncontrollable, impure, and fearful objects. Marks notes that for de Beauvoir, "lack of control [. . .] is a sign of the feminine" (197). In chapter 1, we already saw that the fear of a (feminine) lack of control also informs the question of narrational authority in de Beauvoir's memoirs.

34 Judith Butler has also pointed out this connection between de Beauvoir and Wittig. See "Sex and Gender in Simone de Beauvoir's *Second Sex*," *Yale French Studies* 72 (1986): 46–47.

35 Lynn Higgins, "Nouvelle Nouvelle Autobiographie: Monique Wittig's *Le Corps lesbien*," *SubStance* 14 (1976): 160. In speaking of a "new new autobiography," Higgins is playing on the designation "New New Novel" created during the seventies to describe New Novels written after the first wave of the fifties and sixties.

36 I do not mean to suggest here that Wittig refuses the metaphoricity of language: body and language are not the same thing. Rather, Wittig intimates that language "shapes" our readings of the body, with the latter always already metaphorized. Her attempt lies in wresting the female body from a series of ideologically repressive tropes, through the use of scientific terminology.

37 Monique Wittig, *The Lesbian Body*, translated by David Le Vay (Boston: Beacon Press, 1986): 100–102. It is interesting to note that the translator is an anatomist and surgeon. This text calls for a complete familiarity with the female body, inside and out.

38 "Author's Note" to Wittig, *Lesbian Body*, 10.

39 As Higgins has suggested in her *SubStance* article (165), the blank spaces between sections may well constitute the temptation to remain silent, to renounce a discourse in which the female body could only be a sign of masculine desire. To speak or write is for Wittig the assumption of the fundamental risk: to institute oneself as subject while acknowledging the alienation inherent in that position.

40 "Author's Note" to Wittig, *Lesbian Body*, 11.

41 See Wittig's work, *Lesbian Peoples Material for a Dictionary*, written in conjunction with Sande Zeig, translated by Monique Wittig and Sande Zeig (New York: Avon Books, 1979).

42 Just as Dante turns to Virgil's *Aeneid* as a source of poetic material, Wittig deploys her fiction on the renovated stage of Dante's *Comedy*.

43 See the cover of Wittig's *Virgile, non* (Paris: Editions de Minuit, 1985).

44 Janet Gunn, *Autobiography: Towards a Poetics of Experience* (Philadelphia: Univ. of Pennsylvania Press, 1982), 57.

45 Recourse to classical myth is obviously not new, since many New Novelists (Robbe-Grillet, Butor, Simon . . .) have frequently incorporated Greco-Roman mythemes in their works. In addition, dramatists such as Cocteau, Giraudoux, Sartre . . . etc., of the preceding generations also turned to antiquity for their inspiration. Wittig's work has much in common with the latter, since she too uses the playful combination of daily language and the mythic quest for comic purposes, as well as for proposing a new way to conceive of contemporary issues.

46 "[U]n nulle part qui est soit l'enfer, soit les limbes, soit le paradis." See the cover of Wittig, *Virgile, non*.

47 The examples I give in comparing and contrasting Dante's and Wittig's works do not pretend to exhaust all the intertextual possibilities. I am merely pointing out some of the most salient features.

48 Monique Wittig, *Across the Acheron* (London: Peter Owen, 1987), 7. This English edition describes the trip as "sacred and profane," although the French edition calls it "classique et profane." See Wittig, *Virgile, non*, 7. I have referred to the "classical" quality of the trip because it underscores the intertextual resonances between modern and classical texts.

49 There is one male character in the work with a proper name: the Count Zaroff (36–39), who spends his time tracking down lost souls. In an informal talk at Hunter College (November 1987), Wittig noted that this is not a realistic reference, but rather another intertextual mark: the name comes from a classic old film about the hunting down of humans as if they were animals.

50 In her talk at Hunter College, (1987), Wittig compared the individual, anonymous voices who speak on behalf of the condemned group to a Greek chorus.

51 The British translation, which was carried out without consultation with the author, places headings at the beginning of each chapter, so that the unpredictability of the reading is offset. In the French, however, there are no such chapter headings. Instead, Wittig has placed chapter titles at the end of the book. In this position, the titles seem designed to allow the readers to find sections they wish to *re*read.

52 The color references ("black" and "golden") in this quotation insist upon the fact that this lesbian heaven embraces all races. In Wittig's version of Genesis, Eve (without any Adam) is a beautiful black

woman [see *Les Guérillères*, 52]. Elsewhere in *Across the Acheron* (33), "Wittig" is referred to as a "runaway slave"—the word "maroon" is used (in French "maronne")—which likens her status to that of runaway black slaves in the Antilles.

53   "Wittig" willingly accepts the monstrous visions of her body and turns them around to her advantage: the "long, black glossy hairs" keep her warm, and the "hard, shiny scales" [AA, 15] are beautiful when they gleam in the sun. Similar to her deliberate use of pejorative terms for lesbians (such as "dike"), "Wittig" turns the slanderous into self-affirmation.

54   In an intriguing meeting of "opposites," "Wittig's" role as redeemer or liberator resembles what Toril Moi describes as Hélène Cixous's tendency to cast herself in the role of "prophetess—the desolate mother out to save her people, a feminine Moses [. . .]." See Toril Moi, *Sexual/Textual Politics: Feminist Literary Theory* (New York: Methuen, 1985), 115. The important difference between the two, however, lies in the way Wittig pokes fun at her own image, whereas Cixous appears to take hers more seriously.

55   During her talk at Hunter College, Wittig noted some of the autobiographical dimensions of *Across the Acheron*. She remarked that many of the insults directed against "Wittig" in *Across the Acheron* are not just inventions, but rather abusive comments that have actually been hurled at the author. And the novel's final scene, entitled "The Angels' Kitchen" ["La Cuisine des anges"], was the title of a painting that hung on the wall of the country school that she attended as a child.

56   The English translation (79) unfortunately does not retain the double meaning of this expression.

57   Wittig, "The Straight Mind," 107.

58   Wittig's insistence on lesbianism's political potential, rather than thinking of it as a personal matter of sexual preference, is a provocative position that she shares with Adrienne Rich. Both Rich and Wittig contest the prevailing assumption that heterosexuality is a question of a natural or innate sexual preference and show that heterosexuality as an institution pervasively reinforces male domination in society. Like Michel Foucault, they understand the categories of "sex" as woven into the web of power relations in Western society. According to Foucault, the notion of "sex" has become a causal principle that brings "together, in an artificial unity, anatomical elements, biological functions, conducts, sensations, and pleasures [. . .]." As we have seen, Wittig circumvents

this sort of totalization in her fiction by refusing to define women within an oppositional framework of heterosexuality. In *Across the Acheron*, however, the issue crops up again, as heterosexuality (or, more generally, heterosociality) creates divisions among women. While agreeing to the political force of lesbianism, Rich tends to think of it more as a continuum among women, rather than as a separatist utopia, as has been the case for Wittig. See Adrienne Rich, "Compulsory Heterosexuality and Lesbian Existence," *Signs: Journal of Women in Culture and Society* 5:4 (Summer 1980): 631–60, and Michel Foucault, *The History of Sexuality, Vol.I: An Introduction*, translated by Robert Hurley (New York: Pantheon, 1978), 154.

59   "The Straight Mind" is a translation of "La Pensée Straight," which appeared in issue 7 of *Questions Féministes*, 1980.

60   Emmanuèle de Lesseps, *Questions Féministes* 7 (February 1980): 55–69. For an overview of the whole controversy and some of the responses it elicited from both sides, see *French Connections: Voices from the Women's Movement in France*, edited and translated by Claire Duchen (Amherst, Mass.: Univ. of Massachusetts Press, 1987), 84–110.

61   The British edition refers to "guerrilla warfare" rather than to a token war in translating "de la petite guerre." I have altered the translation in order to remain closer to the spirit of the French. "Guerrilla warfare" in Wittig's terminology would have been too positive a phrase for the context here.

62   I should point out here that I am not concerned with creating a one-to-one correspondence between the literary work and the journal's break-up. Wittig's reading of "One Is Not Born a Woman" at the 1979 conference, "The Second Sex: Thirty Years Later" (held in New York City), elicited similar reactions among certain heterosexual feminists in the audience. (See *Off Our Backs*, 9:11 (December 1979): 24–27.) Rather, I am interested in the way Wittig's fiction articulates personal concerns that are borne out in many occasions of her lived experience.

63   Spivak, "French Feminism," 179.

CHAPTER 5

1   De Beauvoir did, of course, fight racism as a political and social evil. Were she alive and well today, she would no doubt be at the forefront of groups denouncing the racist policies of Jean-Marie Le Pen and his extreme right party in France.

2   Gayatri Chakravorty Spivak, "French Feminism in an International Frame," *Yale French Studies* 62 (1981): 179.

3   Maryse Condé, *Heremakhonon*, translated by Richard Philcox (Washington, D.C.: Three Continents Press, 1982).

4   "On peut retrouver en elle une série de conflits, de contradictions que beaucoup d'Antillaises certainement connaissent, même si elles n'ont pas toujours envie de se les avouer." Interview with Ina Césaire published at the end of Maryse Condé's *La Parole des femmes: Essai sur des romancières des Antilles de langue française* (Paris: Editions L'Harmattan, 1979), 128.

5   Maryse Condé, *Une Saison à Rihata* (Paris: Robert Laffont, 1981).

6   Maryse Condé, *Segu*, translated by Barbara Bray (New York: Viking Press, 1987), originally published in French as *Ségou: Les Murailles de terre* (Paris: Robert Laffont, 1984); the second volume, *Ségou: La Terre en miettes* (Paris: Robert Laffont, 1985), has not yet been translated into English.

7   Marie-Clotilde Jacquey, "'Ségou' est-il un roman malien? Entretien avec Maryse Condé," *Notre Librarie* 84 (1986): 56–60.

8   Jacquey, "'Segou,'" 57.

9   "Dans les précédents romans, j'avais beaucoup parlé de l'Afrique, toujours comme une terre que j'avais beaucoup de difficultés à aimer, que je finissais par aimer, mais qui me demeurait toujours assez étrangère [. . .] le Mali, la région de Ségou, m'ont donné un profond bonheur, une sorte d'éblouissement [. . .]." Jacquey, "'Segou,'" 56–57.

10 "Aucune biographie attentionnée et inspirée recréant ma vie et ses tourments!" Maryse Condé, *Moi Tituba, sorcière noire de Salem* (Paris: Mercure de France, 1986), 172.

11 Condé, *La Parole des femmes*, 49.

12 In a footnote to remarks by Duras about witchcraft, Elaine Marks and Isabelle de Courtivron, the editors of *New French Feminisms* (New York: Schocken Books, 1981 [175]), point out that Jules Michelet's *La Sorcière* [The Sorceress] of 1862 is "a text that has been assimilated by many new French feminist writers, particularly Cixous, Clément, and Gauthier."

13 Teresa de Lauretis, "Feminist Studies/Critical Studies: Issues, Terms, and Contexts," in *Feminist Studies/Critical Studies*, edited by Teresa de Lauretis (Bloomington: Indiana Univ. Press, 1986), 17.

14 "Expliquez l'importance de la connaissance de son passé pour une société et un peuple." Maryse Condé, *Le Roman antillais*, vol.2 (Paris: Fernand Nathan, Collection "Classiques du monde," 1977), 57.

15 In *La Parole des femmes*, 113, Condé makes it quite clear that she

favors independence for Guadeloupe and Martinique. She also is concerned with a collective *Antillean* vision rather than just a disparate series of local perspectives from individual islands.

16   Maryse Condé, "Négritude césairienne, négritude senghorienne," *Revue de littérature comparée* 3–4 (July–December 1974): 409–19.

17   Condé would probably agree with Bell Hooks, who asserts in her book, *Feminist Theory: From Margin to Center* (Boston: South End Press, 1984), 69, that "the life experiences of poor and working class women, particularly non-white women," have often "shown them that they have more in common with men of their race and/or class group than bourgeois white women."

18   "La couleur de la peau de John Indien ne lui avait pas causé la moitié des déboires que la mienne m'avait causée." Condé, *Moi, Tituba*, 159.

19   "Tout ce qui touche à la femme noire est objet de controverse. L'Occident s'est horrifié de sa sujétion à l'homme, s'est apitoyé sur ses 'mutilations sexuelles,' et s'est voulu l'initiateur de sa libération. A l'opposé, une école d'Africains n'a cessé de célébrer la place considérable qu'elle occupait dans les sociétés traditionnelles, le statut dont elle jouissait et [. . .] en est arrivée à une totale idéalisation de son image et de ses fonctions. Nous nous garderons bien de défendre l'une ou l'autre thèse [. . .]." Condé, *La Parole des femmes*, 3.

20   Condé, *La Parole des femmes*, 113.

21   In a recent article, Sidonie Smith has qualified the "quest" as a characteristically male story that cannot "fit" the woman's experience. It seems to me, however, that women can quite fruitfully adopt and adapt this mode when shaping their stories. This repetition in difference, the ability to play with, alter, parody, and transform such "masculine" narrative models constitutes a good deal of both Wittig's and Condé's narrative force. See Sidonie Smith, "The Impact of Critical Theory on the Study of Autobiography: Marginality, Gender, and Autobiographical Practice," *a/b: Auto/Biography* 3:3 (Fall 1987): 3.

22   Virtually none of the novels Condé discusses in *La Parole des femmes* and *Le Roman antillais* anchors the protagonist in a middle-class milieu.

23   Condé makes this discovery about Antillean women writers in *La Parole des femmes* (44), and interprets the heroines' refusal to bear children as a nuanced feminine protest. Her own later character, Tituba, aborts her child when faced with an impossible future for the child and herself.

24 In an interview, Condé professes her admiration for Paule Mar-
    shall, Alice Walker, and black American women novelists in gen-
    eral. See Condé's interview with Ekanga Shungu, "La Bibliothèque
    de . . . Maryse Condé," *Jeune Afrique* 1216 (April 25, 1984): 67.
    Critic Susan Willis points out that the admiration between the
    Caribbean and the U.S. goes the other way, too: "The Caribbean,
    for Morrison as well as for Marshall, is often posited as the New
    World home and culture source for black Americans." See Susan
    Willis: "Black Women Writers: A Critical Perspective," in *Making a
    Difference: Feminist Literary Criticism*, edited by Gayle Greene and
    Coppélia Kahn (New York: Methuen, 1985), 215.

25 In the introduction to *La Parole des femmes* (4), Condé makes this
    point via the translation and explanation of a Creole proverb.

26 Condé uses here the famous image of the black gazelle from
    Léopold Senghor's poetry.

27 "[L]es Antilles sont des créations totalement artificielles du système
    capitaliste." Marie-Clothilde Jacquey and Monique Hugon, "L'Af-
    rique, un continent difficile: Entretien avec Maryse Condé," *Notre
    Librairie* 75 (April–June, 1984): 24.

28 I have cited the original, because the remarks are more clearly
    clichés in French than in English. See *Hérémakhonon* (Paris: Union
    Générale d'Editions, Collection 10/18, 1976), 149–50.

29 This ironic overlapping of the "black" and "white" points of view
    confuses color positions and can be troubling for the reader who
    expects sharply defined color lines. In her 1984 interview, Condé's
    interviewers, failing to see the profound irony in Veronica's situa-
    tion, take the author to task for presenting Africa through a stereo-
    typical "white" view. See Condé's interview with Jacquey and
    Hugon, "L'Afrique," 22.

30 Gallop, *Daughter's Seduction*, xii.

31 "Inutile d'inventer un mythe d'origine pour les Antilles quand on
    sait qu'en 1492 Christophe Colomb arrive en Guadeloupe, et que
    quelques années plus tard un vaisseau négrier débarque des cen-
    taines d'Africains." See Condé's interview with Jacquey and Hu-
    gon, "L'Afrique," 25.

32 "Les termes de son identité lui sont dictés." Jacquey and Hugon,
    "L'Afrique," 24.

33 Gallop, *Daughter's Seduction*, 94.

34 *Feminine Sexuality: Jacques Lacan and the Ecole freudienne*, edited by
    Juliet Mitchell and Jacqueline Rose, and translated by J. Rose (New
    York: W. W. Norton, 1985), 32.

35   It is useful to remember that Condé has characterized the African family saga as male-centered and the Antillean one as female-centered. See Condé's interview with Jacquey, 58.

36   Veronica has also been forced to recognize that her indifference toward learning at least some of the local languages has kept her from being able to interpret the political and social signs around her.

37   Condé adopts precisely the same attitude when she defends her right to speak about women's issues, despite the topic's popularity. See *La Parole des femmes*, 6.

38   "Tout ce que l'on écrit a des racines autobiographiques. Mais l'histoire de Véronica n'est pas la mienne et je n'ai aucune envie de raconter ma vie." Interview with Ina Césaire in Condé, *La Parole des femmes*, 124.

39   "[S]implement un artifice d'écriture." Condé, *La Parole des femmes*, 124.

40   "[F]abriqué à partir de ce que je ne suis pas ou peut-être de ce que je crois ne pas être." Condé, *La Parole des femmes*, 125.

41   "J'avais à raconter une histoire précise et très triste de camarades africains emprisonnés, en fuite, en exil [. . .]." Condé, *La Parole des femmes*, 125.

42   Because she is so leery of positive images that lull the individual or group into self-satisfaction, Condé is sometimes inclined to go the other way, that is, to promote exceedingly negative images of herself or of groups that she associates with. Her statement that the only Antillean writer she likes is V.S. Naipaul—a novelist whom I consider to be anti-black, anti-African . . .—is indicative of her ambivalence toward herself. See her interview with Ekanga Shungu, "La Bibliothèque de . . . Maryse Condé," *Jeune Afrique* 1216 (April 25, 1984): 67.

43   "IC: Est-ce que ne transparaît pas à travers Véronica une sorte de provocation dans l'absence d'engagement tout de même? Avoue que tu voulais choquer un certain militantisme? D'extrême gauche? MC: Bien sûr, parce qu'un certain militantisme qui devient sectarisme, m'ennuie prodigieusement. Au fond de moi, j'ai beaucoup de sympathie pour l'anarchie . . . ." Condé's interview with Césaire, *La Parole des femmes*, 128.

44   Jonathan Ngate's excellent article, "Maryse Condé and Africa: The Making of a Recalcitrant Daughter?" *A Current Bibliography on African Affairs* 19:1 (1986–87): 5–20, shows Condé's torturous ambivalence toward Africa and the Antilles. I am stressing that the

ambivalence is already an internalized conflictual mode directed toward the subject's own sense of self.

45 "C'est une ambiguïté que j'ai vécue et que j'ai eu très vite envie de résoudre en allant chercher des gens qui soient vraiment des Nègres, qui aient le droit de dire: 'Soyons fiers d'être des Nègres' [. . .]." Condé's interview with Césaire, *La Parole des femmes*, 126.

46 "[L]e reflet de questions que je posais moi-même à mon personnage." Condé, *La Parole des femmes*, 127.

47 Condé says her heroines seek to affirm themselves, "as women and as colonized people, in relation to social and political problems of the world" ("en tant que femmes et en tant que colonisées, par rapport aux problèmes politiques et sociaux du monde"). See Condé's interview with Jacquey and Hugon, "L'Afrique," 22.

48 Condé did publish two plays prior to *Heremakhonon: Dieu nous l'a donné* (Paris: Editions Pierre-Jean Oswald, 1972), and *Mort d'Oluwemi d'Ajumako* (Paris: Editions Pierre-Jean Oswald, 1973), but neither of these focuses on *feminine* identity.

49 Condé's interview with Jacquey and Hugon, "L'Afrique," 22.

50 Monique Wittig, *Les Guérillères*, translated by David Le Vay (New York: Viking Press, 1971), 89.

51 "Le paradoxe, c'est qu'en fin de compte, né d'une création vraiment artificielle, le peuple antillais existe." Condé's interview with Jacquey and Hugon, "L'Afrique," 24.

CONCLUSION

1 Barbara Smith, "Toward a Black Feminist Criticism," *The New Feminist Criticism: Essays on Women, Literature and Theory*, edited by Elaine Showalter (New York: Pantheon Books, 1985), 183–84. I would like to thank Sandy Petrey for pointing out this wonderful quotation during a talk he gave at Amherst College, April 1989.

2 I have placed the word "between" in quotation marks because autobiography can never really choose "between" fact and fiction or between experience and language . . . . They are always already intertwined.

3 Like Michel Beaujour's self-portraitists, de Beauvoir, Sarraute, Duras, Wittig, and Condé all deal with guilt in their autobiographical texts. Their works also respond to many of the classical rhetorical categories that Beaujour says replace chronological narrative in the self-portrait (categories including sin and merits, virtues and vices, race, milieu, moment . . .). Beaujour successfully shows that the most modern (and personal) self-portraits use the oldest (im-

personal) forms of classical strategy. But while Beaujour's argument is quite compelling, it is noteworthy that he does not include gender in the array of discursive formula dictating the self-portraitist's choices. I would argue that one's relationship to the classical *topoi* described by Beaujour is not only historically bound (he seems to accept this), but that it is also affected by the subject's implicit or explicit articulation of gender. Gender's role vis-à-vis the classical topics of the self-portrait is not clear in Beaujour's work: the question of gender characteristically disappears as the critic considers only male writers. In similar fashion, issues of race and class readily disappear when white writers or bourgeois writers are being discussed in critical works. It seems to me that as critical readers, we must be careful not to overemphasize the rhetoric of "nothing new under the sun" when that means subsuming crucial distinctions bound to historical situation, gender, class, and race. See Michel Beaujour, *Miroirs d'encre* (Paris: Seuil, 1980).

4 "Nathalie Sarraute," interview with Pierre Boncenne, *Lire* (June 1983): 90.

5 I might add that the way Duras separates women's personal issues from general political positions in *The Lover* can be construed as an objectionable, if not dangerous, move. And Julia Kristeva's article, "The Pain of Sorrow in the Modern World: The Works of Marguerite Duras," *PMLA* 102:2 (March 1987): 138–52, suggests that in the postmodern period we need to move beyond the Durasian universe involving an unhealthy "malady of pain."

6 In Wittig's recent interview in *Yale French Studies*, the tensions between Wittig's radical lesbian politics and her vision of a universal writing resurface. Again, Wittig tries to separate a political content from a literary play on form, and categorically negates the pertinence of gender to her (or anybody's) writing. In remarks very much reminiscent of Sarraute's denial of the writer's specificity, Wittig states: "I can no more say I am a lesbian writer than I can say I am a woman writer. I am simply a writer." While such a denial of a marked writing does not hamper the textual borrowing in a male literary tradition, it *does* render the new version's ability to signify highly problematic because (in the case of *Across the Acheron*) it cuts the allegory off from its political dimensions. See Alice A. Jardine and Anne M. Menke, "Exploding the Issue: 'French' 'Women' 'Writers' and the 'Canon'? Fourteen Interviews," *Yale French Studies* 75 (1988): 257–58.

7 Already in *The Opoponax*, it was abundantly clear that the lesbian

subject came into being through masculine cultural artifacts. The love relationship between two girls is articulated through the recitation of male poets addressing their female lovers. The words don't change, but their effects certainly do.

8   I am indebted to Marie-Hélène Huet for help in presenting a systematic formulation of the authors' borrowings in the conclusion.

Selected Bibliography

T he following listing contains only those works cited or referred to in the text and other works that are of immediate relevance to the topic. Because I have referred to translations of primary book sources whenever possible, I list the English translation first and then the French edition. In the first part of this bibliography are listed the works by and about each of the writers discussed at length in the text. The second part of the bibliography consists of general works of criticism.

SIMONE DE BEAUVOIR

Primary Sources

Adieux: A Farewell to Sartre. Translated by Patrick O'Brian. New York: Pantheon, 1984. *La Cérémonie des adieux, suivi d' Entretiens avec Jean-Paul Sartre*. Paris: Gallimard, 1981.
All Said and Done. Translated by Patrick O'Brian. New York: G. P. Putnam's Sons, 1974. *Tout Compte fait*. Paris: Gallimard, 1972.
Brigitte Bardot and the Lolita Syndrome. New York: Arno Press, 1972. (Unpublished in France.)
Force of Circumstance. Translated by Richard Howard. New York: G. P. Putnam's Sons, 1965. *La Force des choses*. 2 vols. Paris: Gallimard, 1963.
"Littérature et métaphysique." *Les Temps Modernes* 1 (April 1946): 1153–63.
The Long March. Translated by Austryn Wainhouse. Cleveland: World Publishing, 1958. *La Longue Marche*. Paris: Gallimard, 1957.
The Mandarins. Translated by Leonard M. Friedman. New York: Popular Library, 1956. *Les Mandarins*. Paris: Gallimard, 1954.
Memoirs of a Dutiful Daughter. Translated by James Kirkup. London:

André Deutsch and Weidenfeld and Nicholson, 1959. *Mémoires d'une jeune fille rangée*. Paris: Gallimard, 1958.

The Prime of Life. Translated by Peter Green. New York: World Publishing, 1966. *La Force de l'âge*. 2 vols. Paris: Gallimard, 1960.

The Second Sex. Translated by H. M. Parshley. New York: Random House, 1974. *Le Deuxième Sexe*. 2 vols. Paris: Gallimard, 1949.

She Came to Stay. Translated by Yvonne Moyse and Roger Senhouse. London: Martin Secker & Warburg, 1949. *L'Invitée*. Paris: Gallimard, 1943.

A Very Easy Death. Translated by Patrick O'Brian. New York: Penguin Books, 1983. *Une Mort très douce*. Paris: Gallimard, 1964.

Secondary Sources

Bair, Deirdre. "'My Life . . . This Curious Object': Simone de Beauvoir on Autobiography," in *The Female Autograph*. Edited by Domna C. Stanton and Jeannine Parisier Plottel. New York: New York Literary Forum. Vols. 12–13 (1984): 237–45.

Bieber, Konrad. *Simone de Beauvoir*. Boston: Twayne, 1979.

Butler, Judith. "Sex and Gender in Simone de Beauvoir's *Second Sex*," *Yale French Studies* 72 (1986): 35–49.

Cottrell, Robert D. *Simone de Beauvoir*. New York: Frederick Ungar, 1975.

Evans, Martha Noel. "Murdering *L'Invitée*: Gender and Fictional Narrative." *Yale French Studies* 72 (1986): 67–86.

Evans, Mary. *Simone de Beauvoir: A Feminist Mandarin*. New York: Tavistock, 1985.

Francis, Claude, and Fernand Gontier. *Les Ecrits de Simone de Beauvoir*. Paris: Gallimard, 1979.

Idt, Geneviève. "La Cérémonie des adieux de Simone de Beauvoir: rite funéraire et défi littéraire." *Revue des Sciences Humaines*. 4:192 (1983): 15–33.

Jardine, Alice A. "Interview with Simone de Beauvoir." *Signs* 5:2 (1979): 224–36.

Jeanson, Francis. *Simone de Beauvoir ou l'entreprise de vivre*. Paris: Seuil, 1966.

Marks, Elaine. "The Dream of Love: A Study of Three Autobiographies," in *Twentieth Century French Fiction: Essays for Germaine Brée*. Edited by George Stambolian. New Brunswick: Rutgers Univ. Press, 1975, 72–88.

———. *Simone de Beauvoir: Encounters with Death*. New Brunswick, N.J.: Rutgers Univ. Press, 1973.

―――. "Transgressing the (In)cont(in)ent Boundaries: The Body in Decline." *Yale French Studies* 72 (1986): 181–200.

Okely, Judith. *Simone de Beauvoir.* New York: Random House, Virago/Pantheon series, 1986.

Portuges, Catherine. "Attachment and Separation in *The Memoirs of a Dutiful Daughter.*" *Yale French Studies* 72 (1986): 107–18.

Roy, Claude. "Beauvoir, par Simone." *La Nef*, 22 (1958): 75–78.

MARYSE CONDÉ

Primary Sources

Dieu nous l'a donné. Paris: Editions Pierre-Jean Oswald, 1972.

Heremakhonon. Translated by Richard Philcox. Washington, D.C.: Three Continents Press, 1982. *Hérémakhonon.* Paris: Union Générale d'Editions, Collection 10/18, 1976.

Moi Tituba, sorcière noire de Salem. Paris: Mercure de France, 1986.

Mort d'Oluwemi d'Ajumako. Paris: Editions Pierre-Jean Oswald, 1973.

"Négritude césairienne, négritude senghorienne." *Revue de littérature comparée* 3–4 (July–December 1974): 409–19.

La Parole des femmes: Essai sur des romancières des Antilles de langue française. Paris: Editions L'Harmattan, 1979.

"Pourquoi la Négritude? Négritude ou révolution?" in *Les Littératures d'expression française: Négritude africaine, négritude caraïbe.* Université Paris-Nord: Centre d'Etudes Francophones, La Francité, 1973, 150–54.

Le Roman antillais. 2 vols. Paris: Fernand Nathan, Collection "Classiques du monde," 1977.

Segu. Translated by Barbara Bray. New York: Viking Press, 1987. *Ségou: Les Murailles de terre.* Paris: Robert Laffont, 1984.

Une Saison à Rihata. Paris: Robert Laffont, 1981.

Ségou: La Terre en miettes. Paris: Robert Laffont, 1985.

Secondary Sources

Baudot, Alain. "Maryse Condé ou la parole du refus." *Recherche, Pédagogie & Culture* 57 (1982): 30–35.

Bruner, Charlotte and David. "Buchi Emecheta and Maryse Condé: Contemporary Writing from Africa and the Caribbean." *World Literature Today* 59:1 (Winter 1985): 9–13.

Jacquey, Marie-Clotilde. " 'Ségou' est-il un roman malien?' Entretien avec Maryse Condé." *Notre Librairie* 84 (1986): 56–60.

Jacquey, Marie-Clotilde, and Marie Hugon. "L'Afrique: un continent difficile: Entretien avec Maryse Condé." *Notre Librairie* 75 (April–June 1984): 21–25.

Ngate, Jonathan. "Maryse Condé and Africa: The Making of a Recalcitrant Daughter?" *A Current Bibliography of African Affairs* 19:1 (1986–87): 5–20.

Shungu, Ekanga. "La Bibliothèque de . . . Maryse Condé." *Jeune Afrique* 1216 (April 25, 1984): 66–67.

MARGUERITE DURAS

Primary Sources

Agatha. Paris: Minuit, 1981.

"Le Bureau de poste de la rue Dupin." With François Mitterand. *L'Autre Journal* 1 (February 26–March 4, 1986): 32–40.

Le Camion, suivi de Entretien avec Michelle Porte. Paris: Minuit, 1977.

Destroy, She Said. Translated by Barbara Bray. New York: Grove Press, 1970. *Détruire, dit-elle*. Paris: Minuit, 1969.

L'Eden Cinéma. Paris: Mercure de France, 1977.

Emily L. Paris: Minuit, 1987.

Eté 80. Paris: Minuit, 1980.

"L'Homme assis dans le couloir." *Les Cahiers du Cinéma*, 312/313 (June 1980): 32–33.

L'Homme atlantique. Paris: Minuit, 1982.

The Lover. Translated by Barbara Bray. New York: Harper & Row, 1986. *L'Amant*. Paris: Minuit, 1984.

The Malady of Death. Translated by Barbara Bray. New York: Grove Press, 1986. *La Maladie de la Mort*. Paris: Minuit, 1982.

Moderato Cantabile. Translated by Richard Seaver. New York: Grove Press, 1960. *Moderato Cantabile*. Paris: Editions de Minuit, 1958.

Outside: Selected Writings. Translated by Arthur Goldhammer. Boston: Beacon Press, 1986. *Outside: Papiers d'un jour*. Paris: Albin Michel, 1981.

"The Places of Marguerite Duras." With Michelle Porte. Translated by Edith Cohen. *Enclitic* 7:1 (1984): 54–61 and 7:2 (1984): 55–62. *Les Lieux de Marguerite Duras*. With Michelle Porte. Paris: Minuit, 1977.

La Pute de la côte normande. Paris: Minuit, 1986.

The Ravishing of Lol V. Stein. Translated by Richard Seaver. New York: Grove Press, 1966. *Le Ravissement de Lol V. Stein*. Paris: Gallimard, 1964.

The Sailor from Gibraltar. Translated by Barbara Bray. New York: River-
run, 1980. *Le Marin de Gibraltar.* Paris: Gallimard, 1952.
The Sea Wall. Translated by Herma Briffault. New York: Harper & Row,
1986. *Un Barrage contre le Pacifique.* Paris: Gallimard, 1950.
"The Seated Man in the Passage." Translated by Mary Lydon. *Contempo-
rary Literature* 24 (1983): 268–75. *L'Homme assis dans le couloir.*
Paris: Minuit, 1980.
The Vice-Consul. Translated by Eileen Ellenbogen. London: Hamish
Hamilton, 1968. *Le Vice-consul.* Paris: Gallimard, 1966.
La Vie matérielle. Paris: P.O.L., 1987.
The War. Translated by Barbara Bray. New York: Pantheon, 1986. *La
Douleur.* Paris: P.O.L., 1985.
Whole Days in the Trees and Other Stories. Translated by Anita Barrows.
New York: Riverrun, 1984. *Des Journées entières dans les arbres.* Paris:
Gallimard, 1954.
Woman to Woman. With Xavière Gauthier. Translated by Katharine A.
Jensen. European Women Writers Series. Lincoln, Nebr.: Univ. of
Nebraska Press, 1987. *Les Parleuses.* With Xavière Gauthier. Paris:
Minuit, 1974.

Secondary Sources

Borgomano, Madeleine. "Une Ecriture féminine? A propos de Mar-
guerite Duras." *Littérature* 53 (February 1984): 59–68.
———. "Romans: La Fascination du vide." *L'Arc* 98 (1985): 40–48.
Brée, Germaine. "An interview with Marguerite Duras." *Contemporary
Literature* 13:4 (1972): 401–22.
Foucault, Michel, and Hélène Cixous. "A propos de Marguerite Duras."
Cahiers Renaud-Barrault 89 (1975): 8–22.
Gosselin, Monique. "Voyage au bout de la féminité: Figures féminines
dans quelques romans de Marguerite Duras," in *Figures féminines et
roman,* 143–68. Edited by Jean Bessière. Paris: Presses Univer-
sitaires de France, 1982.
Kristeva, Julia. "The Pain of Sorrow in the Modern World: The Works of
Marguerite Duras," *PMLA* 102.2 (March 1987): 138–52.
Lydon, Mary. "Translating Duras: 'The Seated Man in the Passage.'"
Contemporary Literature 24 (1983): 259–68.
Makward, Christiane. "Structures du silence/du délire: Marguerite
Duras/Hélène Cixous." *Poétique* 35 (1978): 314–24.
Marini, Marcelle. "L'Autre Corps," in *Ecrire dit-elle: Imaginaires de Mar-
guerite Duras,* 21–48. Edited by Danielle Bajomée and Ralph
Heyndels. Brussels: Editions de l'Université de Bruxelles, 1985.

Murphy, Carol J. *Alienation and Absence in the Novels of Marguerite Duras*. Lexington, Ky.: French Forum, 1982.

Pierrot, Jean. *Marguerite Duras*. Paris: José Corti, 1986.

Pivot, Bernard. Interview with Marguerite Duras on French television program "Apostrophes." September 28, 1984.

Saporta, Marc. "Le Regard et l'école." *L'Arc* 98 (1985): 49–50.

Schuster, Marilyn R. "Reading and Writing as a Woman: The Retold Tales of Marguerite Duras." *French Review* 58:1 (October 1984): 48–57.

Vircondelet, Alain. *Marguerite Duras*. Paris: Seghers, 1972.

Willis, Sharon. *Marguerite Duras: Writing on the Body*. Chicago: Univ. of Illinois Press, 1987.

NATHALIE SARRAUTE

Primary Sources

Between Life and Death. Translated by Maria Jolas. New York: Braziller, 1969. *Entre la vie et la mort*. Paris: Gallimard, 1968.

"Ce que je cherche à faire." Followed by a panel discussion with Sarraute. In *Nouveau Roman: hier, aujourdhui*. Vol.2. Edited by Jean Ricardou and Françoise von Rossum-Guyon. Paris: Union Générale d'Editions, 1972, 25–57.

Childhood. Translated by Barbara Wright. New York: Braziller, 1984. *Enfance*. Paris: Gallimard, 1983.

Do You Hear Them? Translated by Maria Jolas. New York: Braziller, 1973. *Vous les entendez?* Paris: Gallimard, 1972.

"fools say". Translated by Maria Jolas. New York: Braziller, 1977. *"disent les imbéciles."* Paris: Gallimard, 1976.

The Golden Fruits. Translated by Maria Jolas. New York: Braziller, 1964. *Les Fruits d'or*. Paris: Gallimard, 1963.

Izzum, in *Collected Plays of Nathalie Sarraute*. Translated by Maria Jolas and Barbara Wright. New York: Braziller, 1981. *Isma ou ce qui s'appelle rien*. Published with *Le Silence* and *Le Mensonge*. Paris: Gallimard, 1970.

Martereau. Translated by Maria Jolas. New York: Braziller, 1959. *Martereau*. Paris: Gallimard, 1953.

"New Movements in French Literature: Nathalie Sarraute Explains Tropisms." *The Listener* 65:1667 (March 9, 1961): 428–29.

The Planetarium. Translated by Maria Jolas. New York: Braziller, 1960. *Le Planétarium*. Paris: Gallimard, 1959.

Portrait of a Man Unknown. Translated by Maria Jolas. New York: Braziller, 1958. *Portrait d'un inconnu*. Paris: Robert Marin, 1948.

Tropisms and *The Age of Suspicion*. Translated by Maria Jolas. London: Calder, 1964. *Tropismes*. Paris: Denoël, 1939. *L'Ere du soupçon: Essais sur le roman*. Paris: Gallimard, 1956.

The Use of Speech. Translated by Barbara Wright. New York: Braziller, 1983. *L'Usage de la parole*. Paris: Gallimard, 1980.

Secondary Sources

Besser, Gretchen R. "Sarraute on Childhood—Her Own," *French Literature Series* 12 (1985): 154–61.

Boncenne, Pierre. "Nathalie Sarraute." Interview in *Lire* (June 1983): 87–92.

Brée, Germaine. "Nathalie Sarraute." Interview in *Contemporary Literature* 14:2 (1973): 137–46.

Ezine, Jean-Louis. "Nathalie Sarraute: Sartre s'est trompé à mon sujet." Interview in *Nouvelles Littéraires* 2552 (September 30–October 6, 1976): 5.

Fauchereau, Serge, and Jean Ristat. "Conversation avec Nathalie Sarraute." *Digraphe* 32 (April 1984): 9–18.

Knapp, Bettina L. "Interview avec Nathalie Sarraute." *Kentucky Romance Quarterly* 14:3 (1967): 283–95.

———. "Nathalie Sarraute's *Between Life and Death*: Androgyny and the Creative Process," in *Women in Twentieth Century Literature: A Jungian View*. University Park, Pa.: Pennsylvania State Univ. Press, 1987.

Minogue, Valerie. *Nathalie Sarraute and the War of the Words: A Study of Five Novels*. Edinburgh: Edinburgh Univ. Press, 1981.

Munley, Ellen W. "I'm Dying but It's Only Your Story: Sarraute's Reader on Stage." *Contemporary Literature* 24:2 (1983): 233–58.

Pingaud, Bernard. "Dix Romanciers face au roman." *La Pensée française* (December 12, 1956): 56.

Saporta, Marc. "Portrait d'une inconnue." Interview in *L'Arc* 95 (1984): 2–23.

Sturrock, John. "The Way of Disobedience." *Times Literary Supplement* (June 10, 1983): 596.

Watson-Williams, Helen. *The Novels of Nathalie Sarraute: Towards an Aesthetic*. Amsterdam: Editions Rodopi BV, 1981.

Wittig, Monique. "Le Lieu de l'action." *Digraphe* 32 (March 1984): 69–75.

MONIQUE WITTIG

Primary Sources

Across the Acheron. London: Peter Owen Publishers, 1987. *Virgile, non*. Paris: Minuit, 1985.

Les Guérillères. Translated by David Le Vay. New York: Viking Press, 1971. *Les Guérillères*. Paris: Minuit, 1969.

The Lesbian Body. Translated by David Le Vay. Boston: Beacon Press, 1986. Paris: Minuit, 1973.

Lesbian Peoples Material for a Dictionary. Written in conjunction with Sande Zeig. Translated by Monique Wittig and Sande Zeig. New York: Avon Books, 1979. *Brouillon pour un dictionnaire des amantes*. Paris: Bernard Grasset, 1976.

"One Is Not Born a Woman," *Feminist Issues* 1:2 (Winter 1981):47–54.

The Opoponax. Translated by Helen Weaver. New York: Simon & Schuster, 1966. *L'Opoponax*. Paris: Minuit, 1964.

"The Point of View: Universal or Particular?" *Feminist Issues* 3:2 (1983): 63–69.

"The Straight Mind." *Feminist Issues* 1:1 (Summer 1980): 103–11.

"The Trojan Horse." *Feminist Issues* 4:2 (Fall 1984): 45–49.

Le Voyage sans fin. Appeared as supplement to issue 4 of *Vlasta* (June 1985).

Secondary Sources

Crowder, Diane Griffin. "Amazons and Mothers? Monique Wittig, Hélène Cixous and Theories of Writing," *Contemporary Literature* 24:2 (1983): 117–44.

Duras, Marguerite. "A Brilliant Work: *L'Opoponax*, by Monique Wittig," in *Duras: Outside: Selected Writings*. Translated by Arthur Goldhammer. Boston: Beacon Press, 1986, 228–31.

Higgins, Lynn. "Nouvelle Nouvelle Autobiographie: Monique Wittig's *Le Corps lesbien*." *SubStance* 14 (1976): 160–66.

Lesseps, Emmanuèle de. "Hétérosexualité et féminisme." *Questions Féministes* 7 (February 1980): 55–69.

Marks, Elaine. "Lesbian Intertextuality," in *Homosexualities and French Literature*. Edited by George Stambolian and Elaine Marks. Ithaca, N.Y.: Cornell Univ. Press, 1979, 353–77.

McCarthy, Mary. "Everybody's Childhood," in *The Writing on the Wall and Other Literary Essays*. New York: Harcourt, Brace, 1970, 102–111.

Ostrowsky, Erica. "A Cosmogony of O: Wittig's *Les Guérillères*," in *Twen-*

tieth Century French Fiction. New Brunswick, N.J.: Rutgers Univ. Press, 1975, 241–51.

Simon, Claude. "Pour Monique Wittig," *L'Express* (November 30–December 6, 1964): 69–71.

Wenzel, Hélène Vivienne. "The Text as Body/Politics: An Appreciation of Monique Wittig's Writings in Context." *Feminist Studies* 7:2 (Summer 1981): 264–87.

GENERAL

Barthes, Roland. *Image-Music-Text*. Translated by Stephen Heath. New York: Hill & Wang, 1977.

———. *Mythologies*. Translated by Annette Lavers. New York: Hill & Wang, 1972.

———. *Sade/Fourier/Loyola*. Translated by Richard Miller. New York: Hill & Wang, 1976.

———. *Writing Degree Zero*. Translated by Annette Lavers and Colin Smith. New York: Hill & Wang, 1981.

Beaujour, Michel. *Miroirs d'encre: Rhétorique de l'autoportrait*. Paris: Seuil, 1980.

Berg, Elizabeth L. "The Third Woman." *Diacritics* 12:2 (1982): 11–20.

Bruss, Elizabeth. *Autobiographical Acts: The Changing Situation of a Literary Genre*. Baltimore: Johns Hopkins Univ. Press, 1976.

Butor, Michel. *Change of Heart*. Translated by Jean Stewart. New York: Simon & Schuster, 1958.

Camus, Albert. *The Stranger*. Translated by Stuart Gilbert. New York: Vintage Books, 1958.

Césaire, Aimé. *Return to My Native Land*. Translated by Emil Synders. Paris: Présence Africaine, 1968.

———. *The Tragedy of King Christophe*. Translated by Ralph Manheim. New York: Grove Press, 1970.

Chapsal, Madeleine. *Quinze Ecrivains*. Paris: Juillard, 1963.

Char, René. *Commune Présence*. Paris: Gallimard, 1964.

Chodorow, Nancy. *The Reproduction of Mothering: Psychoanalysis and the Sociology of Gender*. Berkeley: Univ. of California Press, 1978.

Dante Alighieri. *The Divine Comedy*. 3 vols. Translated by John D. Sinclair. New York: Oxford Univ. Press, 1972.

de Lauretis, Teresa, editor *Feminist Studies/Critical Studies*. Bloomington: Indiana Univ. Press, 1986.

de Man, Paul. "Autobiography as De-facement." MLN 94:5 (1979): 919–30.

―――. *Blindness and Insight: Essays in the Rhetoric of Contemporary Criticism*, 2nd edition revised. Minneapolis: Univ. of Minnesota Press, Theory and History of Literature Series, vol.7, 1983.

Derrida, Jacques. *The Ear of the Other: Otobiography, Transference, Translation.* Texts and discussions with Jacques Derrida. Translated by Peggy Kamuf. Edited by Christie V. McDonald. New York: Schocken Books, 1985.

Duchen, Claire. *Feminism in France: From May '68 to Mitterand.* Boston: Routledge & Kegan Paul, 1986.

―――, editor and translator. *French Connections: Voices from the Women's Movement in France.* Amherst, Mass.: Univ. of Massachusetts Press, 1987.

Eisenstein, Hester, and Alice Jardine, editors. *The Future of Difference.* New Brunswick, N.J.: Rutgers Univ. Press, 1985.

Evans, Martha Noel. *Masks of Tradition: Women and the Politics of Writing in Twentieth Century France.* Ithaca, N.Y.: Cornell Univ. Press, 1987.

Fanon, Frantz. *Black Skin, White Masks.* Translated by Charles Lam Markmann. New York: Grove Press, 1967.

"Feminist Readings: French Texts/American Contexts." Special issue of *Yale French Studies* 62 (1981).

Féral, Josette. "Antigone or the Irony of the Tribe." *Diacritics* 8 (September 1978): 2–14.

Foucault, Michel. *The History of Sexuality, Vol. I: An Introduction.* Translated by Robert Hurley. New York: Pantheon, 1978.

―――. *The Order of Things: An Archaeology of the Human Sciences.* Translated by Alan Sheridan-Smith. New York: Random House, 1970.

Freud, Sigmund. "On Narcissism: An Introduction." Edited by James Strachey, *The Standard Edition of the Complete Psychological Works.* Vol.14. London: Hogarth Press, 1953, 67–102.

Gallop, Jane. *The Daughter's Seduction: Feminism and Psychoanalysis.* Ithaca, N.Y.: Cornell Univ. Press, 1982, reprinted 1983.

―――. *Reading Lacan.* Ithaca, N.Y.: Cornell Univ. Press, 1985.

Gardiner, Judith Kegan. "On Female Identity and Writing by Women," in *Writing and Sexual Difference.* Edited by Elizabeth Abel. Chicago: Chicago Univ. Press, 1982, 177–92.

Gasché, Rodolphe. "Autobiography and the Problem of the Subject." *MLN* 93:4 (1978)· 573–74.

Greene, Gayle, and Coppélia Kahn. *Making a Difference: Feminist Literary Criticism.* London: Methuen, 1985.

Gunn, Janet. *Autobiography: Towards a Poetics of Experience.* Philadelphia: Univ. of Pennsylvania Press, 1982.

Haley, Alex. *Roots*. Garden City, N.Y.: Doubleday, 1978.

Hooks, Bell. *Feminist Theory: From Margin to Center*. Boston: South End Press, 1984.

Irigaray, Luce. "One Doesn't Stir without the Other." Translated by Hélène Vivienne Wenzel, *Signs* 7:1 (1981): 56–67.

———. *The Speculum of the Other Woman*. Translated by Gillian Gill. Ithaca, N.Y.: Cornell Univ. Press, 1985.

———. *This Sex Which Isn't One*. Translated by Catherine Porter and Carolyn Burke. Ithaca, N.Y.: Cornell Univ. Press, 1985.

Jacobus, Mary. "The Law of/and Gender: Genre Theory and the Prelude." *Diacritics* 14:4 (1984): 47–57.

Jardine, Alice A. *Gynesis: Configurations of Woman and Modernity*. Ithaca, N.Y.: Cornell Univ. Press, 1985.

Jardine, Alice A., and Anne M. Menke. "Exploding the Issue: French 'Women' 'Writers' and 'the Canon'? Fourteen Interviews." *Yale French Studies* 75 (1988): 229–58.

Johnson, Barbara. "My Monster/My Self." *Diacritics* 12:2 (Summer 1982): 2–10.

Kamuf, Peggy. "Replacing Feminist Criticism." *Diacritics* 12:2 (Summer 1982): 42–47.

Knapp, Bettina L. *Off-Stage Voices: Interviews with Modern French Dramatists*. Edited by Alba Amoia. Troy, N.Y.: Whitson, 1975.

Kofman, Sarah. *The Enigma of Woman: Woman in Freud's Writings*. Translated by Catherine Porter. Ithaca, N.Y.: Cornell Univ. Press, 1985.

Kristeva, Julia. *Desire in Language: A Semiotic Approach to Literature and Art*. Translated by Leon S. Roudiez. New York: Columbia Univ. Press, 1980.

———. "Héréthique de l'amour." *Tel Quel* 74 (1977): 30–49.

———. *Polylogue*. Paris: Seuil, 1977.

———. *Revolution in Poetic Language*. Translated by Margaret Waller. New York: Columbia Univ. Press, 1984.

Lacan, Jacques. *Ecrits: A Selection*. Translated by Alan Sheridan. New York: Norton, 1977.

Lang, Candace. "Autobiography in the Aftermath of Romanticism." *Diacritics* 12:4 (1982): 2–16.

Lejeune, Philippe. *L'Autobiographie en France*. Paris: Armand Colin, 1971.

———. *Le Pacte autobiographique*. Paris: Seuil, 1975.

Lévi-Strauss, Claude. *The Elementary Structures of Kinship*. Translated by James Harle Bell, John Richard von Sturmer, and Rodney Needham. Boston: Beacon Press, 1969.

Marivaux, Pierre de. *The Virtuous Orphan or the Life of Marianne, Countess* *of ******. Translated by Mary Mitchell Collyer. Edited by William Hartin McBurney and Michael Frances Shugrue. Carbondale, Ill.: Southern Illinois Univ. Press, 1965.

Marks, Elaine. "Women and Literature in France." *Signs* 3:4 (1978): 832–42.

Marks, Elaine, and Isabelle de Courtivron, editors. *New French Feminisms: An Anthology*. New York: Schocken Books, 1981.

McConnell-Ginet, Sally, Ruth Borker, and Nelly Furman, editors. *Women and Language in Literature and Society*. New York: Praeger, 1980, 258–73.

Miller, Nancy K., editor. *The Poetics of Gender*. New York: Columbia Univ. Press, 1986.

———. "The Text's Heroine: A Feminist Critic and her Fictions." *Diacritics* 12:2 (Summer 1982): 48–53.

Mitchell, Juliet, and Jacqueline Rose, editors. *Feminine Sexuality: Jacques Lacan and the Ecole freudienne*. Translated by J. Rose. New York: W. W. Norton, 1985.

Moi, Toril. *Sexual/Textual Politics: Feminist Literary Theory*. New York: Methuen, 1985.

Nadeau, Maurice. *Le Roman depuis la guerre*. Paris: Gallimard, 1970.

Olney, James, editor. *Autobiography: Essays Theoretical and Critical*. Princeton N.J.: Princeton Univ. Press, 1980.

"'Race,' Writing, and Difference." Special issue of *Critical Inquiry* 12:1 (1985).

Rich, Adrienne. "Compulsory Heterosexuality and Lesbian Existence." *Signs* 5:4 (Summer 1980): 631–60.

Richman, Michele. "Sex and Signs: The Language of French Feminist Criticism." *Language and Style* 13 (1980): 62–80.

Rousseau, Jean-Jacques. *The Confessions*. Translated by J. M. Cohen. Harmondsworth, Middlesex, England: Penguin, 1953.

Sartre, Jean-Paul. *Being and Nothingness*. Translated by Hazel E. Barnes. New York: Citadel Press, 1964.

———. *Nausea*. Translated by Lloyd Alexander. New York: New Directions, 1964.

———. *What Is Literature?* Translated by Bernard Frechtman. New York: Philosophical Library, 1949.

"The Second Sex: Thirty Years Later." *Off Our Backs* 9:11 (December 1979): 24–27.

Shapiro, Stephen. "The Dark Continent of Literature: Autobiography." *Comparative Literature Studies* 5 (1968): 421–54.

Sherzer, Dina. *Representation in Contemporary French Fiction*. Lincoln: Univ. of Nebraska Press, 1986.

Smith, Barbara. "Toward a Black Feminist Criticism." *The New Feminist Criticism: Essays on Women, Literature, and Theory.* Edited by Elaine Showalter. New York: Pantheon Books, 1985, 168–85.

Smith, Sidonie. "The Impact of Critical Theory on the Study of Autobiography: Marginality, Gender, and Autobiographical Practice." *a/b: Auto/Biography* 3:3 (Fall 1987): 1–12.

———. *A Poetics of Women's Autobiography: Marginality and the Fictions of Self-Representation.* Bloomington: Indiana Univ. Press, 1987.

Spivak, Gayatri Chakravorty. "French Feminism in an International Frame." *Yale French Studies* 62 (1981): 154–84.

Stambolian, George, and Elaine Marks, editors. *Homosexualities in French Literature.* Ithaca, N.Y.: Cornell Univ. Press, 1979.

Stanton, Domna C., and Jeannine Parisier Plottel, editors. *The Female Autograph.* New York: New York Literary Forum. Vols. 12–13, 1984.

Yaeger, Patricia. *Honey-Mad Women: Emancipatory Strategies in Women's Writing.* New York: Columbia Univ. Press, 1988.

Index